In *Queer fictions of the past*, Scott Bravmann explores the
complexity of lesbian and gay engagement with history
and considers how historical discourses animate the
present. Characterizing historical representations as
dynamic conversations between then and now, he demon-
strates their powerful role in constructing present identities, differences, politics, and communities. In particular,
his is the first book to explore the ways in which lesbians
and gay men have used history to define themselves as
social, cultural, and political subjects. In his opening
chapters, Dr. Bravmann elaborates the theoretical and
political stakes of such a project before turning to analyses of how historiography, ancient Greek history, the
Stonewall riots, and postmodern historical texts both
inform and reflect the race, gender, class and political
dimensions to queer subjectivity.

Queer fictions of the past

Cambridge Cultural Social Studies

Series editors: JEFFREY C. ALEXANDER, *Department of Sociology, University of California, Los Angeles, and* STEVEN SEIDMAN, *Department of Sociology, University at Albany, State University of New York.*

Titles in the series

ILANA FRIEDRICH SILBER, *Virtuosity, charisma, and social order*

LINDA NICHOLSON and STEVEN SEIDMAN (eds.), *Social postmodernism*

WILLIAM BOGARD, *The simulation of surveillance*

SUZANNE R. KIRSCHNER, *The religious and Romantic origins of psychoanalysis*

PAUL LICHTERMAN, *The search for political community*

ROGER FRIEDLAND and RICHARD HECHT, *To rule Jerusalem*

KENNETH H. TUCKER, *French revolutionary syndicalism and the public sphere*

ERIK RINGMAR, *Identity, interest and action*

ALBERTO MELUCCI, *The playing self*

ALBERTO MELUCCI, *Challenging codes*

SARAH M. CORSE, *Nationalism and literature*

DARNELL M. HUNT, *Screening the Los Angeles "riots"*

LYNETTE P. SPILLMAN, *Nation and commemoration*

MICHAEL MULKAY, *The embryo research debate*

LYNN RAPAPORT, *Jews in Germany after the Holocaust*

CHANDRA MUKERJI, *Territorial ambitions and the gardens of Versailles*

LEON H. MAYHEW, *The New Public*

VERA L. ZOLBERG and JONI M. CHERBO (eds.), *Outsider art*

Queer fictions of the past

History, culture, and difference

Scott Bravmann

CAMBRIDGE
UNIVERSITY PRESS

PUBLISHED BY THE PRESS SYNDICATE OF THE UNIVERSITY OF CAMBRIDGE
The Pitt Building, Trumpington Street, Cambridge CB2 1RP, United Kingdom

CAMBRIDGE UNIVERSITY PRESS
The Edinburgh Building, Cambridge, CB2 2RU, United Kingdom
40 West 20th Street, New York, NY 10011-4211, USA
10 Stamford Road, Oakleigh, Melbourne 3166, Australia

© Scott Bravmann 1997

First published 1997

Printed in the United Kingdom at the University Press, Cambridge

Typeset in 10/12½ Monotype Times [SE]

A catalogue record for this book is available from the British Library

Library of Congress Cataloguing in Publication data
Bravmann, Scott, 1964–
Queer fictions of the past: history, culture, and difference
/ Scott Bravmann.
    p.   cm. – (Cambridge cultural social studies)
Includes bibliographical references and index.
ISBN 0 521 59101 5 hardback
ISBN 0 521 59907 5 paperback
1. Fiction – History and criticism.   2. Homosexuality in
literature.   3. Literature and history.   4. Identity (Psychology) in
literature.   I. Title.   II. Series.
PN3352.H65B73   1997
809'.93353–dc21   96–54613   CIP

Contents

Preface

This book engages the abiding significance of the past across a range of lesbian and gay discursive practices. Rather than endeavoring to reconstruct any particular historical moment, series of events, or social change, I engage in close readings of rich and varied textual evidence and offer theoretical elaboration to explore the multiple, complex, and inconsistent ways that historical arguments motivate gay and lesbian identities, communities, and politics. Because I believe these diverse practices deserve and need to be taken seriously as social/cultural texts that produce, contest, and destabilize historically contingent fictive identities, I seek to expand what counts as history for gay and lesbian studies. Like much gay and lesbian history writing, however, my argument reiterates the value of historical inquiry as a means of addressing important, often contested and divisive, issues confronting lesbian and gay communities in the present. Yet I also want to reevaluate the terms of that assertion. For that reason, this study refuses to treat "history" as either a stable, completed temporal locus or as a value-free, mimetic representation of the past.

Recent scholarship both in gay and lesbian history and in queer theory has powerfully problematized a wide range of socially constructed and arbitrary regimes of the "normal" and the "natural." Rather conspicuously, however, these inquiries have not been accompanied by an interest in looking at the discourse of history itself as one such regime. Nonetheless, there are compelling theoretical, epistemological, and political reasons to remain skeptical of academic history writing as has been demonstrated by recent critical theoretical work that has sought to make historiography's codes of representation as much an object of analysis as an instrument of it. On the one hand, in response to the crisis in historical studies that this work has responded to and helped provoke, the mode of analysis I pursue in this project regards historiography as a culturally privileged system of signification and rethinks the familiar, confident invocations of history that animate multiple gay and lesbian cultural practices. On the other hand, in light of cogent critiques of both humanist conceptions of subjectivity and of identity politics, I reconsider questions of identity, community, and history from a perspective that acknowledges multiple socially constituted differences among gay and lesbian subjects in order to resist the powerful pull of historical self-representations that gravitate toward "sameness." In this double sense, then, I recognize the need to develop a project of queer cultural studies of history that focuses on the politics and the poetics of historical discourses – on, in other words, queer fictions of the past.

I begin by tracing the modernist narrative logic of social constructionist historical accounts of gay identity formation. Focusing on the ways this logic elides the multiple differences among gay men and lesbians, the first chapter sets the stage for the theoretical elaboration and the substantive arguments developed in the following chapters. The second chapter articulates the project's double theoretical approach to what I call queer historical subjects. Drawing on queer, feminist, and cultural theories, I foreground the intractability of identity and difference that make the subjects of gay and lesbian studies – queer historical subjects – problematic. From there, I move in the latter half of that chapter to theoretical and political critiques of historical representation in order to reassess – indeed, to queer – the place of history in gay and lesbian studies.

Developing these two themes through analyses of historical practices, chapters 4, 5, and 6 read past histories to explore specific, albeit large and weighty, instances of gay and lesbian historical imaginations. My treatment of these highly consequential examples as sites of hermeneutic and political struggle rather than as natural, true, or inevitable, is intended to make possible a substantially more problematic *and* problematically more substantial assessment of the lasting presence of gay and lesbian pasts. Before turning in that direction, however, I consider in chapter 3 a more recent generation of lesbian and gay historiography that has developed the heuristic breakthrough of social constructionist arguments in a more refined way.

In chapter 4 I read past the abiding resonance of the imagined cultural geography of ancient Greece in white gay and lesbian historical fictions. Arguing that these conceptual models of Greek antiquity are neither inevitable nor innocent, I begin by looking at the salience of gender as an axis of differentiation in these "returns" to ancient Greece; then, I move on to develop an explicitly non-essentialized conception of cultural difference and positionality through which we might consider the reflexive constitution of contemporary gay and lesbian identities in relation to racial formation. The next chapter examines the construction of a paradoxical queer "common sense" across social differences effected through the symbolic dimensions of the Stonewall riots. At the same time that they work to construct a collective gay and lesbian identity, I suggest, representations of Stonewall also challenge that construction. In particular, I focus on race, gender, and politics as crucial points of difference and antagonism among queer historical subjects. Without diminishing the significance of Stonewall, these particular differences effectively challenge understandings of the riots that imagine them as moments in a narrative of queer redemption and that regard their yearly commemorations as periods of reconciliation of queer differences, rather than as staging grounds for insisting on those differences.

The sixth chapter pushes the project of queer cultural studies of history further by turning to several provocative texts by lesbians and gay men of color. Contesting the elision of difference in narratives of the queer past while also exploiting the problematic nature of historical representations themselves to address how those representations construct notions of self, community, and politics, these texts' specific re/writings of community, nation, and the body make promising interventions into the cultural politics of history and offer suggestive alternative models for queer historical representation.

I end with a return to historical representation and the question of subjectivity at the vexing crossroads between the past and the future which we call the present.

During the period of writing this book, I have continually been struck by an insistent paradox. Although I firmly believe that all writing is in some sense autobiographical, I have also felt that it would be necessary – for me – in a critical study of queer fictions of the past to transgress the limitations imposed on and by a kind of "autobiographical" writing in which my own subject position became the sole focus of my attention. In responding to abiding and pointed concerns about my attempt to write collectively of gay male and lesbian historical imaginations, I have found myself arguing that were I to abandon my attempt – not to write a co-gendered revisionist gay and lesbian history, but rather to look at how gender matters to queer fictions of the past – I ought to give up my inquiries into race matters as well and, indeed, into any other category of social differentiation. Under these conditions, the most inclusive book I could have written would have concerned itself exclusively with white gay male cultural practices, the least expansive with some version of my personal history. Although I do think both autobiography and studies of white male identity are valuable and necessary, I seriously doubt whether the particular form of "autobiographical" writing that I have tried to resist in this study would have been sufficient to sustain a critical understanding of queer fictions of the past. The narrowness of such a project, it seems to me, is not only untenable in the world of complex and intersecting differences that inform queer social relations, but is also unsuitable to my private needs – thus, the paradoxical return of autobiography. Instead of focusing narcissistically, solipsistically on myself, I wanted to write – and hope to have written – a book that imagines the subjects of lesbian and gay studies as embodied, multiple, historical, fictive – and, yes, problematic. I return to the question of autobiographical writing in chapter 6. For an important study of white male subjectivity, see Fred Pfeil (1995).

To imagine the subjects of lesbian and gay studies in this way is to propose a very particular kind of collective difference. This *queer heterosociality* retains the irreducible differences between gay men and lesbians as historical subjects, for it is from difference itself that heterosociality derives its own troubled and troubling identity; queer heterosociality's queerness is to be found in its resolute refusal to remove differences from the necessary historical identities it puts into conversation. (I have adapted the term "heterosociality" from Marc Stein who used it in a paper entitled "Doing It Together: When Homosexuals Heterosocialize," which he presented at a conference on lesbian, bisexual and gay studies at the University of Illinois in 1992. In my revision, gender is a central but not the sole axis of differentiation among queer historical subjects.) The dialogical relationship among queer historical subjects fostered by this understanding of collective difference, I believe, can help reconstruct the late twentieth-century public sphere by enabling us to look critically at the particular ways we imagine ourselves, our communities, and our relationships to each other. In her essay "Out of the Past," addressing the collectivizing experiences of gay and lesbian political and cultural developments in the post-Stonewall period, Jewelle Gomez offers the crucial reminder that "[o]ur movement is different from others; we have little shared, public history or culture." Without ever once allowing it to diminish her critical stance toward the persistent racisms and sexisms that have informed and undercut gay and lesbian movements, Gomez manages as well to retain the special significance of the ways in which "[o]ur gayness gives us a connection we would otherwise never have in heterosexual society" (Gomez, 1995: 18, 20). Her observant hypothesis is, I think, an instructive example that impels us toward critical engagements with the difficult hybridity of queer heterosociality.

Even as I (guardedly) view it as harboring a democratic promise for the future, I also want to give voice to certain reservations regarding such a project. I need, that is, to acknowledge not only my own continuing ambivalence (notwithstanding my desire to move beyond "autobiography") but also the very real concerns of other participants in this often contentious dialogue. In a powerful reassertion of the need for a sustained feminist critique of "queer studies," Jacquelyn Zita reads "the cosexual nature of lesbian and gay studies" as "a new heterosexual contract" (Zita, 1994: 258). However necessary such a "marriage" might be for creating a field of inquiry that looks most closely at homosexual oppression, she argues that "if this [new academic enterprise] entails submerging the differences between the sexes and erasing over two decades of feminist work on gender, race, class, and heterosexuality, the effort may not be worth it" (p. 259). Though bitter and angry about exclusionary practices, historical amnesia regarding feminist writings on the social construction of gender, and "postfeminist" male dramas in the academy, Zita ends her essay on a note of cautious optimism, "see[ing] some hope in the healthy tensions and contradictions of a lesbian and gay intellectual endeavor: namely, the possibility of reopening a wider discussion on gender, sexuality, class, race, and other differences in the context of queer experience" (p. 268). I share this hope, and it is as a contribution to such a wider discussion that I offer this book.

Acknowledgements

A number of readers have offered a wide variety of helpful, if not always heeded, criticism and advice at various stages of this project. For their input early on, I would like to thank Tomás Almaguer, Gloria Anzaldúa, Jim Clifford, Jeffrey Escoffier, Jackie Goldsby, Donna Haraway, Karl Knapper, Teresa de Lauretis, José Limón, Ming-Yeung Lu, and Carter Wilson. Hayden White, my dissertation advisor in the History of Consciousness Program at the University of California at Santa Cruz, provided necessary assistance in developing, writing, and completing the project from which this book developed. Two people in particular were essential to the transformation from dissertation to book: Catherine Max at Cambridge University Press, who provided necessary guidance along the way, and Avery Gordon, who read a draft of the manuscript and offered enormously helpful, provocative, and generous comments and suggestions for revisions that spurred me to sharpen my argument, alter its presentation, and expand its scope. I would also like to thank Rex Ray for designing the cover image and Jo North for copy-editing the manuscript. I owe my largest debt of gratitude to Steve Seidman whose initial interest in my project, practically since before it was begun, and continued suggestions and support have been critical to bringing this book to fruition.

   The library and archival collections of several institutions proved invaluable to the research of this project. The University of California libraries at both the Santa Cruz and the Berkeley campuses, the library of San Francisco State University, and both the Main and Eureka Valley/Harvey Milk branches of the San Francisco Public Library collectively provided me with excellent opportunities to conduct my research. The Gay and Lesbian Historical Society of Northern California (GLHSNC) gave me access to a number of important documents in their archives. Bill Walker at the GLHSNC was especially helpful and quite willing to share his knowledge; he and Mary Boone Bowling in the manuscripts division of the New York Public Library went out of their way to furnish me with copies of several key texts on very short notice.

Several pieces of this book have appeared as works-in-progress in a number of publications. I am thankful for the helpful suggestions and feedback that the readers and editors of the following publications offered and for permission to use that material here: *Gender, Place, and Culture: A Journal of Feminist Geography*; *Outlook: National Lesbian and Gay Quarterly*; *per*versions: *The International Journal of Gay and Lesbian Studies*; *Queer Theory/Sociology*, ed. Steven Seidman (Cambridge, MA: Blackwell, 1996); and *Socialist Review*.

Finally, I never would have been able to complete this book without the loving companionship and necessary distractions of Cashman Kerr Prince and the feline attentions of Meisje (who was always able to sleep even when I could not and whose playful curiosity explains one way of reading the epigraph to chapter 7).

PART I

Queer cultural studies of history

1

Metanarrative and gay identity

An exclusive focus on the emergence of *the* lesbian or gay identity skews our understanding of the complexity of homosexual experiences.
(Susan K. Cahn)[1]

Identities are the names we give to the different ways we are positioned by, and position ourselves within, the narratives of the past.   (Stuart Hall)[2]

I define *postmodern* as incredulity toward metanarratives . . . Postmodern knowledge . . . refines our sensitivity to differences and reinforces our ability to tolerate the incommensurable.   (Jean-François Lyotard)[3]

Very much an "essential" domain of queer discursive practices, history has had persistent and multiple significances in gay and lesbian studies both inside and outside the academy. Yet we can also discern vital and productive engagements with the past in the larger cultural and political work of lesbian and gay communities. Recurrent fascination with various aspects of ancient Greek culture, biographies of famous homosexuals from the past, and a recovery of Native American *berdache* and other third-gender traditions, as much as the yearly celebrations of the Stonewall riots, the circulation of images and texts of the Harlem Renaissance, lesbian reclamations of pre-Stonewall butch-femme relationships, and the redeployment of the pink – and increasingly black – triangle as a symbol of defiance of, rather than acquiescence to, the historical and contemporary oppression of gay men and lesbians, to offer just a few relatively familiar examples, permeate the themes and styles of gay and lesbian self-representations.[4]

This book returns to the shared point of departure of these disparate, uneven, and at times contradictory projects traversing the various terrains of lesbian and gay studies and communities – their insistent engagement with history. Yet, rather than doing so to undertake a project of historical reconstruction, I return to this complex site to begin a critical study of queer fictions of the past as important social/cultural texts in the articulation of lesbian and gay identities and differences. As historians Martin Duberman, Martha Vicinus, and George Chauncey suggest in their introduction to an anthology of articles on "reclaiming the gay and lesbian past," "some of the most important issues facing, agitating, and sometimes dividing [gay and lesbian communities] today, personally and collectively, are best addressed historically."[5] In addition to its critical, descriptive, explanatory, and strategic uses, however, history also helps circumvent the censorship, denial, and amnesia that have continued to inform so much of lesbian and gay existence. Public celebrations such as the commemorations of the Stonewall riots, the annual Harvey Milk memorial march in San Francisco, and various AIDS-related memory projects such as the Names Project Quilt provide gay men and lesbians with powerful collective forms of historical recollection that animate the present in a variety of complex ways. In other words, though the study of gay and lesbian history provides cogent ways of addressing questions of identity, politics, community, and difference, historical events and memories of them also continue to imbue the present with meaning and give the past a surplus of signification that is itself in need of critical analysis.

In the chapters that follow, I will argue that lesbians and gay men, individually and collectively, have a relationship to history that is not only complex but also contradictory. In making that proposal and addressing its implications for queer historical subjects, I will read past histories to look at how some of the many cultural claims, public celebrations, and political debates that traverse, animate, and divide gay and lesbian communities do not merely reference the past but are actually strongly motivated by historical argument. The importance of history to gay men and lesbians goes beyond the lessons to be learned from the events of the past to include the meanings generated through retellings of those events and the agency those meanings carry in the present. Lesbian and gay historical self-representations – queer fictions of the past – help construct, maintain, and contest identities – queer fictions of the present. For this reason, we need to look at how the images of the gay and lesbian past circulating among us animate the present and to read lesbian and gay historical self-representations as sites of ongoing hermeneutic and political struggle in the formation of new social subjects and new cultural possibilities. Thus, while *Queer fictions of the past* reiterates the value of history as a means to address a range of pressing issues confronting lesbian and gay communities, it also reevaluates the terms of that assertion.

Before proceeding along the double trajectory of this book's principal argument, however, I need to look closely at an important generation of gay and lesbian historical scholarship that has recounted the story of the modern homosexual and the rise of a specifically gay identity. In this chapter, I use this complex and contradictory relationship to history to rethink "the making of the modern homosexual" from a position of relative skepticism towards such narratives that has been opened up by the general political, cultural, and theoretical projects of postmodernism.[6]

Over the past decade and a half, numerous historical, sociological, and theoretical studies have explored the emergence of lesbian and gay identities, subcultures, communities, and politics.[7] The historicizing project of this generation of research has revealed not only the discontinuities between cultural conceptions of homosexuality across time and space but also the ways in which the various sustained attempts to gain knowledge of sexuality are themselves constitutive of that bodily domain of pleasure, power, and personal identity now regarded as sexuality. While enabling a more careful and specified diachronic analysis of the development of, on the one hand, heterosexist and homophobic institutions of domination and, on the other, celebratory and resistant gay and lesbian cultural practices, these texts have in turn tended to reify certain current conceptions of homosexuality which are unified and stabilized by contrasting them to those of an utterly different past. That is, they have created categories of bodily, psychic, social, and political experience on either side of this divide between past and present that are not only fundamentally different from each other but are also fundamentally similar to themselves, and they have constructed coherence, cohesion, and stability against the multiply fractured subject positions that constitute the lives of lesbian and gay individuals. Although social constructionist theory is dynamic and promising in relationship to understanding both the past and the present, these studies of the emergence of lesbian and gay identity have been relatively unsuccessful at recognizing race, gender, and class (among other) antagonisms "within" that identity. In foregrounding diachronic or historical ruptures between social constructions of "homosexuality," these related projects have underemphasized the synchronic or contemporary ruptures between social constructions of homosexuality and their own specific histories, rife with contradictions of their own. Moreover, the developmental model of history on which these accounts are based paradoxically unifies the past histories of "gay identity," a process that their genealogical strategy seemingly attempts to resist.

Though varying in the emphasis they place on specific historical processes, social structures, crystallizing events, and public and private discourses, these arguments agree that a distinctive homosexual identity has emerged only in the last century or so; they use this argument of the comparatively recent formation of a homosexual identity as an expression of individual desire within the available discourses in order to explain the emergence of gay and lesbian subcultures, communities, and social movements in Europe, the United States, and elsewhere at different moments in the twentieth century. As John D'Emilio has pointed out in a survey of research on gay history, however, "of all national histories being investigated, that of the United States most clearly confirms the argument of [Jeffrey] Weeks and [Michel] Foucault concerning the emergence of a distinctive gay identity."[8] For this reason, both the analysis and the critique that follow are decidedly and purposefully US-centered.

In these arguments, several factors stand out among the various conditions that enabled the existence of gay and lesbian worlds, especially the growth of industrial capitalism and its attendant impact on kinship and family life, gender roles, urbanization, and ideologies of accumulation, ownership, and individualism. D'Emilio makes this argument most forcefully in his article "Capitalism and Gay Identity" (a force that perhaps reflects the greater latitude for critique afforded by its site of publication). In that essay, D'Emilio "argue[s] that lesbians and gay men have *not* always existed." Rather "we are a product of" a particular historical period whose "emergence is associated with the relations of capitalism." Specifically, it is the free labor system "that has allowed large numbers of men and women in the late twentieth century to call themselves gay" (p. 102). The growth of capitalism and the spread of wage labor, D'Emilio and others argue, transformed the structure, functions, and relationships of family life. Having previously been both a system of consumption and a system of household production, the family began to lose its economic self-sufficiency by the nineteenth century when men and women became increasingly involved in and dependent on the capitalist free labor system. (Of course, this monolithic version of the "family" is also highly contested and reiterates the long-existing ideology of the yeoman farmer in America which marginalizes such central familial economic forms as slave families, the white plantation economies dependent on the slave-labor system, and the US government's attempt to construct patriarchal, land-owning Native American nuclear families with the implementation of the General Allotment Act in 1877.) This change effected a shift in the significance of the family away from a materially productive institution towards an affective unit which brought with it changes in the meaning of sexual relations between men and women. As D'Emilio points out, whereas offspring had once been necessary contributors to the household economy, with the growth of wage labor and the socialization of production "it became possible to release sexuality from the 'imperative' to procreate" (p. 104). Within this new set of experiences, heterosexual expression gradually began to be conceived of as a way to achieve intimacy, happiness, and pleasure rather than substantially and perhaps most importantly as a (re)productive act. By removing the productive aspect from the household economy and fostering a separation of (hetero)sexuality from procreation, capitalism, D'Emilio contends, made it possible for "some men and women to organize a personal life around their erotic/emotional attraction to their own sex" (p. 104) and "survive beyond the confines of the family" (p. 105).

These new possibilities for personal life, however, were inscribed with and through highly salient marks of difference. In her article "Patriarchy, Sexual Identity, and the Sexual Revolution," Ann Ferguson focuses directly on the question of how these new and changing economic possibilities affected the life choices available to and pursued by women. Ferguson also stresses the importance of "nineteenth-century industrial capitalism . . . for women [in particular] in that it eventually weakened the patriarchal power of fathers and sons." While "this relative gain in freedom was not an instant effect of capitalism," she argues, not only did the "acquisition of an income g[i]ve women new options" but so too did "commercial capital's growth [spur] the growth of urban areas, which in turn gave feminist and deviant women the possibility of escaping the confines of rigidly traditional, patri-archal farm communities for an independent, if often impoverished, life in the cities" (p. 156). Ferguson's attention to the particular place of women in the economy points to a set of ruptures across gay and lesbian identities that undermine the logic of these theoretical accounts. I will return to these problems at the end of this chapter.

These accounts of a specifically "gay identity" contrasted to past construc-tions of homosexuality emphasize and reinterpret broad-based trans-formations in the social structure that are part of a much longer, much larger process of modernization, and they provide focused discussions of the changes both in such "personal" aspects of life as sexuality, gender, identity, and love and such "public" areas as cities, the economy, medicine, and culture. In *All That Is Solid Melts into Air*, an approving reappraisal of "the experience of modernity," Marshall Berman identifies these less specified processes and posits a "truth" about modernity that anticipates the problems of the gay identity thesis. "Modern environments and experi-ences," Berman proclaims in an unironic hyperbole, "cut across all bound-aries of geography and ethnicity, of class and nationality, of religion and ideology: in this sense, modernity can be said to unite all mankind."[9]

Ultimately, then, on Berman's analysis, *modernity is indifferent to difference.* The experience of modernity, however, is not marked solely by vastly new and profound changes in social organization and material forces carrying out their changes on an impersonal society and unwitting, passive humans. The "world-historical processes" of change have also enabled, even required, a wide range of cultural responses. These cultural responses, which Berman identifies as "modernism," consist of "an amazing variety of visions and ideas that aim to make men and women the subjects as well as objects of modernization, to give them the power to change the world that is changing them, to make their way through the maelstrom [of modern life] and make it their own" (p. 16).

Several points in Berman's reconstructed story of the interrelated projects of modernization, modernism, and modernity parallel the specific accounts of gay and lesbian identity formation in social constructionist historical-theoretical work. The most direct link between Berman's analysis and the arguments of this gay and lesbian research is "the process of economic and social development [which] generates new modes of self-development, ideal for men and women who can grow into the emerging world" (p. 66). Both arguments also focus on the vast rural-to-urban migration that has caused as well as emerged from large-scale social disruption over the past 200 years. The individual move from the "closed social system[s]" (p. 66) of small communities to the unrealized urban promise of "great cities" (p. 59), Berman argues, has been motivated by the desire for "action, adventure, an environment in which [one] can be . . . free to act, freely active (p. 66). A related feature of this urban promise, both for Berman's view of modernity as an undifferentiated project and for the more focused histories of gay identity formation as an aspect of modernity, is the change in consciousness effected by the collapse of "order and complete content" that had been provided by small-town "little worlds" (p. 55). Urban environments, Berman argues as do gay historians, have afforded anonymity through which one can escape "the surveillance of family, neighbors, priests . . . all the suffocating pressures of the closed small-town world" (p. 54).

In part the collective cultural projects of modernism, as Berman sees them, promise the security of individual development and a stable self-identity in "the maelstrom" of an ever-changing world. For many gay men and lesbians, coming out of the closet has reflected these twin desires and has played a decisive role in the politicization of homosexuality since Stonewall. As a powerful way to develop and claim "who we really are," coming out meets the modernist promise of stability in a world characterized by change. However, the security of a stable, "real" gay or lesbian self is an illusion produced through the strong personal and political value invested in the process of coming out.[10] In addition to fostering this illusory personal safety, coming out contributes to the notion of a stable, unified, uncontradicted "community" and suggests a larger emergence of "gay identity" which reconstructs the historical past around modernist criteria of authenticity and development. As Jeffrey Weeks explains:

> "Coming out" is usually seen as a personal process, the acceptance, and public demonstration, of the validity of one's homosexuality. But it can also be seen as an historic process, the gradual emergence and articulation of a homosexual identity and public presence.[11]

By emphasizing the fundamental structural reorganization of society associated with the rise of capitalist economies as a grand, universalizing historical process, this generation of research on homosexuality has obscured recognition of effective and meaningful difference within that overarching process of change. Eve Sedgwick has rightly pointed out that "these historical projects . . . still risk reinforcing a dangerous consensus of knowingness about the genuinely *un*known, more than vestigially contradictory structurings of contemporary experience." This generation of research, she argues, has "counterpos[ed] against the alterity of the past a relatively unified homosexuality that 'we' *do* 'know today.'"[12] Additionally, however, these texts have counterposed against the alterity – the difference, the newness – of current conceptions of homosexuality a relatively unified past that "they" *did* "know then." The paradigm of "the making of the modern homosexual" denies or subsumes under the privileged sign of gay identity whatever antecedent forms of difference might have existed; that is, within the logic of these accounts, these differences are just as indifferent in the historical development of gay and lesbian identities as the differences dismissed by Berman are to modernity itself.

I want to suggest, however, that we begin thinking about "the making of the modern homosexual" not as a "fact" but as an argument, fundamentally as a narrative with serious implications for addressing issues historically. Rather than simply describing an historical process, these accounts of the past themselves help "make" or "construct" the fiction of the modern homosexual. In this sense, they are themselves part of what Foucault has termed the reverse discourse (curiously, problematically, and inaccurately in the singular) on homosexuality and are themselves agents in the reformulations and contestations of the meanings of homosexuality.[13] Specifically, we need to regard the "modernist" tendencies within this collective body of research as a rhetorical practice closely allied with those experiences of modernity the work investigates.

Most importantly, these arguments about gay identity need to be read in relation to Berman's hyperbolic statement on modernity's indifference to geographic, ethnic, class, national, religious, and ideological differences which itself reiterates this very indifference to difference. Berman's framework for ascribing creative agency to the human subjects of modernization does not recognize the ways in which these vital differences inform the "amazing variety of visions and ideas" of the "modernist" cultural projects he champions. In its indifference to difference, the totalizing sweep of modernist histories and cultural theories anchors present identities in a stable, coherent personal and social past (the family, capitalism, cities); overrides, disallows, and denies other experiences; and implicitly grounds conceptions of gay identity within the specific experiences of urban, middle-class white men. For the history of industrialization – the material base of the modernity championed by Berman and the catalyst that propelled the wholesale changes in family life preceding the emergence of urban gay subcultures – has a complex, exploitative "underside" that belies the inevitability of "the real social movement toward economic development" (p. 40), thus problematizing "the cultural ideal of self-development" (p. 40) whose ideological underpinnings are in fact connected to the economic *under*development of whole populations of people. While these gay history texts recount somewhat different versions of the modernity yielded by modernization, we need to take seriously Berman's reminder that these processes of historical change are connected to, reflected in, *and* addressed by modernist cultural practices. More than simply describing the modernisms of the past, the relationship between modernization and modernism is also reiterated in the historical narratives they recount. As Berman says, they, too, are "visions and ideas that aim to make men and women the subjects as well as objects of modernization" (p. 16).

Within these modernist narratives, the cultural and political constructions of gay identity and a social movement are built upon the mutual experience of homosexuality, a mutual experience subject to (eventual) mediation by multiple differences, including those of race, gender, class, and nationality which the ostensible "unity" of modernity cuts across. Jeffrey Escoffier, for instance, makes the following observation about the historical emergence of "difference" within gay and lesbian identity-based political movements (in the early 1980s).

In gay politics not only has the affirmation of shared experience resulted in the consolidation of homosexual differentness, but in the lesbian and gay-male communities' drive for affirmation differences have emerged among the members of both communities that cannot be eradicated.[14]

Escoffier's observation, however, suggests a contemporary fracturing of an historically unified gay identity, as if there had been no past heterogeneity, conflict, and autonomy within these "communities." This assessment retains modernism's indifference by recontaining difference as an *emergent* element within its dialectical fiction and thus preventing the destabilization of the narrative of the emergence of "gay identity."

Two principal categories of social "difference" – gender and race – raise fundamental questions about the indifferent logic of these accounts. Permanently inscribed in discussions of lesbian and gay history, "the mark of gender" makes problematic any effort to locate historical emergences solely in changes in the social relations of production, economic developments, and restructurings of family life.[15] As Martha Vicinus has recently argued, this structural model is inadequate for explaining "the historical roots of the modern lesbian identity."

A lesbian identity did not result from economic independence, nor from an ideology of individualism, nor from the formation of women's communities, although all of these elements were important for enhancing women's personal choices.[16]

Vicinus also argues that developing "an explanation of the sources of a lesbian identity" is a baffling project "because there is no agreement about what constitutes a lesbian" (p. 177). This lack of consensus on the (historical) meaning of the substantive "lesbian" also clearly compounds the complex problems of trying to locate the historical relationship between the construction of lesbian and gay male identities.

In addition to reframing the question of the historical development of a lesbian identity within a gender-based, female-specific critical analysis, Vicinus's insistence on this point raises another vexing problem. If a gay identity for men and a lesbian identity for women resulted from different historical, material, and ideological factors, as her essay would seem to suggest, why then did these separate and different identities begin to appear at roughly the same period – or did they? How, in other words, do we recognize what these (partially) distinct identities might share in terms of their historical development without either reiterating a position that denies gender specificity and difference or regarding this significant historical detail as purely coincidental? How "different" is the difference of gender? Further, we need to address the extent to which "difference" is salient *within* the historical development of these two gender-based categories of sexual identity. How have such social experiences and economic circumstances as those structured by age, class, race, and ethnicity, among others, inflected the specific histories of gay and lesbian identities not only "across" gender but also "within" each gender?

Though it only receives brief and indirect mention, the existence of a lesbian and gay subculture in Harlem during the Renaissance – a complex moment in black gay history that has received a relatively significant amount of attention – is clearly problematic for D'Emilio's narrative account of the development of gay identity in the USA.[17] In an attempt to explain the class-bound possibilities for the creation of lesbian and gay social spaces in the early part of this century, D'Emilio posits the cultural value of the family (rather than the material factors such as a lack of privacy in overcrowded living conditions which would make more obvious sense within his argument) as the primary restriction facing women and men who might otherwise have sought a niche in which they could safely pursue their same-sex desires. In "Capitalism and Gay Identity," in contrast to working-class, white immigrant communities, he writes:

> *for reasons not altogether clear,* urban black communities appeared relatively tolerant of homosexuality. The popularity in the 1920s and 1930s of songs with lesbian and gay male themes – "B. D. Woman," "Prove It on Me," "Sissy Man," "Fairey Blues" – suggest an openness about homosexual expression at odds with the mores of whites.   (p. 106, emphasis added)

Without explicitly enumerating them, D'Emilio makes two (not necessarily related) points here: (1) a certain measure of tolerance of homosexuality in urban black communities such as Harlem during the 1920s and 1930s which suggests that, unlike the case in European immigrant communities, gayness was somehow *not* "a difficult option to pursue" in black communities; and (2) in light of this relative tolerance, the actual pursuit of that option by men and women within those communities. What most needs to be noted about this brief reference to urban black constructions of homosexuality, however, is the problem it poses for D'Emilio's argument, both historically and theoretically.

Both urban black gay subcultures of the 1920s and 1930s *and* the relative tolerance they apparently were met with in the larger black communities are anomalous features not only in relationship to "standard" heterosexist and racist histories which would ignore or deny both black and gay experiences but also in relationship to D'Emilio's own revisionist social history.[18] Perhaps ironically, D'Emilio calls attention to the inadequacy of his account for making sense of the "contrast" between white and black communities by marking his surprise at the latter's ostensible tolerance towards homosexuality with the phrase "for reasons not altogether clear." From one perspective, to insist that the reasons why an urban black lesbian and gay subculture could exist during the 1920s and 1930s in the USA are "not altogether clear" reveals the tenacity of his paradigm by suggesting that future research might not only reveal what these reasons were but would also reconfirm the paradigm's explanatory power. From a different perspective, however, the "failure" of D'Emilio's account to make clear what these reasons were could be viewed as a particularly effective challenge to the paradigm's implicit reinforcement of the idea that "difference" – and especially differences of race, the most salient organizer of politics, social space, and identity in the USA throughout the century in which "the making of the modern homosexual" occurred – has not always been central to the multiple strategies of the reverse discourses (emphatically in the plural) on homosexuality.[19]

Although social constructionist arguments have made significant theoretical contributions to our understanding of sexuality and above all have worked to destabilize ahistorical, naturalizing, ethnocentric, and ultimately homophobic readings of lesbian and gay sexualities, the presence of "difference" in contemporary lesbian and gay communities, "moments" from the queer past that are incommensurable with these abstract arguments, and a (developing) discourse of "difference" within lesbian and gay studies raise pressing questions about the linear trajectory of these materialist social histories. As a way to recenter "difference" in gay and lesbian history and to draw out the recent valuable work on "queer differences" in the present, I want to suggest a turn towards a postmodern writing of the past that would make such singular, linear, narratively complete accounts of the construction of "gay identity" impossibly problematic by directly challenging the modernist drive for unity, in Berman's terms, "across the bounds of ethnicity and nationality, of sex and class and race" (p. 6).

These questions of identity and difference – metaphysical, epistemological, ontological, even political – also provoke reflection on how historical representation "works." In part, the shortcomings of this generation of historical scholarship are to be explained – although not explained away – by the limited but still important scope of their project. Rather than offering full historiographical studies, these studies set out to develop, as D'Emilio puts it in "Capitalism and Gay Identity," "a new, more accurate *theory* of gay history" (p. 101, emphasis added) that would replace the invented mythologies of the gay liberation era. The importance of "theory" to historical representation, however, points to another central aspect of postmodern history-writing. Such a project seeks also to retheorize historical representation in order to problematize and reframe the very meaning of history itself, something that is already powerfully present in queer cultural practices. In the next chapter I look at the problem of identity and difference and at the question of theory and history, both of which are integral to my proposal for postmodern queer cultural studies of history that address these larger questions of historical representation in relation to specific practices in queer contexts.

2

Queer historical subjects

Identities, differences, and queer heterosociality; or, the problematic subjects of lesbian and gay studies

Identity must continually be assumed and immediately called into question.

(Jane Gallop)[1]

Lesbian and gay identities are both constructed and essential, constructed in the sense that they are historically moulded and therefore subject to change, essential in the particular sense that they are necessary and in the end inescapable.

(Jeffrey Weeks)[2]

The primary aim of this book's project of queer cultural studies of history is to look at how identities and differences construct and are constructed through queer fictions of the past. These intractable and mutually constitutive aspects of queer heterosocial subjectivity – identities and differences – are the very substance of lesbian and gay communities, movements, and theories, and they at once inform and disrupt a myriad of cultural, political, and intellectual practices. Complex and partial, these *queer fictions of the present* must be seen as contradictory *and* supplemental – either/or as well as both/and. As hybrid and syncretic cultural formations, however, queer identities and differences point directly to the problematic subjects of lesbian and gay studies.

When I speak of the problematic subjects of lesbian and gay studies, I refer most obviously to the question of gender borne by the way these projects are named. Although its current usage ostensibly remarks the (gender-based) differences between gay men and lesbians, the practice of linking lesbians and gay men together can just as effectively elide the very differences it intends to point out. Because lesbian and gay studies is permanently inscribed with "the mark of gender," any hypothetical identity ascribed to its problematic subjects is always already vexed by difference.[3] When undertaken as separate, gender-specific endeavors, however, gay studies and lesbian studies have at least partially reproduced "sexual difference" – in this case the difference of (gay) men from (lesbian) women – and have made other differences, certain similarities, and a variety of political alliances and cultural affinities difficult if not impossible to conceptualize and pursue. Perhaps less obvious because not remarked by the process of naming such a project, my unspecified suggestion of "other differences" further problematizes the subjects of lesbian and gay studies in ways that will occupy much of the argument and analysis presented in the chapters that follow.

I turn now to two attempts to address the problem of gender for queer heterosociality, a problem which can be read as the paradigmatic, though decidedly not exclusive, instance of differences among queer historical subjects. From that discussion I move on to look at the productive and worrisome relationship of "queer" to lesbian and gay theory and politics. Next, I consider the partial and specific nature of identity as a fiction that enables the unsettled certainty with which I recognize queer historical subjects, a category of people that the readings developed in subsequent chapters both assume and deeply problematize. Finally, I draw on theoretical and political critiques of historiography to suggest the kind of queer/ed understanding of historical representation that is central to my project of queer cultural studies of history.

Eve Kosofsky Sedgwick and Diana Fuss have drawn out some of the key dimensions of gay and lesbian studies' gender-marked inscription. Although not entirely successful at mapping the terrain of queer heterosociality, and less so its democratic promise, their arguments have important implications for the development of lesbian and gay politics and theory and are useful for rethinking identity and difference, identity across difference, even identity as difference. For both Sedgwick and Fuss, the relationship between gay and lesbian subjects is a conflicted but nonetheless – or even for that very reason – a crucial point for investigation. In spite of certain significant differences between them, each of their analyses delineates ways that theoretical arguments on homosexuality have reproduced the gender difference between (gay) men and (lesbian) women. Perhaps the most significant dissimilarity between their formulations is Fuss's willingness to hold both gay male and lesbian studies accountable for the shortcomings of their gender-separatist inquiries while Sedgwick seems unwilling or unable to find fault with gay male theories of sexuality.

Focusing squarely on the presumptive relationship between gay and lesbian subjects, Sedgwick seeks to initiate a "gay theory" that moves beyond the impasse of gender-separatist inquiry, a separatism which she locates fundamentally within lesbian-feminist theory and practice without, alas, locating anything similar to it within gay male theory. Sedgwick's formulation of the basis for this new project of gay theory substantially displaces the usefulness of (a remarkably unspecified, though implicitly cultural) feminist theory to gay studies. This displacement is both possible and necessary, Sedgwick argues, because feminist theory is "an optic calibrated in the first place to the coarser stigmata of gender difference."[4] Sedgwick's new trajectory of gay theory is inclusive of lesbian theory to the extent that the latter "(a) isn't simply coextensive with feminist theory (i.e., doesn't subsume sexuality *fully* under gender) and (b) doesn't a priori deny all theoretical continuity between male homosexuality and lesbianism" (p. 39). Because the study of sexuality and the study of gender cover different areas, Sedgwick assumes as axiomatic the impossibility of "an a priori decision about how far it will make sense to conceptualize lesbian and gay male identities together. Or separately" (p. 36).

Though all of her subsequent chapters focus centrally on male sexual definition in canonical late nineteenth- and early twentieth-century literary representations, Sedgwick's theoretical project in the introduction to *Epistemology of the Closet* seeks to problematize – but not eliminate – "the separatist-feminist [framework] that emerged from the 1970s." This framework, she argues, has tended to deny any "grounds of commonality between gay male experience and identity" and lesbian experience and identity (p. 36). Although Sedgwick acknowledges the radical assumptions behind this separatist framework, she also calls into question "the powerful impetus of a gender-polarized feminist ethical schema [that] made it possible for a profoundly antihomophobic reading of lesbian desire (as a quintessence of the female) to fuel a correspondingly homophobic reading of gay male desire (as a quintessence of the male)" (p. 37). In Sedgwick's analysis, feminist theory has reproduced, in a modified, gender-separatist form, the "logical" entailments of what Judith Butler has termed "the compulsory order of sex/gender/desire" in which there is a "[p]resumption of a binary gender system [that] implicitly retains the belief in a mimetic relation of gender to sex,"[5] although in this revision desire is homo- rather than heterosexual and the stark polarization is structured solely in terms of gender difference.

Yet Sedgwick also attenuates the scope and impact of her rather strong dismissal of feminist theory's usefulness to gay theory by positing feminist theory as a highly instructive model for this new co-gendered project of gay theory to emulate, at least in part. On her reading, gay theory would profit by asking the same sorts of questions as those asked by feminist inquiry but not with the expectation of receiving the same sorts of answers. Her principal concern in retaining some aspects of feminist theory for gay theory derives from the productive ways the former has addressed questions of "how a variety of forms of oppression intertwine systematically with each other; and especially how the person who is disabled through one set of oppressions may *by the same positioning* be enabled through others," questions which "we aren't yet used to asking as antihomophobic readers" (p. 32).[6] By positing at once an essential sameness as well as an essential difference between them, however, this proposition – which tends to defer (perhaps rightly) to feminist reading strategies as a guide or a necessary starting point for antihomophobic or gay theory – blurs some of the distinction between gay and feminist modes of inquiry that Sedgwick seeks to establish. Indeed, Sedgwick's attempt to differentiate gay and feminist theories stumbles on the differences within feminist theory which her dismissal of (an implicitly "cultural") feminism fails to acknowledge.

Exploring a similar set of concerns in her essay on lesbian and gay theory and identity politics, Diana Fuss's analysis of these issues is firmly embedded in the context of the larger discussions of feminism, nature, and difference that she engages in her book *Essentially Speaking*.[7] Although Fuss links lesbian theory and gay male theory together at the outset of her chapter, she quickly calls attention to the multiple problems embedded in making this move. Since gay and lesbian subjects very often inhabit different social worlds, have different political concerns, and operate within different intellectual traditions, Fuss suggests that "a certain adversarial relation between them (first and foremost, perhaps on the level of theory) cannot be easily ignored" (p. 98). From this position of gender-based difference, Fuss offers the tentative generalization that "current lesbian theory is less willing [than gay male theory] to question or to part with the idea of a 'lesbian essence' and an identity politics based on this shared essence" while the latter body of works, "following the lead of Foucault, ha[s] been quick to endorse the social constructionist hypothesis and to develop more detailed analyses of the historical construction of sexualities" (p. 98). Toward the end of her chapter, Fuss returns to this concern to identify "the emergence of a lesbian/gay binarism within homosexual politics and theory" as one of two areas particularly rich in promise for future work in lesbian and gay studies (p. 110).[8]

Reminding us that homosexuality is not a singular, uniform subject-position, Fuss calls attention to the ways both the gay pole and the lesbian pole of this binarism tend to erase the other side by failing to consider the irreducible differences between and among lesbians and gay men. The work of self-identified gay male writers, she maintains, either "effects a complete and total silence on the subject of lesbianism while implicitly coding homosexuality as male" (Michel Foucault) or, somewhat more sympathetically, "situates lesbianism as a footnote to gay male history – the subordinated other in a newly constructed gay/lesbian binarism" (John D'Emilio). For their part, however, lesbian-feminist theorists such as Luce Irigary, Monique Wittig, and Adrienne Rich "have . . . inverted this binarism and erected a lesbian identity on the rejection and repression of a male hom(m)o-sexual economy" in which "the exchange of women between men" serves "as culture's inaugural institution of oppression." In substantial agreement with Sedgwick's reading of such projects, Fuss contends these feminist theorizations of male homosociality either end up erasing the male homosexual as an embattled subject (position) or leave gay men "bear[ing] the burden of a cultural homophobia designed to mask the determinative power of gay male relations" (pp. 110–111).

Frustrated by lesbian and gay studies' failure to "progress beyond the adversarial relations where each side persistently plays out the erasure of the other," Fuss urges us "to begin the hard work of investigating some of these structuring tensions *within the general field of gay and lesbian theory*" (p. 111, emphasis added). Yet Fuss's reference to a "general field of gay and lesbian theory" merely indicates its existence without explicitly identifying what the domain of that co-gendered field of inquiry does, could, or might even have to look like. It is unclear from her position whether moving beyond the antagonistic relations between lesbian and gay male theoretical work requires thinking beyond "these structuring tensions" or merely exploiting them to theoretical or political advantage at strategic, unpredictable moments. By broaching the topic of these structuring tensions, however, Fuss's treatment of the issue importantly challenges lesbian and gay studies to focus on the irreducible differences in which its multiple subjects are always already inscribed.

Although neither Sedgwick nor Fuss is engaged in an historiographical project, they both make gestures towards historicizing the terms of their discussion. In their separate analyses, the differences between gay male and lesbian theories that Fuss identifies and those between gay and feminist theories that Sedgwick delineates, are (in part) historically rooted in what John D'Emilio has called "the gendered seventies."[9] Their attention to the discourses that both clarified and constructed the highly differentiated social relations between gay men and lesbians in the 1970s is suggestive of new reading strategies. As both Sedgwick and Fuss indicate, these discursive formations created substantially reworked realities for queer historical subjects. A distillation of their most important insights, however, reveals ways of nurturing what I have suggested might be the democratic promise that adheres to the heterosocial relationships among queer historical subjects. Taking this suggestion seriously, including the lessons to be learned from the histories and theories of the gendered seventies, I turn now to ponder what we might learn from the new and emergent social, cultural, and political practices of the queer nineties, where queer means trouble as much as it means gay and lesbian.

Operating under the trope of queerness, recent attempts to problematize the problem of this queer heterosocial connection between men and women have begun to raise new sets of political and theoretical questions about the relationship between lesbian and gay identities, sexualities, histories, politics, and communities. Because queer has been theorized variously: as a way of "deconstructing our own discourses and their constructed silences" (Teresa de Lauretis); of "foreground[ing] same-sex desire without designating which sex is desiring" (Sue-Ellen Case); and of remarking "difference" (Allan Bérubé and Jeffrey Escoffier); both its uses and its usefulness are multiple and open-ended.[10] Whether or not it has been fully adequate in its deployment, this decade's race for queer theory in gay and lesbian studies has been instructive and productive in so far as it has made us quite uncomfortable with once comfortable notions of opposition, hierarchy, and cultural privilege.[11] As a heuristic device, "queer" has helped focus attention on how culturally sanctioned versions of the normal and the natural have been constructed and sustained, revealing them to be cultural fictions enabled only through their dependent relationship with the abnormal and the unnatural which these fictions themselves construct. In addition to exposing the arbitrary, albeit powerful and abiding, cultural privileges ascribed to the normal and the natural, the critical projects developed by queer theorists have also sought to problematize gay and lesbian identity categories as aspects of stable and unified subjects. Yet, while this transition from antecedent terms such as gay and lesbian to the term queer has significantly altered the scope of inquiry to include a larger range of deviant sexualities and has focused its inquiry on the problem of heteronormativity, queer theories and practices have not abandoned all ties to those earlier forms. It is, however, less the case that this transition is incomplete, than that queer historical subjects have inescapable gay and lesbian pasts.

   By shifting the grounds of theory, these new projects neither deny nor accept the continuity between lesbian and gay experiences "across" gender. Rather, they seek in part to investigate – or at least to allow the investigation of – the intricacies of these relationships as historical, discursive, and fictive formations. Yet as suggested by Sue-Ellen Case's cautious advocacy of "queer" as a non-gendered heuristic, theoretical, and political device in which she maintains her feminist skepticism of such projects and warns of the historical and theoretical "problems that congregate at this site" where gender is not specified, the term cannot by itself resolve the divisive, difficult, and dire differences that are everywhere felt throughout society, even as our queerness connects us in ways that do not exist in straight worlds.[12]

For both Sedgwick's and Fuss's analyses as well as those of other theorists who have taken up what Fuss calls the "gay/lesbian binary within homosexual theory and politics," it is precisely the tension of gender as the sexual difference between (lesbian) women and (gay) men that constitutes the fundamental difference informing "queer" theories and practices, but what about other differences? While the primary impact of coupling gay men and lesbians or replacing the gender-marked phrase gay and lesbian with the ungendered term queer is the (possible) elision of differences that are specific to gender, differences of race, class, generation, geographic location, and political ideology, for instance, retreat to a secondary status in, become imperceptible under, or altogether disappear from both of these analytical frameworks. Neither privileging the mark of gender nor foregrounding an ungendered same-sex desire guarantees that we will see the multiple social differences which are always there right alongside of gender and which are themselves integral to sexual identities and the performativity of gender.

The bracketing of difference enabled by the use of the term "queer" creates voids that are at once productive *and* dangerous. On the one hand, the term seems to offer a certain kind of reconstructed identity by positing the sexual difference of gay men and lesbians (and perhaps bisexuals, transsexuals, and other sex/gender outlaws) from straights. On the other hand, because "queer's" lack of specificity is multiple, its use has responded to and helped proliferate discussions of queer differences – sometimes deferring endlessly to a place of further differences and generating problems that are frustrating, often excruciatingly painful to deal with, and reflective of the difficulty of maintaining a pronounced and insistent critique of the vastly complex structures of homophobia and heterosexism (which is due in large part to the very vastness and complexity of homophobia and heterosexism, including often substantial disagreement as to what they "are"). Yet, the various kinds of stalemates that arise around differences among queer historical subjects are substantially less troubling than the persistent, if at times latent, refusal to acknowledge and address those differences. For this reason, I would advocate a reading of the trope of queerness that expands rather than eliminates the lesbian-feminist critique of gay liberation and reconnects us to the historical importance of the split that developed between gay and lesbian-feminist liberation in the early 1970s. As Jewelle Gomez remarks in regard to that split, "[f]eminism remained a difficult issue for gay organizations because it asked that members struggle internally with their own privilege as well as externally with other causes of oppression."[13] Gomez's point echoes Eve Sedgwick's advice that gay theorists learn from feminist theory how to approach the multiple, contradictory social positions in which queer historical subjects are situated and reminds us that queer difference is itself internal as well as external. But her assessment of the historical split between gay and lesbian politics, cultures, and theories during the gendered 1970s *also* supports continued separatism*s* along the varied lines of differentiation and identification in lesbian and gay communities during – and after – the queer 1990s.

Although each of these articulations of difference might operate on foundationalist assumptions that seek to stabilize social relations and our knowledge of them by rooting them outside of history and discourse (something that is no less true of attempts to foreground sexuality than it is of efforts to foreground race or gender), it is also important to consider how the multiplication of differences among queer historical subjects *recombines* overlapping, mutually constituting categories of social organization and identification to create particular and temporary social positionings. On such a reading, differences among queer historical subjects do not irrevocably obviate any simultaneous basis for identity as a particular instead of a general necessity, so long as one does not subscribe to a narrow, and therefore fragile, sense of identity.

When I began this chapter with the suggestion that identities and differences – which I referred to as the very substance of gay and lesbian communities, movements, and theories – are complex *and* partial, contradictory *and* supplemental, intractable *and* mutually constitutive, I had in mind an understanding that derives from recent treatments of identity in the overlapping literatures of cultural studies and social movement theory as well as lesbian and gay studies and feminist theory. These works have proposed looking at identity as a point of suture, as a temporary, non-exclusive, and political point of identification – and, more by implication than by direct discussion, regarding difference as a point of rupture, as a temporary, non-inclusive, and political point of differentiation. In Stuart Hall's statement of this position, identities are "the necessary fiction of politics," and they are "always representations" that "can never be adequate

to the subjective processes which are temporally invested in them."
Recalling Benedict Anderson's study of the rise of nationalism, *Imagined Communities*, Hall argues that political collectivities based on identity "are of necessity *imaginary* communities." From his perspective on identity as a "holding operation," multiple versions of identity-based politics nonetheless remain viable and powerful social formations, yet just as importantly, this argument makes impossible the construction of such politics on the basis of a "fixed" notion of identities "which have some relationship to 'what one really is,' or around interests which can be constructed or mobilised without understanding that they are always partly the result of an imaginary investment."[14]

The key terms of Hall's formulation – especially its anti-essentialist emphasis on subjectivity, imagination, instability, and impermanence – are echoed in a range of writings specific to queer historical subjects, including Eve Sedgwick's and Diana Fuss's psychoanalytically inflected post-structuralist views of gay and lesbian identities, and more recently the supplementary work of queer social theorists that looks critically at the *social* dynamics implicated in the politics of identification and differentiation.[15] These latter projects in particular have insisted on regarding collective queer identities as temporary but compelling fabrications that are remade through the actively inventive projects of political mobilization and social movements, rather than as antecedent, immutable, essential truths. By placing dissent, ambivalence, and uncertainty at the center of queer heterosociality's democratic promise in the reconstruction of the public sphere, these various investigations of the fictive and consolidating processes of identification, how movements refashion identities, and the specific necessities of identity politics allow a more cogent and flexible understanding of the uneasy and troubled affiliations that mark queer activism of the past decade.

In the readings of specific places, moments, and texts undertaken in chapters 4, 5, and 6, I draw upon and expand these arguments by focusing on how queer fictions of the past themselves construct identities and differences. Before undertaking those particular analyses, however, I need to look directly – albeit queerly – at the question of history.

Queer/ed History

What is history? Judging by what we hear around us that is a question that needs to be asked again.   (Paul Veyne)[16]

Naturally, *our* relationship to history is very different from *theirs*.
(Stefan Dudink)[17]

In the rest of this chapter, I work to draw out some important implications of recent critical studies of historical representation that have collectively, though not in unison, radically defamiliarized our ways of knowing the past and have responded to as well as provoked a significant crisis in historical studies. I suggest that the idea of history itself is problematic, various, and unstable and lay the groundwork for subsequent chapters in which I take advantage of the consequences of that argument for understanding the complex identifications of queer historical subjects and compound the already contradictory relationships of queer heterosociality. Speaking in terms of gay and lesbian historical imaginations rather than simply historiography, I seek to develop a conception of history in lesbian and gay studies and queer theory that takes individual, collective, and popular memory practices seriously as cultural and political interventions into everyday life and that recognizes representations of the past as powerful social/cultural texts in their own right. From this perspective, lesbian and gay historical imaginations can themselves be read as central and important aspects of the multiple "reverse" discourses on homosexuality.[18] Assessing and pursuing these multiple resonances requires a suspension of our (dis)beliefs – a suspension that forms part of the destabilizing and defamiliarizing promise of the ways in which the term "queer" has been revitalized in recent years.

In one of the few explicit attempts to bring the challenges and interventions provoked by the term "queer" to bear on gay and lesbian historical studies, Donna Penn has recently argued for a historiography that upsets conventional categories of identity. "Just as 'queer' politics intends an oppositional relationship to the normal," she writes, "so too must queer history."[19] Specifically, although she is also concerned with revealing the shortcomings of a queer revisionist history that regards (previous) gay and lesbian activism, organizing, and scholarship as assimilationist or conservative, Penn draws on queer theory's interest in cultural representation, discourse, subjectivity, and the workings of the normal to reframe lesbian history. In so doing, she hopes to circumvent "the production of knowledge on homosexuality [based] on definitions that depend upon homosexual identity" (p. 29) and the "invisibility of lesbians in much of the historical record" (p. 35). "A queer approach" to documentary evidence and cultural texts, she argues,

might permit reading lesbianism where, initially, it doesn't seem to be. An application of queer theory to the historical investigation of lesbianism need not require sources that are explicitly about lesbianism for them to shed light on the operations of the normal. (p. 35)

Penn's particular use of the term "queer," in fact, works to circumvent one of its critics' most insistent and important claims – namely, that by eliding the gender differences inscribed in the earlier distinction between gay and lesbian, queer (once again) makes lesbians invisible.

Penn's lively assessment and substantial remapping of deviant historiography, however, also suggest their own lacunae in relation to what she refers to as "the way in which we conceptualize history and the subject(s) of inquiry" (p. 34). I want to draw attention to another valence of the trope of queerness – of queer's "oppositional relationship to the normal" – that amplifies important questions about history writing raised by a number of scholars in diverse disciplines. This other reading of the trope of queerness is partially anticipated by my crucial difference with Penn on what she calls "Queer and the Historical Imagination" (p. 32) and "the way in which we conceptualize history" (p. 34). Whereas Penn writes in the singular, I would – quite emphatically – insist on the plural to retain the social/cultural significance of the vast array of queer historical imaginations and the ways "we" conceptualize history.

Queer theory's quick and powerful problematization of a phenomenally wide range of constructed and arbitrary regimes of the normal has not been accompanied by an interest in looking at historiography itself as one of these regimes. There are, however, compelling reasons to remain suspicious of historiography. The "bourgeois science" of history as practiced in the academy and elsewhere can – I would argue that it *must* – just as readily be regarded and investigated as an aspect of the culture of heteronormativity against which queer subjects (ostensibly) align ourselves.[20] As Michael Warner points out, "'[q]ueer' gets a critical edge by defining itself against the normal rather than the heterosexual, *and normal includes normal business in the academy*."[21] By engaging this oppositional relationship to the normal practice of proper historical representation, the remainder of this chapter delineates the second key operation involved in the theoretical project of queer cultural studies of history. In reevaluating lesbian and gay historical studies from a queer perspective, we need to remain skeptical of "history proper" (without dismissing it) so that we can reflect critically on the multiple, discordant, and inconsistent nature of queer historical practices and the stakes involved in such historical representations.

Gay and lesbian historians have consistently maintained that the study of the past provides cogent means of addressing many of the concerns of the present. Penn also makes such an argument at the end of her essay, suggesting that "the practice of history . . . must . . . delineate how [social, cultural, and political] changes are produced, when and by whom, if they are to serve as 'lessons of history.'"[22] Her argument reiterates John D'Emilio's assertion in his influential 1983 article "Capitalism and Gay Identity" that "a new, more accurate theory of gay history" is essential to any "political enterprise" enabling lesbians and gay men "to preserve our gains and move ahead."[23] D'Emilio seeks to move away from the conception of the past used by gay liberationists of the late 1960s and early 1970s who, he contends, in the absence of a "history that [they] could use to fashion [their] goals and strategy," invented a "mythical history" based on their personal experiences "which [they] read backward in time" (p. 101).

Part of this mythology, D'Emilio argues, is the idea that "until gay liberation, gay men and lesbians were always the victims of systematic, undifferentiated, terrible oppression" (p. 101). D'Emilio also challenges the widely accepted "myth of the 'eternal homosexual'" that claims that "[w]e are everywhere; not just now, but throughout history, in all societies and all periods" (p. 101). Against this static, universalizing myth, D'Emilio asserts that "gay men and lesbians have not always existed" but "have come into existence in a specific historical era" (p. 102). Myths such as these, D'Emilio stresses, "have limited our political perspective" and "locked our movement in place" (p. 101). Interestingly, however, D'Emilio does acknowledge that "lesbians and gay men won significant victories in the 1970s and opened up some safe social space in which to exist" (p. 108) despite the persistence of homophobic and heterosexist oppression. In making this evaluation of the 1970s, D'Emilio implicitly recognizes the profoundly consequential point that, however outdated by the early 1980s, the invented mythologies that formed the basis for gay liberation-era historical self-representations were on some level politically effective for more than a decade.

Though part of D'Emilio's project is to join with other scholars, writers, and community-based historians in making information about the lesbian and gay past available to a number of diverse readerships, his "theory of gay history" is also intended to interpret this past, to generate understanding of it, to derive meaning from it. For such a theoretical project, gay and lesbian history is not merely the chronicling of past events that had some bearing on lesbian and gay lives or of historical issues pertaining to homosexuality; significantly, "history" is also a way of making sense of that historical material in order to draw conclusions from it, to make it "useful." D'Emilio wants, as he puts it in his theoretical essay, "to suggest some political lessons we can draw from this *view of history*" (p. 102, emphasis added). In other words, D'Emilio proposes that there is a strategic, even a moral, teaching to be learned from the study of gay and lesbian history, but we need to have a system of understanding – what he calls a "theory of gay history" – through which we can evaluate the past before we can determine what it means for us in the present and how it might help us in the future.

Gay and lesbian historians' understandable desire to derive political lessons from the study of the past recalls some of the arguments developed in recent critical studies of historical representation. As Hayden White observes,

A specifically *historical inquiry* is born less of the necessity to establish *that* certain events occurred than what certain events might *mean* for a given group, society, or culture's conceptions of its present tasks and future prospects.[24]

White's claim is part of a larger body of recent works by a number of literary and historical theorists who have argued that historiography is a privileged system of signification for representing the past, highly rule-governed and decidedly unnatural. The kind of understanding provided by a specifically historical inquiry, they maintain, is itself a construction that is subject to a whole series of questions regarding interpretation, representation, and narrative.[25] Situating historians' representations of the past within these literary-theoretical critiques of historiography as method allows us to focus attention on those aspects of history-writing which can be neglected, begged, avoided, or disavowed in its practice – namely, as White puts it, "the extent to which the discourse of the historian and that of the imaginative writer overlap, resemble, or correspond with each other."[26] These displacements or concealments of its codes of representation are central to historiography's process of representing the past. As Michel de Certeau has succinctly and forcefully put it in an essay on the science and fiction of historiography, "[r]epresentations are authorized to speak in the name of the real *only if they are successful in obliterating any memory of the conditions under which they were produced.*"[27]

These formal theoretical critiques of historical method have coincided with the complex and varied intersections of multiple emergent intellectual and political projects: for instance, women's movements and feminist theories, Third World liberation struggles and post-colonial literatures, civil rights movements, Marxist cultural critiques, multicultural scholarship, as well as gay and lesbian practices. By forcing an awareness that, as Linda Hutcheon puts it, "history cannot be written without ideological and institutional analysis, including analysis of the act of writing itself,"[28] these theoretical and political arguments provide us with a critical vantage point for rethinking the notions of "history" that are so confidently invoked by lesbian and gay historians and in the larger arena of queer self-representations. My use of the term "gay and lesbian historical imaginations" is, in part, an attempt to respond to these theoretical and political challenges to formal history-writing, neither dismissing the crucial work of politically engaged revisionist historiography nor remaining beholden to such research.

In developing this project of rethinking gay and lesbian historical imaginations, I am also interested in interrogating what the short-lived British collective Popular Memory Group in the Centre for Contemporary Cultural Studies has called the "implicitly non-popular effects of focusing on formal history-writing, a practice largely colonized by academic and professional norms," as a way of presenting the past.[29] The group's interest in "popular memory," which they "define first as an *object of study*, but, second, as a *dimension of political practice*" (p. 205), echoes my own interest in developing a conception of queer historical studies that takes lesbian and gay representations of the past seriously as political and cultural interventions in(to) the present. Although popular memory retains certain aspects of inherited social practice, it also manifests an oppositional form that resists the public representations and dominant memory practices sanctioned by the conservative reliance on tradition or official history. Both the paradoxical politics of visibility manifested in Gay and Lesbian Freedom Day Parades and the lasting scholarly interest in gay and lesbian history, for example, are in part attempts to refuse the abiding denial and censorship of homosexuality in the dominant culture that claims territorial rights over tradition and official history as its exclusive, and unified, domain. In addition, such popular memory projects can have both individual and collective dimensions simultaneously, as is the case with the Names Project quilt that serves in part as a catharsis for those still living, as remembrance of those now dead, and as a way to "bear witness" to the complex collective losses of the global AIDS epidemic.[30]

Approaching historical representations through popular memory is particularly important for directing our attention to historical subjects' various locations in the present; the concern with memory focuses our attention on the relationship between past and present rather than the past alone as a distant, discrete object. "It is because 'the past' has this living active existence in the present," Popular Memory Group points out, "that it matters so much politically" (p. 211). Stressing "the need to expand the idea of historical production well beyond the limits of academic history-writing . . . to include *all* the ways in which a sense of the past is constructed in our society," Popular Memory Group calls for "the recognition of a larger social process in which 'we ourselves are shaped by the past' but are also continually reworking the past which shapes us" (p. 207, quoting

Christopher Hill). The point I wish to make, however, is not that popular memory is somehow a "better" or "more authentic" representation of the past than historiography – that, lacking professional status, popular memory is not just as much encoded as history proper. Indeed, in so far as they set out to establish a pan-cultural lesbian and gay existence, certain "popular" texts that seek to reclaim a "lost" gay and lesbian history can be criticized for reiterating culturally specific identity categories as universal.[31] Addressing history on the larger scale that includes "*all* the ways in which a sense of the past is constructed in our society," however, would allow us to consider the differences *and* the similarities between representations of the past and might yield valuable insights into the formation of historical meaning.

Though I want to maintain that the past really did happen – or, as Fredric Jameson puts it in *The Political Unconscious*, that "history is not a text" – the analysis of historical representation as an act of writing acknowledges Jameson's immediate qualification of his claim. This qualification reframes historical questions in terms of our access to the past "in textual form" only, whether as archival documents, published memoirs, oral history interviews, public celebrations, or any other form of historical memory.[32] Rather than merely revealing "facts" about the reality of the past, these various sorts of historical texts actually rework it and in the process construct the facts they represent and the relationships among them. For this reason, historical truths – the strategic lessons to be drawn from history – might well be approached through a literary historiography that draws on the dissolution of the distinction between realistic and fictional representations as proposed by recent theories of discourse and locates "factual" as well as "subjective" truths in the ways we understand, interpret, and write about the past.

The Popular Memory Group collective also argues that the theories and methods of historical inquiry are useful "as an element in strategic analysis. We start from the need to understand contemporary political problems. We seek to examine the conditions on which contemporary dilemmas rest" (p. 212). Echoing D'Emilio's position, they recognize that the study of history can offer "salutary 'lessons.'" This approach to history sees "[t]he link between past and present . . . [a]s in essence an exhortatory one . . . warning, for instance, against returns to past disasters" or "identifying 'traditions' which then become resources for present struggles" (p. 212). Adding to these two conceptions of the relationship between past and present, however, Popular Memory Group further insists that "all political activity is intrinsically a process of historical argument and definition . . . all political programmes involve some construction of the past as well as the future, and . . . these processes go on every day" (p. 213). For their part, philosophical and tropological analyses of formal history-writing make somewhat similar or analogous claims regarding the political or ideological entailments of historical representation. As White puts it, "every historical narrative has as its latent or manifest purpose the desire to moralize the events of which it treats."[33] Or, in Michel de Certeau's formulation, "history is always ambivalent: the locus that it carves from the past is equally a fashion of *making a place for the future*."[34]

In demanding accountability for how history is written and how the past is represented, these literary, philosophical, tropological, and political critiques of historiography allow and encourage us seriously to entertain doubts about the "normal" practice of proper history. These critical approaches to representations of the past are particularly relevant to queer historical subjects. From the perspective afforded by such investigations, we might discern an analogous relationship between, on the one hand, the "regimes of the normal" which privilege the constructed categories of heterosexuality *and* historiography and, on the other hand, the disruptive challenge to both of these regimes posed by "queer." Just as the powerful strand of queer theory energizing so many recent gay and lesbian studies projects draws complexly and not complacently on psychoanalytic and poststructuralist theories of subjectivity, queer cultural studies of history as I envision them are deeply indebted to these also quite substantial critical theories of historical representation.

Like the "utilitarian" arguments for gay and lesbian historical studies made by others that insist on their critical, descriptive, explanatory, and strategic uses, I also recognize that history lends meaning to individual and collective experiences, suggests answers to urgent questions, and offers directions for social movements. My interest in regarding gay and lesbian historical imaginations as hermeneutically and politically charged sites for constructing, maintaining, and contesting queer identities, however, is intended to problematize the construction of such meanings, answers, and signposts by insisting that historical understandings are subject to questions of interpretation, representation, authority, textuality, and narrative and by resisting the cultural power historiography ascribes to itself through its concealed codes of representation. Although queer historical subjects' interventions into the past are themselves powerful social practices in the construction of identity, community, and politics, the various ways "we" imagine ourselves historically also serve to problematize and contest those identities, communities, and politics. The nuanced, often contradictory, highly charged conceptions of queer subjectivities articulated by these multiple fictions of the past compound the stakes involved in gay and lesbian historical studies. It is, however, precisely in order to take these individual, collective, and popular memory practices seriously as interventions into the politics and culture of everyday life that lesbian and gay studies needs to consider how queer fictions of the past reconstruct the present moment.

Because history refuses to be disciplined into univocality, rather than "a" theory of gay history, we need to develop many complementary, even contentious, theories. Initially, multiplying queer theories of history will foster the recognition, production, and analysis of the surplus of significations of queer fictions of the past. The particular project that I am calling for – queer cultural studies of history – is one trajectory in the multiplication of these theories. But it is an important one, for it facilitates (connected) oppositional critiques of heteronormativity, the constraints of modernist historical narratives, and naturalized representations of the past. Recognizing that the relationship between past and present allows no suggestion of finality, queer cultural studies of history rely on and draw out the postmodern interventions that encourage an incredulity towards metanarratives, trouble closure and resolution, valorize instability, and remain suspicious of coherence. As postmodern practices, queer cultural studies of history alter – or, better, amplify – the urgency of the ongoing conversations on gay and lesbian histories that we hear around us. From this perspective, queer fictions of the past are not sites of latent meaning. Rather, they are dynamic rhetorical performances that engage in specific dialogues between past and present to offer, as Dana Polan suggests, "some possible meanings" of history and that therefore demand readerly participation in the construction of those shifting, fluid, and inconsistent possibilities.[35] Moreover, queer cultural studies of history must also look at the relations between texts and the contexts of reading and writing in order to pursue a critical assessment of the role of queer fictions of the past in historical processes themselves. Such a project would, for instance, allow us to raise new questions about gay liberationist mythologies of the past and how their specific reworkings of history enabled, and perhaps hindered, particular kinds of political organizing.

Although I argue that queer fictions of the past need to be regarded as performative rather than literal or descriptive retellings of history, this way of reading and writing about the past is nonetheless consonant with the possibility of evaluating claims to, and arguments over, historical representations. By refusing to understand identities as singular, fixed, or pre-existing, however, queer heterosociality's complex articulation of the problematic subjects of lesbian and gay studies makes it impossible to base these evaluations on a straightforward or comfortable understanding of interests that are self-evidently and eternally linked to particular individuals or social groupings. It is, in fact, a central element of queer fictions of the past to articulate the construction of those interests and to historicize the complex intersections of identities and differences. Certainly, the interpretive challenge created by the expansion of historical languages, the articulations of new relationships to the past, and reconsiderations of the possibility for history in the absence of universals compound the tasks of historical argument for gay and lesbian subjects as much as they do for anyone else. Yet, although queer cultural studies of history presume the problematics of historical representation and knowledge, such projects are equally committed to addressing the construction of current meanings from the traces of the past that are sutured together by gay and lesbian historical imaginations – historiography, community celebrations, political action, film and video, invented traditions, and so forth. No less than history proper, queer fictions of the past make strong claims for the importance of history – recounting, explaining, and interpreting the past. Without evacuating the pressing need to select, evaluate, and come to terms with historical representations, however, queer cultural studies of history seek to investigate how these projects present their arguments and to rethink their specific claims to the past in light of the troubled criteria on which such selections, claims, and evaluations are made.

Finally, like all representations, queer fictions of the past are *partial* perspectives, in the fullest sense of that word: susceptible to reinterpretation and revision, they are both incomplete and value-laden, telling us something but not everything about the world and doing so at a certain cost. As problematic subjects marked by the multiple differences inscribed in queer heterosociality, queer historical subjects are interested in and represent the past in ways that are also fraught with multiple differences. Under these conditions, the meaning of "history" – readily recognized as an "essential" domain in queer knowledges – itself becomes problematic and open-ended. We need, therefore, to analyze queer fictions of the past and the kinds of identities and differences they produce in much the same ways as we analyze any of the other practices within lesbian and gay cultures. To anticipate somewhat and to borrow Stanley Aronowitz's characterization of postmodern thought's denial of "impartial competence," queer cultural studies of history regard historical representations as "bound to discourse," as incomplete and value-laden narratives about the world, and as instances of the close configuration between knowledge and interest.[36] In the sense that they are bound to discourse, however, queer fictions of the past are also bound to displease as well as please, to challenge as much as confirm.

The next four chapters are intended to do precisely that, looking in turn to recent work in US gay and lesbian historiography, the recurrent place of ancient Greece in white gay and lesbian historical imaginations, the importance of Stonewall as a queer cultural text, and the promising re/writings of the past by gay men and lesbians of color which have made dramatic interventions into the production of historical meanings.

PART II

Reading past histories

3

Re: reading queer history

Although social constructionist historical–theoretical accounts of gay identity formation have tended to reiterate overlapping stories of modernity, modernization, and modernism, they have also been integral (if often neglected) parts of a series of postmodern cultural, political, and historical practices that distrust and disrupt universalizing and deterministic metanarratives. Not only have these historically based theoretical arguments about gay identity disputed naturalized views of heterosexuality, the family, and reproduction while objecting to homophobic assumptions embedded in multiple cultural, social, and political practices, but they have also challenged false universals that derive from humanist notions of an eternal, immutable human nature or essence. In addition, these projects have laid the groundwork for critical historiographies of the contingent construction of sexual differences that integrate and build upon anti-essentialist analyses of gender, race, class, and other forms of social power, domination, and resistance. Indeed, as their own kind of postmodern interventions, social constructionist projects in lesbian and gay historical studies might themselves be better understood as open-ended and contingent works-in-progress that refuse to accept or make arguments about "the final analysis." In this sense, these historicizing investigations encourage ongoing revisitation and reconsideration. Notwithstanding the contingency of such arguments, however, their analyses of multiple discursive regimes also leave them open to re-reading as social/cultural texts that reconstruct queer identities, histories, politics, and communities in particular ways and with particular consequences.

As I point out presently, the continued investigation of queer pasts within a constructionist framework has resulted in important revisions, clarifications, and reinterpretations of some of the arguments of this first generation of gay and lesbian social history. Recently, a newer generation of gay and lesbian historical research has begun undertaking projects that trouble this earlier work's tentative generalizations about gay identity formation by looking at the intersection of multiple social differences in the construction of queer heterosociality. Because these newer investigations of the varied histories of gay men and lesbians include looking at how queer historical subjects have made *and made sense of* their cultures, they have begun to recognize the important role of popular memory, mythologies of the past, and gay and lesbian historical imaginations in the reverse discourses on homosexuality. Accordingly, although neither sanctioning nor foreclosing them, these studies indirectly point to the possibility of critical analyses of *contemporary* queer fictions of the past. It is the project of queer cultural studies of history to carry out these kinds of analyses by reading past histories.

Gay and lesbian historiography as works-in-progress

This newer generation of US gay and lesbian historiography has pursued substantially more focused, specified, and detailed research agendas than the earlier social constructionist histories of gay identity formation. Yet these later studies are also deeply informed by the principal heuristic strength of the earlier social constructionist theoretical arguments. Several of these studies – in particular George Chauncey's *Gay New York*, Lillian Faderman's *Odd Girls and Twilight Lovers*, Elizabeth Kennedy and Madeline Davis's *Boots of Leather, Slippers of Gold*, and Esther Newton's *Cherry Grove, Fire Island* – have made "gay and lesbian historiography" much more complex and subtle.[1] Their complexities and subtleties have modified some of the grander, more tentative claims of the accounts of the social construction of *the* "modern" *homosexual*, while retaining and building upon the proposition that sexual identities are "made" or "constructed" through and in relation to social practices and discursive regimes and are therefore malleable and historically contingent.

Each of these four studies utilizes oral as well as archival sources, but there are also important differences in their approaches. Chauncey, Kennedy and Davis, and Newton analyze communities in specific locations; all of them combine, as Kennedy and Davis explain of their project, "ethnography – the intensive study of the culture and identity of a single community – with history – the analysis of the forces that shaped how that community changed over time" (p. 2). In contrast to these local ethnographic accounts, Faderman's book offers a comprehensive survey of the variety of lesbian experiences in twentieth-century America that pays particular though not exclusive attention to "the development of lesbian subcultures" (p. 7). Also, although each book draws on material and makes arguments pertaining to both lesbians and gay men, three of them – Chauncey's, Faderman's, and Kennedy and Davis's – develop principally along gender separatist lines of inquiry and analysis. Surely responding to (without explicitly acknowledging) criticism of male-authored social constructionist accounts of gay identity formation for inadequately addressing lesbian subjectivity and the gender dynamics of discourses on sexuality, Chauncey explains his decision based on "the differences between gay male and lesbian history and the complexity of each [which] made it seem virtually impossible to write a book about both that did justice to each and avoided making one history an appendage to the other" (p. 27).[2] Because they are situated within feminist discourses and women's history, however, the separatist investigations pursued by Faderman's and Kennedy and Davis's studies might be seen as articulating this difference differently and drawing on highly resonant political as well as academic reasons for their choices. Yet despite strong historical and political reasons for pursuing separatist accounts, such decisions also articulate the mark of gender in ways that are different from, perhaps even inconsistent with, its particular articulation in the place and period under investigation. As Kennedy and Davis note in their book, for instance, "there was no ideological commitment to [gender] separation" in the lesbian community they studied; nonetheless, "there was some [gender-based] difference in culture and consciousness, as expressed most clearly by rough and tough lesbians who had little to do with gay men" (p. 381).

While these separatist strategies not only make analytic sense for such focused research and also help circumvent the shortcomings of previous "gender-blind" materialist historical frameworks, they postpone consideration of what remains the substantial historical coincidence of the two gender-separated social constructions, "gay" and "lesbian." In the introduction to his book, Chauncey explicitly remarks the significance of this (temporary) pause in co-gendered research, noting that "it will ultimately prove important to theorize [the] historical development [of lesbian and gay cultures and representations] in conjunction, but it may take another generation of research on each before an adequate basis for such theories exists" (p. 27). In contrast to these three separatist studies, Newton employed a co-gendered approach to writing about "America's first gay and lesbian town" – a remarkably ambitious undertaking given the long-existing "male framework" (p. 288), which has reinforced the "impression of a gay male, not a lesbian [or shared] space" (p. 1). This decision, however, was necessitated by the fact that "women have played a critical role in every era [of Cherry Grove's queer history] but the 1960s" (p. 8). In part, then, when read in conjunction with the other three studies, Newton's book details how gender-separatist accounts unified around exclusive categories of male and female might overestimate the social and cultural ruptures between gay men, lesbians, and "our" respective histories, yet Newton also problematizes her co-gendered analysis of queer heterosociality in Cherry Grove by pointing out that lesbians "remained a distinct and separate group whom gay men recognized as alien kin, sisters yet strangers" (p. 203).

Both Kennedy and Davis's and Chauncey's texts clearly depict working-class lesbian and gay subcultures that contradict "[t]he old dogma" (Chauncey, p. 10) that has continued to locate the initial development of queer identities in middle-class white (male) social worlds. Although there is a marked difference between the portrayal of the working-class lesbians in Kennedy and Davis's study who "built a community in bars or at house parties" (p. 8) and that of the working-class gay men in Chauncey's study who forged their gay world in New York's streets (ch. 7), both books contest the extent to which material constraints and close-knit family relations made it difficult for working-class women and men to make lesbian and gay life-choices. Relatedly, these two texts problematize the central importance of the promise of anonymity afforded by cities that marks the earlier literature. "To focus on the supposed anonymity of the city," Chauncey argues,

is to imply that gay men remained isolated from ("anonymous" to) one another. The city, however, was the site not so much of anonymous, furtive encounters between strangers . . . as of an organized, multilayered, and self-conscious gay subculture, with its own meeting places, language, folklore, and moral codes.   (p. 133)

For working-class lesbians, as Kennedy and Davis argue, butch-femme roles "were a powerful social force. They were the organizing principle for this community's relations with the outside world" and worked to make lesbians visible "to one another *and* to the public" (p. 152, emphasis added).

Not only do Chauncey and Kennedy and Davis reconstruct the urban environments of New York City and Buffalo as complex, fractured, and contested sites that have allowed multiple possibilities for queer historical subjects to intervene in, expand, and redefine the public sphere. Drawing on these and other conceptions of urban space, they also propose that their particular findings might be extendable to other cities, whether to "other thriving, middle-sized US industrial cities with large working-class populations" (as Kennedy and Davis say, p. 10) or as "*prototypical*" of "the urban conditions and changes that allowed a gay world to take shape" (as Chauncey argues, pp. 28–29). Of course, urban life has only been part of the history of gay and lesbian communities in the United States. Indeed, as

Newton maintains in her study, the "ills" associated with life in large urban areas helped foster the class-based seasonal exodus of gay men and lesbians from the cities to Cherry Grove "where gay men and women began building their summer capital." "The first gay Grovers," she explains, "seem to have sought both a more authentic experience in nature and an escape from the controls imposed by their (relatively privileged) work and social lives" and "settled in a spot . . . on the far margin of metropolitan life" (p. 13). This temporary migration or "escape" from the city, however, was also fueled by the pervasive homophobia and heterosexism of even the most viable urban areas in which gay men and lesbians could exist publicly. "Resorts like Provincetown, Massachusetts, Key West, Florida, and the Grove," Newton observes, "were (and to a large degree still are) the *only* places gays could socialize and assemble without constant fear of hostile straight society" (p. 2).

Despite the ways they complicate notions of "gay identity" and show how there is no such unitary phenomenon as "the" homosexual, all of these studies remain deeply concerned with questions of same-sex sexuality, a concern that lends the texts themselves distinctively gay and/or lesbian identities. In other words, though revealed as internally differentiated, the "modern" category of homosexuality nonetheless provides the thread that sutures together the diverse, unstable, contradictory, and shifting histories recounted within each book and also ties all four texts together. Kennedy and Davis, for instance, provide a "comprehensive survey of the lesbian community in Buffalo, New York" (p. xvi) and address "problematic issues about boundaries" (p. 3) to look at "questions about the changing forms of [lesbian] identity and community" (p. 7). Central to the forms of lesbian identity they explore, however, is women's explicit acknowledgment of "their erotic interest in women" (p. 12). In thus differentiating their study from previous lesbian-feminist formulations that "privileged passionate and loving relationships over specifically sexual relationships in defining lesbianism" (p. 12), Kennedy and Davis return to "sexuality as an *essential* ingredient in lesbian life" (p. 13, emphasis added). Although understood differently, Faderman's pursuit of change and diversity in twentieth-century lesbian experiences is also organized on the basis of an "essential" sexuality, so that her history includes women "whose lives were lived primarily or exclusively within heterosexual communities and who may be considered lesbian only by virtue of their secret sexual identification" (p. 7).

Somewhat differently, Chauncey's book is focused both on the multiple forms of male sexual identity in the period between 1890 and World War Two and on a nascent "gay identity" coming into full emergence. "The ascendancy of *gay*" as term of identification, he argues, reflected . . . a reorganization of sexual categories and the transition from an early twentieth-century culture divided into "queers" and "men" on the basis of gender status to a late-twentieth-century culture divided into "homosexuals" and "heterosexuals" on the basis of sexual object choice.   (p. 22)

Although this "transition from one sexual regime to the next was an uneven process, marked by significant class and ethnic differences" (p. 13), Chauncey speaks consistently of "a" gay world "because almost all the men in those networks conceived of themselves as linked to the others in their common 'queerness' and their membership in a single gay world, no matter how much they regretted it" (p. 3). Chauncey's supposition of discontent among the members of the imagined community of gay men in New York City is of grave concern for contemporary considerations of queer identity politics, for the ambivalence it suggests points both to the (seeming) intractability of identity and to the rejection of static or comfortable notions of who "we" are, raising significant questions about how, why, and to what degree same-gender desire transcends other social differences, particularly race and class. Furthermore, his suggestion that "[t]he limited convergence of lesbian and gay life in the 1920s . . . marked an important stage in the emergence of the social category of the homosexual" (p. 228) raises provocative questions about how future generations of research will address the historical construction of a queer heterosociality across gender with its own unsatisfactory kinds of identification.

In a series of autobiographical, theoretical, and historiographical presentations, Allan Bérubé has also begun to address questions of class and homosexuality. Focused especially on the working-class dimensions of gay and lesbian political history in a way that includes a strong commitment to race and gender analysis as well, however, his work-in-progress is rather different from the studies discussed above.[3] The conception of homosexuality as a primary political identity developed by such homophile organizations as the Mattachine Society and the Daughters of Bilitis, Bérubé argues, has tended to require a significant amount of "fitting in." "Coming out," in other words, can be *not only* the twin processes of personal disclosure and the development of a public homosexual presence identified by Jeffrey Weeks *but also* a process of reidentification structured by preexisting middle-class norms, values, and attitudes that require abandoning, denying, or hiding working-class backgrounds, experiences, and allegiances. For working-class gay people, however, other political movements have existed that have advanced gay rights through a committed cross-sexual class solidarity without privileging gay identity over other identifications and social experiences. To find and understand specifically working-class gay political history, Bérubé maintains, we have to look at the centrality of work itself in the lives of working-class people and, especially, the social, political, and economic movements of labor unions.

In a case study of one such movement, Bérubé has been investigating the gay male networks that were a central part of the West Coast Marine Cooks and Stewards Union (MCSU). From the early 1930s to the 1950s, the communist, multiracial, and queer-positive MCSU effectively organized its members and maintained a "controversial commitment to working-class solidarity, racial equality, and organizing 'queer work' [work that is performed by or has the reputation of being performed by queers, such as that of the MCSU]." In contrast to the Mattachine Society's efforts to fashion a gay identity-based minority political movement beginning in the early 1950s, MCSU members created a multiracial work culture and union-based movement that "developed their own collective strategies to achieve the broad political goal of surviving with dignity as working-class queers."[4] Falling victim to McCarthy-era anti-communism and homophobia, the MCSU was ultimately crushed by the FBI, the Coast Guard, and anti-communist (white) male union members. The MCSU's demise, Bérubé points out, coincided with the emergence of the latter Mattachine Society which had effected its own purges of radical members by exploiting precisely the same anti-communist hysteria over "un-American" activities that had destroyed the once powerful union. Unlike the middle-class white gay men who lost their "movement" in this reorganization, however, the purged and blacklisted MCSU members were unable to find subsequent work, an extreme situation that suggests some of the differences between labor and sexual politics.

By concentrating on working-class solidarity and (implicitly) class antagonism in gay history, Bérubé's research and the tentative conclusions he has drawn from it problematize the drive for unity in modernist narratives of gay identity formation. That the very different fates of the Marine Cooks and Stewards Union and the post-purge Mattachine Society were not only located at the same crucial historical juncture but were also enabled by the same salient political and cultural features critically compromises understandings of gay identity as a point of suture, resolution, and cross-class allegiance. Indeed, the central and effective role that the homophile organizations played in the creation of postwar gay and lesbian communities needs to be seen not as autonomous from but rather as integrally related to the changing nature of social movements in the post-World War Two era, in which the Old Left's preoccupation with the working class as the locus of mobilization and change was decentered by the emergence of the New Left's focus on cultural rather than economic radicalism

exemplified in the shift away from economic- towards identity-based political movements.[5] But, in spite of a number of social and historical forces
that facilitated them (including the limitations of class-based politics), as
Bérubé's study of the MCSU attests, such shifts were given a powerful
helping hand by the collusion of a variety of anti-communist, anti-labor
forces that quite effectively suppressed radical union organizing across
racial boundaries. In other words, John D'Emilio's argument in *Sexual
Politics, Sexual Communities* that the "pioneering . . . [gay and lesbian]
activists had not only to mobilize a community" but in fact "had to create
one"[6] has an important corollary. The legacy of their organizing efforts is
a double-sided coin, for those activists' relative success in making a homosexual minority in the United States might just as plausibly be regarded as
both the creation of one particular possibility for queer historical subjects
and the articulation of a powerful hegemony that eliminated other possibilities for gay political organizing in, as D'Emilio phrases it, their "retreat to
respectability."[7]

The presence of the past

Sharply focused on many of the tensions and contradictions of queer
heterosociality, this recent work in lesbian and gay historiography has
successfully furthered the project of dislodging the modernist meta-
narrative of gay identity formation that glosses over difference, anomaly,
and specificity. Their allegiance to the kinds of evidence and argumenta-
tion that constitute the norms of academic historiography, however,
reconfirms the modernist premise that the past is a knowable object of
study. Although they upset narrative closure and the presumed unity of
identity, these projects' adherence to the codes of proper historical representation precludes them from making a more skeptical assessment of the
nature of historical knowledge or broadening their analyses to rethink the
meaning of the "historical" contingency of queer identities and the ways in
which queer historical subjects continue to use the past to construct notions
of self, community, and politics. I do not, of course, want to overstate this
point; in part, these studies have sought to show that how gay men and
lesbians have understood and articulated their relationships to the past has
had important implications for the development and transformation of
queer public spheres. George Chauncey, for example, devotes several pages
of *Gay New York*'s chapter on "the making of collective identity" to a discussion of gay folklore where he pays particular attention to the
"constructi[on of] historical traditions" as crucial ways that gay men fash-
ioned and interpreted their culture. "By imagining they had collective roots

in the past," he writes, "[gay men] asserted their collective identity in the present."[8]

The project of queer cultural studies of history which I have been discussing extends such investigations from a concern with the past to an interest in the present to examine the past–present relation embodied in and reconfigured by gay and lesbian historical imaginations. These queer popular memory practices, which include but are not limited to historiography, not only attest to the abiding presence of the past and its significance; they also engage history in ways that foster community, expand public and private discourses on sexuality, construct queer subjectivity, and insist on the differences, specificities, and particularities of (queer) historical relations. As postmodern practices that suspend the search for historical certainty, the reading strategies of queer cultural studies of history also mark a shift away from the residual empiricist impulse to determine *what* the past means for lesbians and gay men while turning towards the substantially greater instability of *how* the past's multiple textualizations construct meaning for queer historical subjects.

The case studies presented in the next two chapters – ancient Greece and Stonewall – are only two social/cultural texts that might be read under the critical lens of queer cultural studies of history. Indeed, as evidenced by the rather different projects of Katie King, Stuart Marshall, and Martha Gever, the autobiographical, theoretical, and polemical writings of Audre Lorde, the use of the pink triangle as a symbol of gay resistance, and cinematic representations of lesbian history in the postwar era make complex, conflicted, and compelling interventions into the production, deployment, and circulation of queer historical knowledges.[9] I believe, however, that Greece and Stonewall offer particularly rich, productive, and problematic texts for re-reading under such a lens. In anticipation of the specific arguments about Greece and Stonewall that are developed in the readings in the next two chapters, I want to state briefly my reasons for selecting them. To begin with, I was interested in looking at "large" topics that recur in a variety of textual forms, and the more I considered them, the more I was taken by the rather different consequences or possibilities borne and enabled by these two examples of the abiding presence of the past for queer historical subjects.

Gay men's and lesbians' relationships to ancient Greece cannot be understood apart from the abiding cultural capital that the Classics wield in the academy and their literal and symbolic place in the larger arena of political discourse and "cultural warfare" involving questions of education, "Great Books," multiculturalism, and "civilization." Many – far too many – projects in anthropology, art history and practice, historiography, political

theory and rhetoric, popular culture, and literature have directly contributed to the deep resilience of a constructed, idealized, and imagined ancient
Greek culture in the articulation of Western(ized) conceptions of nation,
race, and citizenship, including the construction of an unacknowledged
white racial identity. But this large, rather general cultural investment is not
the only reason I look at the place of ancient Greece in gay and lesbian
historical imaginations. Greece also matters because of its particular
historical importance in the specific discourses of gay and lesbian subject
formation through which, as Michel Foucault puts it, "homosexuality
began to speak in its own behalf."[10] In other words, investigations of prior
and continuing uses of Greece as a potent social/cultural text in the reverse
discourses on homosexuality have substantial relevance to understanding
how queer historical subjects exist collectively, including how racial politics
are evacuated from or marked within these constructed collectivities.
Despite their drawbacks, which I believe are many and varied, these particular queer fictions of the past are in need of being taken seriously as part
of the problematic relations of queer heterosociality.

Likewise, the Stonewall riots also have enormous cultural salience for
queer historical subjects, but I think with quite different effects. It is hardly,
or perhaps just barely, an exaggeration to say that Stonewall is a ubiquitous
symbol in contemporary US gay and lesbian cultures, and in various other
national contexts as well.[11] The riots, and the strategies of cultural politics
they ostensibly inaugurated, not only signal an historical rupture between
different modes of political activism (pre-Stonewall homophile assimilationist politics versus post-Stonewall gay and lesbian liberation and reform
politics), but they also figure centrally in public definitions of and struggles
over community. In contrast to ancient Greece's problematic recurrence in
queer fictions of the past, the Stonewall riots, it seems to me, possess much
more democratic promise. The promise of queer fictions of Stonewall,
however, does not inhere in some kind of settled, determined meaning;
rather, representations of Stonewall serve as contests for (alternative)
meanings that enable public discussions in which queer heterosocial differences are developed, maintained, and reconstructed.

4

The lesbian and gay past: it's Greek to whom?

Sappho's alright, but she doesn't represent me.   (Alice Yee Hom)[1]

In 1883, John Addington Symonds, British poet and critic as well as argu-
ably the first English-language historian of homosexuality, published a
private edition of his short treatise on "Greek love" bearing the unassum-
ing and unexposing title, *A Problem in Greek Ethics*.[2] As the research of a
number of more recent scholars has begun to show in fuller detail, with
greater theoretical acumen, and at a time of relatively freer political
possibilities, male homosexual relations or *paiderastia*, the gender-specific
focus of Symonds's essay, did indeed constitute a very particular problem
in Greek ethics; more pointedly, however, male homosexual relations also
constituted, as Symonds would refer to it in a subsequent essay, "a problem
in *modern* ethics."[3] Without detracting from Symonds's insights into Greek
history and customs, I want to explore a rather different, more implicit
strand of his thought, a thread which is intricately woven into the larger
web of Western cultural imaginations and which persists in gay and lesbian
writings, yet – as the adjectival phrase "gay and lesbian" would anticipate
– one which bears heavily the mark of gender. Like his compatriot Lord
Byron, who some seventy years earlier had escaped the homophobia of
Georgian England through a self-imposed temporary exile to Greece
enabled in part by the Romanticist movement's conception of classical and
Homeric Greek culture as the pure origin of Western civilization, Symonds
had a class-, culture-, and gender-specific relationship to the ancient Greek
world which brought it readily to mind as a starting point for his groundbreaking and courageous anti-homophobic scholarship.[4] Symonds sought,
as Jeffrey Weeks argues, "to establish, by using the Greek analogy, that
[male] homosexuality *could* be accepted as part of the social mores of
society."[5]

I begin this chapter with a fairly simple premise: in the years since Symonds published his essay, figurations of Greek culture have consistently served as one of the most important points of origin for a conception of homosexuality that differs from the wide-ranging, though often various, divergent, and site-specific, hostile and condemnatory hegemonic religious, popular, medical, and juridical views in the West.[6] In the pages that follow, however, I seek to problematize the status of these queer relationships to ancient Greece. In a preliminary reading, I substantiate and qualify this premise by marking out a central aspect of the salience of gender as an axis of differentiation in these recurrent imaginary "returns" to ancient Greece by gay men and lesbians, highlighting an important difference between certain gay male and lesbian uses of Greek culture in the articulation of a (sexual) subjectivity. In a second reading, I seek to develop an explicitly non-essentialized conception of culture, cultural difference, and position-ality through which we might consider the reflexive constitution of con-temporary gay and lesbian identities in relation to racial formation. While this latter strategy is not meant to unify men and women "across" gender, it is intended both to pull together and to draw out a number of somewhat shared racialized – whether or not unambiguously racist – tendencies in gay and lesbian historical self-representations by white men and women.

One consequence, and I believe a healthy one, of this move towards developing a discourse on race in relation to white racial/identity formation is the positioning of white queers differentially to queers of color as historical subjects. A discourse on race can and needs to be developed in relationship to gender and sexuality, as has been convincingly demon-strated by the emergence, especially since the early 1980s, of a critique of racism, racial representation, and "color blind" analysis within feminist thought and practice. In the context of a co-gendered gay-and-lesbian – or, perhaps, queer – studies, however, such a discourse remains relatively impoverished in comparison with the allied yet different project of feminist inquiry, though to suggest that it has been non-existent or insignificant thus far would slight the vast array of queer theories and texts, especially by people of color, which have deliberately and provocatively made race a central mode of analysis, reflection, contestation, and politics in relation to lesbian and gay cultures.

"It's Greek to whom?" – the question posed by this chapter's title – is meant to remark and to ironize the centrality of these various but recurrent thematizations of ancient Greece in lesbian and gay cultural, historical, and political production. While asked rhetorically, my particular question here is intended to raise some initial points regarding a strategy for reading the histories of lesbian and gay male historical self-representations as contestable, politically saturated texts. In this sense, I am pursuing a rather different trajectory in lesbian and gay historical studies from the one David Halperin develops in his recent collection of "essays on Greek love." Though he recognizes the ways in which representations of the Greeks have provided lesbians and particularly gay men "potentially meaningful 'guide[s] for life,'" Halperin argues that "[i]f we are ever to discover who 'we' really are, it will be necessary to examine more closely the many respects in which Greek sexual practices *differ* from 'our own' – and do not merely confirm cherished assumptions about 'us' or legitimate some of 'our' favorite practices" (pp. 1–2). In the context of this chapter, I argue that it is precisely the effects of these beliefs and "cherished assumptions" in relationship to ancient Greece among other locations and moments which need to be thought through theoretically, historically, and culturally if we are going to take seriously Halperin's diacritical marking of the terms "we," "our own," "our," and "us" which clearly insists on the problematic nature of these concepts of collectivity and selfhood.

In their different projects of using ancient Greece as the raw material for fashioning new possibilities for homosexual existence, these conceptual *models* of Greek antiquity have been neither historically inevitable nor politically innocent. As one of the abiding fictions of so many European and Euro-American gay and lesbian uses of history, these figurations of Greek culture, though remarkably gender-differentiated, are invested in cultural and political practices whose status cannot remain unexamined. This investigation of lesbian and gay uses of the Greek past seems particularly authorized at a time when recent public debates on race, ethnicity, and multiculturalism have so thoroughly problematized notions of culture, identity, and history – both inside and outside of the discourses on lesbian and gay identities. For it is, after all, one of Western culture's most persistent "cherished assumptions" that ancient Greece is somehow "ours" – whether as a "guide for life" or as the society which best elucidates "our" historical "differences" from it in order for us "to discover who 'we' really are."[7]

Integral to this particular assumption about who "possesses" the heritage of ancient Greece is the historically recent origin of currently dominant conceptions of classical civilization. Martin Bernal calls the development of this view of Greek history "the fabrication of ancient Greece," a process which took place during the eighteenth and nineteenth centuries as new notions of progress and racial inequality became paradigmatic in both scientific and historical studies. The construction of Greece "as the epitome of Europe but also its pure childhood," Bernal argues, worked to displace the view of their history conventionally held by the Greeks themselves in the classical and Hellenistic ages, according to which "Greek culture had arisen as the result of colonization, around 1500 BC, by Egyptians and Phoenicians."[8] This latter view, which Bernal refers to as the "ancient model" of Greek history, proved problematic to post-Renaissance and modern European thinkers; the ancient model, Bernal argues, "had placed a barrier in the way of the new faiths that Greek culture was essentially European and that philosophy and civilization had originated in Greece" (p. 31). A far-reaching and compelling aspect of Bernal's hypothesis on "the fabrication of ancient Greece" as the origin of European culture is the necessity, as he puts it, "not only to rethink the fundamental bases of 'Western Civilization' but also to recognize the penetration of racism and 'continental chauvinism' into all our historiography, or philosophy of writing history" (p. 2).

Moreover, although the reverse discourses on homosexuality, such as Symonds's arguments by analogy, seized and transformed the emergent hegemonic discourse on Greece in specific and bounded locations, the very resistance to the operations of power enabled by this repositioning has been just as firmly rooted in England's changing conceptions of race, masculinity, nationhood, and citizenship in the latter half of the nineteenth century. In particular, as Linda Dowling has argued, the study of Greek culture was crucial to the liberal university reform efforts which were intended to provide a secular resolution to the cultural crisis nineteenth-century England faced "by producing a new civic elite to lead Britain out of socio-cultural stagnation and into a triumphal age of imperial responsibility: Britain as a world civilization with Oxford as its intellectual center."[9] Thus, although they have been important forces in the reconstruction of social definitions of homosexuality, the strong resonance of Greek culture in gay and lesbian historical self-representations over the last century and its continued salience in the present cannot be severed from the larger cultural projects of the fabrication of ancient Greece and the particular set of meanings ascribed to it, including the heavy political and cultural baggage of deep-seated theories of civilization, discourses on national survival, and racial belief systems.

By beginning the work of problematizing the histories of identity formation in relation to the manufacture of a mythical "Greek" past, I hope to enable a more cogent analysis of some of the structuring tensions traversing the varied spaces of lesbian and gay politics and theory. How have conceptions of Greece as the "founding myth" of lesbian and gay existence framed contemporary discourses, representations, politics, and possibilities? How, in turn, are the broad, multiple, and highly vocal demands of multiculturalism likely to be negotiated in the formation of new lesbian and gay – or "queer" – political subjects? Before proceeding in this direction, however, I need to give a fuller, if also occasionally speculative, account of the premise framing this project and to point to an important textual and contextual difference between lesbian and gay readings/writings on "Greek" matters.

Although in the latter half of this chapter I implicitly stress certain similarities in the cultural imaginations framing the construction of these images of Greece as salient possibilities for identification, there are important gender-marked differences in the forms they have taken which need to be remarked if we are to begin to understand not only the specificities of lesbian and gay identities but also their relationships to each other. In general, conceptual models of Greek antiquity have been used much more readily by gay men than by lesbians; such a disproportionate use of the Greek past is consistent not only with the overwhelmingly greater availability of male-authored and male-centered discourses but also with the particular textual silences historically imposed on women by men, a kind of silencing which is magnified in the long tradition of male commentaries on Sappho.[10] In broad relief, and not surprisingly, the contours of gay male and lesbian representations of ancient Greece have been symptomatic of the larger social context(s) in which men and women are (sexual) subjects.

A significant aspect in which gay and lesbian discourses are differentiated, and one which I will turn to immediately to highlight their inscription in/through gender, has been that while certain gay male writers have had to attempt a (partial) *de*sexualization of relationships between men, a number of lesbian writers have been faced with the problem of getting outside of the sexual vacuum of what Carroll Smith-Rosenberg has called "the female world of love and ritual."[11] This problem is suggested by Michael Bronski and Judy Grahn, two contemporary writers who consider, respectively, "the making of gay sensibility" and "the lesbian poetic tradition." As Bronski suggests, "[g]ay men in Victorian England prized the classical tradition of male friendship" as "a safe way to express emotions" which served as "both a *cover* for forbidden sexuality and a manifestation of male bonding."[12] By way of contrast, lesbians have regarded Lesbos, in Grahn's words, "as an ideal place, home, where one is central to one's own life, and where the women are bonding, are sisters – *and more than sisters*."[13] For gay men, Greek models have helped attenuate (or "cover") an excess of sexuality, while for lesbians, the more restricted use of Sappho and Lesbos has offered an explicitly sexual model ("more than sisters") for female relationships.

Beginning with late-Victorian homosexual writers and continuing through to the present, idealized forms of male friendship have been recurrent themes in an ever-growing variety of textual articulations of the "meaning" of male homosexuality. Idealized representations of the classical tradition of male friendship worked somewhat to circumvent the climate of hostility towards male homosexual behavior pervasive in late-Victorian society.[14] Speaking on his own behalf during his first trial for "gross indecency," Oscar Wilde, the embodiment of the emerging social category of the male homosexual as a new "type" of sexual actor, claimed precisely such an idealized notion of male relations. In his famous apology for male love (whose "words produced a spontaneous outburst of applause from the public gallery"), Wilde denies the physical aspects of love between men while highlighting its emotional and affectional aspects:

"The love that dare not speak its name" in this century is such a great affection of an elder for a younger man as there was between David and Jonathan, *such as Plato made the very basis of his philosophy*, and such as you will find in the sonnets of Michaelangelo and Shakespeare. It is that deep, spiritual affection which is as pure as it is perfect.[15]

John Addington Symonds and Edward Carpenter, both contemporaries of Wilde, develop his brief allusion to a "pure" and "perfect" "spiritual affection" as an important basis for their own, more elaborate defenses of male homosexuality.

In *A Problem in Greek Ethics*, Symonds argues that the Greeks distinguished between "two separate forms of masculine passion . . . a noble and a base, a spiritual and a sensual" (p. 15). Symonds assures his (possibly quite alarmed) reading audience that his essay is only marginally concerned with "the baser form of paiderastia," because, as he puts it, "vice of this kind does not vary to any great extent, whether we observe it in Athens or in Rome, in Florence of the sixteenth or Paris of the nineteenth century." Rather, Symonds's text addresses "[t]he nobler type of masculine love [which] is, on the contrary, almost unique in the history of the human race." Before proceeding in this direction, however, Symonds hastens to point out that Greek love – "this unique product of their civilization" – while "not free of sensuality, did not degenerate into *mere* licentiousness" (p. 17, emphasis added) and stressed "a code of honour [which] distinguish[ed] the noble from the baser forms of paiderastia" (p. 48). Symonds reiterates this (his or the Greeks'?) somewhat ambivalent or coded attitude towards the "sensuous" aspects of male friendship in his subsequent essay *A Problem in Modern Ethics*. There, in a chapter on "Literature – idealistic," Symonds insists that "it must definitely be stated that [Walt Whitman's poetry] has nothing to do with anomalous, abnormal, vicious, or diseased forms of emotions which males entertain for males" (p. 115). On the following page, however, Symonds tempers his rather hyperbolic – and, one might well suppose, somewhat feigned – disgust for sexual relations between men:

Whitman never suggests that comradeship may occasion the development of phys-ical desires, but then he does not in set terms condemn these desires, or warn his dis-ciples against them . . . Like Plato in the Phaedrus, Whitman describes an enthusiastic type of masculine emotion, leaving its private details to the moral sense and special inclination of the person concerned.   (p. 116)

By invoking a split between the public world and "private details" (a separation which did not exist in England until 1967 when the recommendations of the Wolfenden Report to decriminalize consensual homosexual acts between men over the age of twenty-one were finally passed into law), Symonds effectively conceals the (potentially) sexual aspects of male friendships while still being able to argue that "homosexual passions" have a "spiritual value" which can be "utili[zed] for the benefit of society" (p. 1).[16] On the other hand, Symonds was severely constrained by what was possible at the time, for the mere appearance of his texts was problematic, as their limited publication for private circulation would indi-cate.

Edward Carpenter makes a similar distinction between love as "physical instincts and acts" and love as "the inner devotion of one person to another."[17] A substantial portion of his writings on "the intermediate sex" is devoted to arguing this point with specific reference to then-current atti-tudes towards same-sex love:

It would be a great mistake to suppose that [Uranians'] attachments are necessarily sexual, or connected to sexual acts. On the contrary (as abundant evidence shows), they are often purely emotional in their character; and to confuse Uranians (as is often done) with libertines having no law but curiosity in self-indulgence is to do them a great wrong.   (pp. 193–194)

Carpenter refers to "Polynesian Islanders," "Albanian mountaineers," and "other notably hardy races among whom this affection has been devel-oped" (p. 210), arguing, in fact, that "[t]he annals of all nations contain similar records" of a socially useful "homogenic love." He suggests, however, that "probably among none has the ideal of this love been quite so enthusiastic and heroic as among the post-Homeric Greeks" (p. 201). Carpenter seeks to argue that "Greek love" took a non-sexual form that emphasized a pure, sublimated friendship between men: "the *ideal* of Greek life was a very continent one . . . a base and licentious indulgence was not in line with it" (p. 214). By emphasizing the "ideal" nature of these relationships, however, Carpenter implicitly recognizes the possibility of failing to meet that ideal, of occasionally "slipping," as do Symonds's Greeks, into "sensuality," though presumably still not taking the degenerate form of "mere licentiousness."

In spite of the recent explosive growth of gay and lesbian historical studies, the continued paucity of documentary evidence, personal records from the past, and oral history projects makes it difficult to gauge just how influential specific texts have been in the individual and collective lives of homosexually active men and women outside of certain privileged networks of writers, scholars, and artists. While there do exist a number of archival records and more recent oral history interviews that indicate something of the scope, if not the full depth, of the varieties of lesbian and gay investments in representations of ancient Greek "homosexuality," it remains unclear whether these are in any sense representative of the lives, experiences, and imaginations of other gays and lesbians. Several interviews with older gay men in Britain have begun to shed light on the importance of the small body of writing on homosexuality that was available in the earlier part of this century. Kevin Porter and Jeffrey Weeks, editors of a recently published volume of these interviews, suggest that:

writers such as [Edward Carpenter, Havelock Ellis, and John Addington Symonds] provided a vocabulary through which homosexually inclined people could give meaning to their feelings, and recognize that they were not the only such individuals in the world. The explanations offered in such books . . . provided for some way of understanding difference that proved potent in shaping emergent sexual identities.⑱

In other words, while in no sense actually definitive of homosexual identities, the works of Carpenter, Ellis, Symonds, and other turn-of-the-century sexual theorists opened up various new areas for imagination, dialogue, and organization.[19]

While it is difficult to assess fully the effects these British discursive practices had on "popular" lesbian and gay imaginations in the USA, they have contributed to the formation of new sexual identities here as well. In *Gay American History*, his groundbreaking collection of documentary material on the legal, medical, social, and political aspects of homosexuality in what is now the USA, Jonathan Katz has identified an early instance of Symonds's influence in the USA. Citing a letter from the ongoing though intermittent correspondence between Symonds and Thomas Sergeant Perry – "an American educator, literary, historian, editor, and friend of Henry James" – Katz argues "[t]hat Symonds's homosexual emancipation efforts had some early influence in the United States." Specifically, in a letter to Perry dated March 27, 1888, Symonds referred to his essay on Greek ethics, which he had sent to Perry some time previously, suggesting the possibility of an even larger, but still clandestine readership extending beyond the circle of close friends and colleagues in England among whom Symonds had originally circulated his text.[20]

Katz's more recent collection, *Gay/Lesbian Almanac*, excerpts a case study included in the chapter on homosexuality in Joseph Collins's 1926 book, *The Doctor Looks at Love and Life*. A female music teacher at a Southern college, having been abandoned by her lover Rachel who was beginning to speak of marriage to a man, wrote to Collins in search of advice about the "aberration" of her "homosexual attraction." Distraught over Rachel's increasingly cold and distant treatment of her, the letter writer sought "some way to renew [her] interest in life." By this time, she was already familiar with Edward Carpenter's *Love's Coming of Age* and "knew that [she] belonged to the 'intermediate sex.'" A search of nearby university and medical libraries for additional "information regarding the subject that interested" her proved fruitful, bringing to her attention "the lyrics of Sappho" about whom she "endeavored to find all [she] could" as well as "John Addington Symonds' remarkable book *A Problem in Greek Ethics.*" Yet, having "learned that the Aeolian women had made a degeneracy out of what the Dorian men have made a virtue," she felt "more of an outcast than ever."[21] Thus, while providing lesbians and gay men with the ability to understand their "differences," not only have such texts operated within historically embedded ideologies of gender and representations of men and women, but they have also not been exclusively "liberatory" or "progressive" in their effects. Though an assessment of the full scope of its significance can only remain highly speculative, the continuing overall importance of private library searches by lesbians and gay men looking for information on themselves would tend to suggest that many others besides Perry and the unnamed woman in Collins's study might well have come across Symonds's book – or, given its scarcity, at least references to it – throughout the past century or so.[22]

In contrast to Symonds and Carpenter, who sought in ancient Greece an apology for or an amelioration of the "excess" sexual signification becoming increasingly attendant on male relationships in late-Victorian England, Renée Vivien and Natalie Barney, two ex-patriate anglophone authors living in *fin-de-siècle* Paris and writing in the language of their adopted home, were inspired by the life and work of Sappho (some of whose previously unknown poems had been discovered by archaeologists just before the turn of the century) to imagine new forms of relationships among women. In their social and literary lives, Vivien and Barney, lovers from 1899 to 1901 and again briefly in 1904, sought to wrest control of representations of Sappho specifically and lesbianism generally from male authors to articulate an explicitly female sexual agency free from male-imposed constraints and expectations, this latter project one which was central to Sappho's own work as well.[23] Sappho, Lesbos, and Greek pagan-ism formed a central component of Vivien's and Barney's creative, erotic, and emotional life together. Both Barney and Vivien studied classical Greek: not only a bold move to access what Virginia Woolf would later call the "secret language" of men from which women were by and large excluded, but also a chance for Vivien – the more apt pupil of the two – to read, translate into French, and expand upon Sappho's fragments.[24]

Though it would not be until 1904 that they actually traveled to Lesbos, by 1901 Barney and Vivien had already begun to entertain the idea, suggested by Barney, of "gather[ing] a group of poetesses around us, deriving inspiration from each other, as Sappho did on Mytilène," in a sense attempting to actualize the mythical visions of Lesbos, Sappho, and her circle of poets that they had begun to create in their own work.[25] Vivien, identifying Barney "with her cult of Lesbos," subsequently wrote her enthusiastic response to this suggestion: "Sweet mistress of my songs, let us go to Mytilène" (p. 43). Though their voyage to Lesbos turned out to be somewhat of a disappointment in comparison to the images of Sappho's island that had animated them thus far, Barney and Vivien decided to stay on the island and moved into two adjacent houses where they intended to establish their poetry school.[26] Their endeavor was cut short, however, when Vivien left Mytilène to return to Paris and her new lover, the Baroness de Zuylen.

In her poem "Psappha revit" ("Sappho Lives Again"), published after this first of her trips to Lesbos, Vivien situates herself among a small number of female writers who have inherited and maintained Sappho's poetic tradition: "A few among us have preserved the rites/Of burning Lesbos, as golden as an altar."[27] Yet, not only did Vivien identify herself with/as Sappho, but she also occasionally regarded Barney as Sappho (and not just Atthis, Sappho's beloved), telling Barney that "[t]hat Sappho there is you," while re-reading Barney's *Cinq petits dialogues grecs* (*Five Short Greek Dialogues*) during their trip to Lesbos.[28] As Karla Jay notes in her critical study of the two authors, however, Vivien's and Barney's identifica-tion with and inspiration by Sappho was "less an act of resurrection than one of invention of new modes to suit the requirements of their own situa-tion." Their efforts "to re-empower Sappho . . . also empowered [them] by elevating an appropriate literary foremother."[29] More concerned with developing new possibilities for lesbian existence than with resurrecting Sappho through realist biographical representation, Barney and Vivien challenged heterosexualized versions of Sappho's life and work, in the process creating sharp critiques of misogyny and homophobia.

In Vivien's autobiographical novel *A Woman Appeared to Me*, the character Vally (based on Barney) declares, "Psappha [Vivien's preferred spelling of the poet's name] has certainly been the greatest of the misunderstood and slandered," reserving particular scorn for "the invented legend of a mad infatuation for the handsome Phaon, a legend whose stupidity is equalled only by its lack of historical truth."[30] San Giovanni, Vivien's *alter ego* and "the poetess of Mytilène" (p. 22) who "was certainly once born on Lesbos" (p. 10), also contests the historical veracity of the legend of Sappho's love for Phaon, offering a learned commentary which establishes that a "kind of low humor . . . invented the tale" of her infatuation with a man (p. 9). Following up on San Giovanni's observation, the narrator-protagonist (Vivien) insists on a "common-sense" reading of the tale's fabrication. "Only a vulgar mind," she points out, "could have substituted the bearded faces of Kerkolas and Phaon for the divine smile of Atthis and Eranna" (p. 9). All three characters – San Giovanni, Vally, and the narrator – offer different, but mutually reinforcing, feminist critiques of heterosexual and male-identified representations of Sappho. San Giovanni states her position bluntly:

I neither love nor hate men . . . What I hold against them is the great wrong they have done to women. They are political adversaries whom I want to injure for the good of the cause. Off the battlefield of ideas, I know them little and am indifferent to them.   (p. 11)

For her part, Vally contends that "[i]f there are only a few women writers and poets, it is because women are forced by convention to write about men." Sappho, Vally maintains, achieved immortality as a poet because "she didn't deign to notice masculine existence. She celebrated the sweet speech and the adorable smile of Atthis, and not the muscled torso of the imaginary Phaon" (pp. 48–49). Finally, the narrator expands her previous "common-sense" argument and quickly dismisses Petrus' claim of "the irresistible seduction of the male" as an explanation for Sappho's (alleged) heterosexual infatuation. Inverting heterosexist theories of the natural and the normal, she insists that "[t]hat [Sappho's attraction to Phaon and heterosexuality itself] would be a crime against nature, sir. I have too much respect for our friend to believe her capable of an abnormal passion" (p. 11).[31]

Barney's and Vivien's critique of heterosexism and their defense of homosexuality, though perhaps seen as "inconsistent" from certain contemporary vantage-points, made powerful statements in the early part of this century. While Barney and Vivien were critical of male-defined, heterosexist images of female sexuality, as Karla Jay observes:

their sexual paradigm left a woman with only two choices: to be a virgin . . . almost indistinguishable from the feminine ideal chiseled in marble by the men who had preceded them, or to be the suitor . . . but lacking that actual temporal power conveyed on real men by patriarchal society.[32]

At times, however, their texts did manage to forge a new possibility for female-centered sexual agency, albeit one that "combines" these two conceptions of "masculine" and "feminine" eroticism. In Vivien's "Bona Dea," the Sappho-based narrator declares:

I love you, [Amata]. I, Caia Venantia Paullina . . . love you with a sweet and imperious love. I love you both as a lover and as a sister . . . I shall be at once your master and your possession. *I love you with the frenzy of male desire and with a languid, feminine tenderness.*[33]

On the subsequent page, however, Vivien's narrator (Sappho) complicates this passage by claiming both sides of the dichotomy as dual aspects of the same "female love": "I will reveal to you the strength and the sweetness of female love" (p. 118).

Situating their work historically in relationship to other discourses on homosexuality, Gayle Rubin argues that Barney and Vivien "understood who they were and what they were up against" as lesbians. "There were few homosexuals of either sex who comprehended the dimensions of the homosexual situation."[34] Barney and Vivien were careful to distinguish between lesbianism and male homosexuality, however. "For the love between women," Vivien's Sappho declares in "Bona Dea," "is nothing like the love of men. I love you for yourself and not for myself" (p. 119). Vivien developed this distinction between women's and men's loves more fully in "The Friendship of Women" by desexualizing "the magnificent tenderness of Ruth the Mohabite for Naomi."[35] In contrast to "the affection of David for Jonathan [which] has always seemed more passionate than brotherly" (p. 101), Vivien's first-person narrator insists "[n]o carnal languishing crept into the friendship between these two women" (p. 102). Barney articulated a similar kind of distinction between male and female homosexual desire and practice. While she criticizes André Gide whose "promiscuity reduced to the level of erotic need . . . has done nothing to raise [homosexuality] above the level of heterosexuality," she extols "serial monogamy" among women as a creative practice:

And the great Sappho, did she not live in harmony with not one but several women friends? As one succeeded another they succumbed to that sweet rivalry which is more a source of inspiration than of discord, judging by the fragments that Sappho, the "tenth Muse," has left us . . .[36]

For Barney, herself an adventurous romantic who wrote of relationships that "fidelity is merely the triumph of habit over indiscretion" and "forever is too long a time," the essential difference between these "male" and "female" forms of sexual adventure obtained in a commitment which lasted longer than lust.[37] In any event, by turning to Sappho as a model, Vivien and Barney were enabled to reject masculinist conceptions of how women should be.

On one reading, the importance of Sappho in lesbian literary and historical self-representations is rather peculiar because virtually nothing is known of her life, and the extant poetry is also quite minimal. "Who is Sappho?" Dudley Fitts asks in his foreword to Mary Barnard's English translation of the poet's work. After naming a long list of rumored possibilities, he answers that "[w]e can agree to 'lyrist' and 'Greek' . . . The rest is speculation . . . We have heard a great deal about Sappho, and we know almost nothing."[38] So little record of Sappho exists, in fact, that for the entry under "Sappho" in their *Lesbian Peoples: Materials for a Dictionary,* Monique Wittig and Sande Zeig have left a blank page, a clear invitation to (lesbian) readers to write their own stories and draw their own conclusions from the absent and/or censored historical record.[39] Yet, for writers as different as Susan Gubar and Judy Grahn, it is exactly this possibility for speculation about the "meaning" of Sappho that makes her culturally and politically valuable. As Gubar notes in her "Sapphistries," "[p]recisely because so many of her original Greek texts were destroyed, the modern woman poet could write 'for' or 'as' Sappho and thereby *invent a classical inheritance of her own.*"[40] For her part, Judy Grahn argues that what has survived of Sappho is "enough to form the memory of a tradition" (p. 11). Lesbian poets, she maintains, "have consciously drawn from a tradition leading back to Sappho" because "[h]aving a mythic history . . . is completely necessary to the Lesbian poetic search for . . . a model of a new community, a new relationship of women to the world" (pp. 57–58, 113).

Since Symonds and Carpenter and Vivien and Barney produced their quite different works animated by visions of ancient Greece, Greek cultural practices have continued to be thematized, addressed, claimed, and deployed in a whole range of both antihomophobic and homophobic writings crossing generic and disciplinary boundaries to include fiction, poetry, and art as well as literary, social scientific, historical, and popular non-fiction texts. Although it would be impossible to give an adequate account of their scope and form, it is precisely the banal abundance of such "uses" of ancient Greece to which I want to call attention here as I shift my argument to the culturally problematic nature of the "mythical" backdrop to these discourses. Certainly by the early 1960s, both appropriations of and direct references to Greek sexuality had become a widespread trope for homophiles and homophobes alike to render their own particular conceptions and evaluations of homosexuality. Consider the following several examples of how "Greece" has been salient for queer historical subjects:

1 Lesbian and gay publications from the 1950s and 1960s regularly included articles on ancient Greek society, published excerpts from classical texts, and reviewed books dealing with aspects of Hellenic culture.[41]

2 The Daughters of Bilitis, the first national lesbian organization in the USA, rooted itself in representations of Greece, taking its name from Pierre Louÿs's mock-classical *Chansons de Bilitis* (*Songs of Bilitis*), a literary hoax published in 1894 in which Bilitis is portrayed as a lesbian and a contemporary of Sappho.[42]

3 The titles of certain lesbian pulp novels, such as Valerie Taylor's *Stranger on Lesbos* (1960) and *Return to Lesbos* (1963), not only invoked Sappho's island as a "lesbian space" but also reversed the homophobic implications of Richard Robertiello's *Voyage from Lesbos* (1959).[43]

4 Finally, modern Greece is increasingly being marketed as a destination for gay tourists, as a "site" rich with meaning for lesbians and gay men. One recent gay and lesbian travel guide suggests: "from its history to its myths, [Greece] probably offers more cultural resonance for gay foreigners than any other country. This is, after all, the place that gave its name not only to those Greek active/passive references in the personals, but to all lesbians."[44]

At the outset of *A Problem in Modern Ethics*, Symonds proclaimed that it is "the Greek race . . . to whom we owe the inheritance of our ideas" (p. 1). Nearly one hundred years later, David Halperin implicitly addresses Symonds's claim to a Greek cultural or racial heritage for himself and his unspecified (British? male? educated? white?) contemporaries (or might Symonds's own ideas reject the temporal specificity of the term "contemporaries"?). In his analysis of Harold Patzer's and Michel Foucault's "two views of Greek love," Halperin argues that the Greeks "are all about us," though "not because we are (allegedly) their inheritors."

Rather, the Greeks are all about us insofar as they represent one of the codes in which we transact our own cultural business: we use our "truths" about the Greeks to explain ourselves to ourselves and to construct our own experiences, including our sexual experiences.   (p. 70)

Thus, while earlier distancing himself from the tradition of gay writers who have found in the Greeks "a meaningful guide to life" (p. 1), at this point Halperin works to recuperate them in a similar fashion, albeit one that recognizes – in fact, *insists on* – a reading of cultural "truth" as "fiction." Though no longer valid as "a repressed presence inside us, or a utopian alternative to us," the Greeks, according to Halperin's assessment, are nonetheless still ours, "occupy[ing] an unexplicit margin framing our own self-understanding" (p. 70). For Halperin, in other words, the Greeks remain salient in our cultural imaginations, but now we must understand them in a new light, as a code or metaphor rather than as the kernel of our true being or as our positive elsewhere.

What has happened, then, to the diacritical marking of the terms "we," "our own," "us," and "our" with which Halperin introduced his discussion? Halperin's seemingly revised position confounds me, leaving me to ponder further: Why is Greece still "ours," and, to reiterate a question asked by Ed Cohen in a recent article on "gay" identity politics, who are "we" anyway?[45] The answer to the question of who "we" are, in this instance, seems to lie in the unquestioned – indeed, unquestionable – commitment to the belief that Greece is somehow still "ours." From this perspective, "we" are always already defined as those to whom Greece belongs, or – to retain Halperin's apparent "redefin[ition] of our relation to the Greeks" (p. 70) – "we" are those people for whom images of ancient Greece operate as cultural truths and as margins to self-understanding. That is, even after Halperin's revision of our understanding of ancient Greek sexual practices, "we" are ulti-mately "ourselves" precisely to the extent that Greece continues to inform "our" self-representations, a kind of self-understanding that would seem very much to situate a present-day "us" within the same logic of social reproduction and national regeneration that animated the imperial projects of the Oxford reform movement of the preceding century. Halperin's insis-tence that Greece forms the parameters of "our" self-understanding, in other words, begs the question: the lesbian and gay past is Greek to whom?

One important way of beginning to address this question is to consider alongside these metaphoric and literal "returns" to Greece the use of new, or alternative, or resistant, "national" discourses in the struggle over possible meanings for queer historical subjects. (Re)turning to a larger set of imagined cultural geographies in origin stories of queer subjectivity not only dispels the false (or at least falsely universalizing) characterization of "Greece" as a significant locus of cultural truth for "us," but it also enables a closer inspection of the ways that queer fictions of the past operate as powerful social/cultural texts in the ongoing (re)construction of gay and lesbian identities and differences.

In a recent exploration of "allegories of identity" for Chinese-American gay men published in *Lavender Godzilla*, the quarterly journal of the San Francisco Bay Area Gay Asian Pacific Alliance, Ming-Yeung Lu develops a critical reading of Bret Hinsch's *Passions of the Cut Sleeve: The Male Homosexual Tradition in China*, a book which, in Lu's words, "highlights certain *cultural* dynamics implicit in the discovery of a 'male Chinese homosexual tradition' by an American scholar."[46] While Hinsch's text offers a critique of Western categories of sexuality as essence and specifically their application to Chinese society, it does this, as Lu points out, by "contrast[ing] the West with a 'Chinese' *cultural* identity that appears to be as essentialist as the sexual identity he sets out to problematize" (p. 8). Within the frame of this culturalist argument, Hinsch sees only one viable option for Chinese homosexuals: "he advi[s]es today's Chinese homosexuals to return to their tradition – to the 'examples of antiquity' – [instead of looking] to New York and San Francisco for examples to emulate'" (p. 8).

In response to Hinsch's traditionalist outlook, Lu frames his own discussion to center not only on the question of political efficacy but also on that of positionality. "How useful is it," Lu asks at the outset of his essay, "to claim such a tradition for me, politically, as a Chinese gay man – in particular, one living in America?" (p. 7). Lu's critique hinges precisely on questioning Hinsch's desire "to retrieve a *pure* 'Chinese' sexual subject free of 'Western' influences." Yet such a romanticized "return to a pure point of origin" is clearly impossible, for the "present conditions [of Chinese society] have been affected – irreversibly – by their present and past encounter with the West" (p. 10). Thus, Lu suggests, "[f]or many Chinese homosexuals, 'to look to New York and San Francisco for examples to emulate' is not a confusion of one's cultural identity, nor simply a desire to be like the West, but an attempt to use available political concepts to break the social and political impasse of homophobia" (p. 10). Relatedly, Lu points out that Hinsch's "analysis completely obliterates the 'Westernized Chinese,' who crosses boundaries *the other way* geographically (those of us who are in New York and San Francisco) and/or metaphorically," while securely placing Hinsch himself in the position of the "expert who is capable of traversing cultural boundaries" (p. 10).

Though he seeks to sever his subjectivity from Hinsch's (romantic?) commitment to "traditional" or "authentic" Chinese culture, Lu nonetheless does not abandon the idea of "cultural difference." Rather, he reiterates the urgency of focusing on the historical specificities of racial and national formations, including an analysis of culturally mixed or hybrid forms. "The point is *not* that there is no 'culture,' but that any analysis of it must attend to the contingent social, political, and economic conditions that make up a certain 'culture'" (p. 12). Such attention to the contingency of the material conditions under which "a certain 'culture'" exists might enable a number of readings of Alice Hom's statement which stands as the epigraph to this chapter: "Sappho's alright, but she doesn't represent me." Provoked by the original (mis)placement of her talk on a panel of unrelated research, Hom made this statement in an extended moment of exasperation at what she perceived as the conference organizers' failure to distinguish the particular differences between the issues raised by two papers on canonical anglophone authors (Walt Whitman and E. M. Forster) and her presentation on Asian Pacific lesbians in the USA. In light of her attempt to articulate a specific diasporic history, we might cautiously interpret Sappho's inability to shoulder the burden of representing a Chinese-American lesbian as merely a mark of "cultural difference." After all, although her comment clearly tempers Sidney Abbott and Barbara Love's earlier enthusiastic pronouncement that "Sappho was a Right-On Woman," Hom assures us that Sappho is still at least "alright."[47] On this speculative reading, Hom's position would seem to be closer to Hinsch's than to Lu's: she feels a strong connection to or affinity with "Chinese culture," which is, as Lu reminds us, a culture that "today has much to do with its history of encounter with the West and its current position in a world economy dominated by post-industrial capitalism" (p. 12). Yet, such a reading of Hom's comment promises very little beyond a bland acknowledgement of the salience of "cultural difference" in gay and lesbian historical imaginations. It does not bring us any closer to understanding what processes of identification and disavowal – what systems of representation – make Sappho inadequate for (some) Chinese-American lesbians, nor does it address the specific cultural–historical interventions made by the Asian Pacific Lesbian Network (the focus of Hom's presentation) or by Hom's presentation itself.

Integral to Sappho's inability to represent Hom would be the Greek poet's very status as a representation in historically specific constructions of Western culture. Earlier in this discussion I took issue with David Halperin's revised thesis on "our" relationship to ancient Greece "as an unexplicit margin framing our self-understanding." If we follow through on the argument assumed by this position, however, a dynamic develops in which people for whom images of Greek antiquity do not produce "self-understanding" – people like Hom whom Sappho does not represent – are relegated not simply *to* the margins of "our self-understanding" but, in fact, *beyond* them. Thus, according to the logic of Halperin's argument, the representational relationship between Sappho the Greek poet and Hom the Chinese-American lesbian is indeed only one of pure cultural difference, and the reason Sappho does not represent Hom is simply because she *cannot* represent her – ancient Greece is emphatically *not* "hers" because Hom, or at least her cultural history, is "Chinese," not "Greek" (!). But, it seems to me, this relationship is not merely a banal instance of "cultural difference," for the dynamic implicit in Halperin's analysis actually constructs "our" "Other" through its very deployment: if Greece is not "yours," you are not "us." "You" are not marginalized in, but rather excluded from, "our" discourse.

In terms of the rhetorical question motivating this chapter, this point matters precisely because, following Halperin's argument, ancient Greece does not have an "authentic" or "essential" connection to any of "us." Though "the Greeks are hardly alien or lost to us," he writes, "we are . . . [not] their inheritors," nor "may [we] expect to find vestiges of them buried within ourselves, faintly discernible beneath layers of historical encrustation, transformation, and displacement" (p. 70). If this is in fact the case, if indeed Greece is really not "ours" except as a "neutral" or "historically open" signifier available to anyone, why then can it not be Hom's? If "the Greeks are hardly alien or lost to us," *why* does Sappho not represent her? Is it because Hom fails or chooses not to see herself in (representations of) Sappho, a possibility suggested by the speculative hypothesis that she feels an affinity with Chinese culture? In other words, is Sappho's failure to represent Hom something personal and unique to Hom, or might it be something else – either something about Sappho or something structural, something historical, something rooted in "the social," something specific to how Western culture has constituted itself in and through its relationship to the fabrication of ancient Greece?

Again, Lu's discussion of allegories of identity is useful, directing us to an historicized investigation of the various contemporary situations of Chinese-Americans. "[T]he culture of Chinese in America," Lu points out, "has much to do with their histories of immigration and *alienation*, their political status as Asian/Pacific Americans, and their dispositions today in ethnically, racially, and economically stratified America" (p. 12, emphasis added). Lu's mention of *alienation* certainly harmonizes with Hom's embittered response to the marginalization of her project which seemed to regard it only as an afterthought. The term also implies a certain kind of making or keeping "foreign" that pointedly recalls the histories of Chinese immigration to an "America" in which government policy, official history, and racial discrimination have continued to mark Asian Americans as foreigners.[48] Further, the use of the word *alienation* reminds us of the process of making "Other," of making "you" into someone who is not "us," which is implicit in Halperin's analysis. Perhaps, then, the "openness" of ancient Greece, or any particular ancient Greek figure such as Sappho, as a signifier of "self" is not as unlimited as it might at first seem. From this perspective, ancient Greece's ability to signify, its salience as a "margin framing . . . self-understanding," appears to be deeply intertwined with specific histories of racial formation and, in particular, the limits of white racial definition.

Of course, as I intimated above, ancient Greece is not the only cultural–historical site that has informed queer fictions of the past, and to focus on Greece as "the" site of queer origins in the reverse discourses on gay and lesbian sexualities obscures the variety of writings that make no attempt to situate themselves within a Hellenocentric tradition. Critic Bonnie Zimmerman addresses this issue in relation to the proliferation of "origins stories" in contemporary US lesbian literature. Though "Sappho's Island resonates in our [lesbians'] dreams and fantasies, and is recreated imaginatively in lesbian feminist literature,"[49] such an island of women, she points out, has proven to be problematic as a representation of lesbian origins, for it has consistently elided crucial questions of racial specificity, at once displacing women of color and subsuming them under the sign of the same within white lesbian political and cultural discourses. In response to the restricted notions of community embedded in the white Western model of the Island of Lesbos, Zimmerman suggests, "some [lesbian] writers [have begun to] propose a variety of islands and homelands – a cosmopolitan archipelago – to replace the old exclusivity of Lesbos" (p. 173). She points to the emergence of writings by lesbians of color in which "homelands" such as Carriacou, Jamaica, and Aztlán "all enter into the mythic structure" of lesbian discourses. On Zimmerman's reading, "Lesbian Nation is *becoming* ethnic, particular, and diverse through the politics of identity" (p. 173, emphasis added).

This account of recent lesbian literary history in the USA proposes a certain kind of multicultural stance whose posture is compatible with a pluralist purchase on various lesbian "pasts." In this way, we can read the texts of the Hellenocentric tradition and those of the "cosmopolitan archipelago" as making related if separate arguments about the past, deploying various imagined cultural geographies to construct specific and different historical identities. And, indeed, remapping the globe to make visible these multiple points of origin is a necessary, though not sufficient, step in a multicultural rethinking of lesbian and gay pasts. Yet, I would suggest that these two kinds of projects (those concerned with Greece and those concerned with other homelands) are not parallel or homologous practices: neither are they intended as such, nor do they operate that way. Although it recognizes their representation of alternative, previously excluded or silenced historical claims, Zimmerman's assessment under-estimates the significance of these more recent texts' racial and cultural cri-tiques as specifically political interventions into the discourses on subject formation both within US feminism and American culture generally.[50]

Against such a pluralist version of multiculturalism in which "cultural difference" is "reduced to ethnic nationalism," Lu offers a theory of multi-culturalism as a politically and economically engaged critique of the status quo. "Multiculturalism," as he formulates it,

is supposed to reveal the structures in our society that systematically keep certain *identifiable* groups from having access to power and resources, and thus from becoming speaking and acting subjects in their own right. The goal of multi-culturalism should be to open the way for changing these structures. It should not be merely a substitution of the melting pot with an ever-proliferating menu of novel dishes garnished with exotic meats and spices.   (p. 12)

Rather than regarding the texts of the "cosmopolitan archipelago" as simply addressing the question of equal representation of differences, in other words, we need to understand those texts through and because of their analyses of various, overlapping, mutually constitutive relations of power. Operating in part as sites of resistance to precisely those figurative constructions that insist that "we" – queer and non-queer alike – are still somehow bounded by ancient Greece, these "other" homelands bring to the fore urgent questions bearing on the relationship between the social construction of lesbian and gay identities and historical, political, and cul-tural representations in which ancient Greece is regarded as, in Halperin's words, the "unexplicit margin framing our own self-understanding."

I would, finally, like to suggest that it is this notion of the "unexplicit" that most succinctly renders "ancient Greece" problematic in queer historical self-representations. For, in contrast to the uses of the "other" homelands in what Zimmerman calls "a cosmopolitan archipelago" by writers of color who claim, create, and want a specified cultural/racial identity, the multiple uses of Greece in queer fictions of the past reproduce a certain "us" – white gay men and lesbians – as a racially (but not sexually) unmarked category. By leaving racial difference unmarked, unexplored, and thus perhaps unrecognized, white gay and lesbian fictions of Greece are inscribed in and through a racial *in*difference which prevents a candid consideration of "race" – not merely as a sign of difference but fundamentally as a category of oppression operating through racial formations, racial ideologies, racialized fantasies, and racisms – and how it intersects with the various histories of lesbian and gay identity formation and the multiple reverse discourses of queer historical subjects through which "we" are continually reconstructing "ourselves." The racially limited "access" to ancient Greece, whose genealogy is itself a retrospectively fabricated historical fiction, works simultaneously to determine the substance and significance of racial categories and to reiterate historically embedded racial meanings. If it really is the case that "the Greeks are hardly alien" to (certain) white Americans (and Europeans), the racially specified interventions of people of color recall the histories of racial formation and point to the very real possibility of differences, alienation, specificity, and various forms of resistance that immediately and continuously trouble "us" as queer historical subjects.

5

Queer fictions of Stonewall

> "Stonewall" is *the* emblematic event in modern lesbian and gay history.
> (Martin Duberman)[1]

In indication of the scope and depth of their importance to queer historical subjects, the Stonewall riots have been referred to as "[a] sort of lavender Bastille Day"; "the official start of the gay liberation movement"; "our
Verdun – they shall not pass and all that"; and, in a campy play on that
more famous opening salvo two centuries before, as "the hairpin drop
heard round the world"; as well as, in numerous accounts, the beginning of
the "modern" gay and lesbian movement.[2] Indeed, it is the significance of
"Stonewall" as a symbol – as "*the* emblematic event" – for a wide range of
gay and lesbian political, social, and cultural practices that has occasioned
this chapter, for these multiple practices refuse any facile, consistent, or
coherent summing up, even as they call for critical analysis. There exists, I
want to suggest, a very deep and basic paradox for gay and lesbian communities in relation to those several nights' events, and it is a paradox that
powerfully reiterates the themes of identity and difference framing, motivating, and traversing this book's project of queer cultural studies of
history. Regarded as the catalytic event in the formation of gay militancy,
"Stonewall" is also seen as, on the one hand, a unifying encapsulation of
the diversity within queer heterosociality and, on the other hand, a moment
of rupture "authentically" rooted in the experiences and actions of men
and (some) women marginalized in gay politics as people of color, as drag
queens, as butch dykes, as street people, as counterculturalists.

Queer fictions of Stonewall – the meanings "we" attach to or find in the
riots, the sense "we" make of them – are not isolated social/cultural texts
about some *singular* essence and autonomy of gay and lesbian identity,
community, and history. Rather, these sense-making projects locate the
riots in the larger historical field whose own contours they (implicitly) map
as well. Literally through annual public celebrations that bring "the

community" "together," and symbolically through various naming strategies and institutional structures, representations of Stonewall help to assert
the queer nation of the late-twentieth century. Despite their shared point of
departure, however, queer fictions of Stonewall draw on open-ended representational possibilities that also suggest the problematic and contested
nature of claims about community and identity. Like the widespread
currency of models of Greek antiquity in certain gay and lesbian historical
representations that I engaged in the previous chapter, queer fictions of
Stonewall also need to be taken up as subjects of social, cultural, and political analysis in the historical construction of lesbian and gay identities and
differences, of queer fictions of the present. Several areas (again those made
visible around race and gender and also, in this case, political practice
broadly construed) usefully highlight the paradoxical character of those
investments in Stonewall. Before turning to the principal analysis proposed
for this chapter, however, I want to begin with a relatively extensive discussion of Martin Duberman's recent book *Stonewall*, the first full-length
study of the riots, the political and cultural context in which they occurred,
and their immediate aftermath in New York City.

Reading *Stonewall*

In the preface to his book, Duberman points out that "'Stonewall' has
become an empowering symbol of *global* proportions."[3] He continues,
however, with a critical observation that decisively informs the nearly 300
pages that follow, and especially the middle section of the book called
"1969" (pp. 169–212):

Remarkably – since 1994 marks the twenty-fifth anniversary of the Stonewall riots
– the *actual* story of the upheaval has never been told *completely*, or been *well understood*. We have been trading the same few tales about the riots from the same few
accounts – trading them for so long that they have transmogrified into *simplistic
myth*.   (p. xv, emphasis added)

Suggesting that his book will tell the whole story, Duberman undertakes
the "overdue" project of "grounding the symbolic Stonewall in empirical
reality and placing the events of 1969 in historical context" (p. xv). The
book's epigraph – an excerpt from Clifford Geertz's *The Interpretation of
Culture* that not only situates becoming human in the paradoxical process
of "becoming individual . . . under the guidance of cultural patterns" but
also urges us to investigate "detail" in order to get beyond "misleading
tags" and "empty similarities" – anticipates the way Duberman pursues this
task. "In attempting to [ground the riots in reality and to contextualize
them]," Duberman explains in his preface,

I felt it was important *not* to homogenize experience to the point where individual voices are lost sight of. My intention was to embrace precisely what most contemporary historians have discarded: the ancient, essential enterprise of *telling human stories*.
(pp. xv–xvi, emphasis in original)

This approach explains the "unconventional narrative strategy in the opening sections of the book" which recreate "half a dozen lives with a particularity that conforms to no interpretive category but only to their own idiosyncratic rhythms" (p. xvi).

Duberman is also careful, however, to place his book within the context of professional historiography because "gay men and lesbians – so long denied any history – have a special need and claim on historical writing that is at once accurate *and* accessible" (p. xvii). The book's structure and development tie these concerns about accessibility and accuracy closely together, a connection that demands its reader's critical engagement. Though Duberman deliberately focuses on "individual lives" in order "to make past experience more directly accessible than is common in a work of history," his project is "decidedly not designed as 'popularized' history – by which is usually meant the slighting of historical research or the compromising of historical accuracy" (p. xvii). Indeed, the extensive footnotes to virtually all of the written text of *Stonewall* attest to Duberman's "[diligent search] for previously unknown or unused primary source materials" and suggest his "[scrupulous adherence] to scholarly criteria for evaluating evidence" (p. xvii). Aware of the potential for certain kinds of professional objections to his method of historical representation, Duberman acknowledges the grounds for such criticism:

My emphasis on personality might legitimately be called novelistic but, in contrast to the novelist, I have *tried* to restrict invention and remain faithful to known historical fact.
(p. xvii, emphasis added)

It is precisely this fact–invention distinction that motivates Duberman's research: recognizing that such a "grounding" and "context[ualizing]" are "overdue," Duberman sets out to tell "completely" "the actual story of the upheaval" set off by the police raid on the Stonewall Inn (p. xv). His particular mode of historical representation – "the focus on individuals and on narrative" – is explicitly an attempt to "increase the ability of readers to *identify* . . . with experiences *different* from, but *comparable* to, their own" (p. xvii, emphasis added).

Duberman's preface raises two important points in relation to the questions pertaining to historical representation that form this book's second principal axis of investigation. Though Duberman studiously tries to offer a full accounting of the real story of the riots, I want to suggest that his book is ultimately unable to escape its opening sentence: "'Stonewall' is *the* emblematic event in modern lesbian and gay history." For, as the diacritical marking of the bar's name reminds us, no matter what kind of history is being recounted or, to put it another way, what version of "the ancient, essential enterprise of *telling human stories*" is being employed, "Stonewall" always already means more in gay and lesbian historical imaginations than a mere bar, a routine police raid, and even the exceptional riots of several nights' duration that followed the raid. In contemporary gay and lesbian cultures, "Stonewall" signifies much beyond the "empirical reality" and "historical context" of 1969, though precisely what it signifies has always been a site of contestation. The current value of the "events," even – or especially – to the degree of the urgency of their narration as a complete and actual story, is precisely their mythic proportions, their non-actualness, their partiality.

In spite of the ostensibly objective, unchanging, and universal appeal of "empirical reality" and "historical context," Duberman's account contains a barely concealed wish for diversity in gay and lesbian historical representations, a diversity that is partially belied by the story he tells. Yet Duberman's account leaves unasked and thus unanswered the question of whose reality he is writing about and whose context he is placing those events in. Though he points out that "[n]o group of six could possibly represent the many pathways of gay and lesbian existence" (p. xvi), Duberman maintains that:

they can suggest some of the significant childhood experiences, adult coping strategies, social and political activities, values, perceptions and concerns *that centrally characterized the Stonewall generation.*   (p. xvii, emphasis added)

Neglected in this construction of "reality" and "context" are questions of how and when "Stonewall" has been located within "other" historical accounts, trajectories, ruptures, projects, and locations. Not only do we need to regard the multiple and different histories that inform our locations in the world as integral to the construction of our "reality" and "context" but also how (dominant) representations of "reality" and "context" construct silences, gaps, and discontinuities.

The latter third of Duberman's book recounts the riots' effects on his six narrators, gay and women's liberation politics in New York City, and the organizational efforts behind the first anniversary march (pp. 215–280). With less than one-fifth of its pages devoted to the entire year of 1969, and less still to the riots themselves, however, how much of his book is really about the narrowly construed notion of "Stonewall" – a "Stonewall" stripped of its mythology – that Duberman wants to articulate? How much, on the other hand, is about efforts then and now to articulate a political movement grounded in a spontaneous "nay-saying" that evokes both an innocence and a collective consciousness? These questions are related to questions that might be asked about the way Duberman presents his account. Duberman's oral history method of "*telling human stories*" places him as the (invisible) transmitter and editor of his subjects' voices but not their source, and he acknowledges that his "greatest debt is to the six people who trusted me to tell their stories and endured the multiple taping sessions which made that possible" (p. xi). Yet, although those interviews are "the source of most of the quotations" in the text, he "could not surrender to [his six subjects] the authorial responsibility to interpret the evidence" (p. xi). To have surrendered this responsibility would not only have compromised his "adhere[nce] to scholarly criteria for evaluating evidence" (p. xvii) but it would, in effect, also have inserted his account back into the realm of popular memory or mythology from which Duberman set out to rescue representations of Stonewall in the first place.[4]

Although I agree with Duberman about the urgency of providing lesbians and gay men with "access" to the past, I want to take issue with his project as well. Duberman's reliance on "an unconventional narrative strategy" (p. xvi), his refusal to "[conform] to [any] interpretive category" (p. xvi), his "belief in democracy: the importance of the individual, the commonality of life" (p. xvi), his attempt to "restrict invention and [to] remain faithful to known historical fact" (p. xvii), and finally his appeal to "individual experience" (p. xvi) and "lively human representation" (p. xvii) as antidotes to the "simplistic myth" (p. xv) of the riots that continues to circulate through gay and lesbian networks calls for critical investigation. Such a reevaluation is especially urgent in light of the recent philosophical, tropological, and political critiques of historiography discussed in chapter 2, the peculiarities oral sources present for historiography, and the problematic use of "experience" as historical evidence. I want to dwell briefly on these latter two points.

For his part, Duberman makes a paradoxical appeal to narrative and experience. On the one hand, in an oddly mixed metaphor, he tells us he wants to prevent "individual voices [from being] lost sight of" without, on the other hand, "foreclos[ing] speculation about patterns of behavior" (p. xvi). Duberman insists that the life stories of his subjects offered in the opening sections of his book are recreated "with a particularity that conforms to no interpretive category but only to their own idiosyncratic rhythms" (p. xvi), yet he makes no particular or explicit claim about the mode of interpretation he uses in the latter half of the book, except that he "ha[s] tried to remain faithful to known historical fact" and has "scrupulously adhered to scholarly criteria for evaluating evidence" (p. xvii). Even if we allow Duberman the possibility of an unmediated historical representation in which he merely collects, organizes, and edits the life stories of his subjects, it remains questionable whether his six narrators told their stories without using "interpretive categories" – consciously or unconsciously. Indeed, as Alessandro Portelli reminds us, it is precisely narrators' desires, imaginations, and reconstructions – *their interests* – that make oral history a valuable, and unique, way of producing knowledge about the past. Accordingly, however, because "[o]ral sources are *narrative* sources . . . the analysis of oral history materials must avail itself of some of the general categories developed in the theory of literature" such as those that address "the velocity of narration," and also "distance," "perspective," and "distinctions between narrative genres."[5] In other words, the "idiosyncratic rhythms" of Duberman's narrators' stories both contribute to our understanding of how "Stonewall" animates particular lives *and* suggest the need for thinking critically about them in terms of the "novelistic" against which Duberman contrasts his account (p. xvii).

Yet Duberman's book does reveal, to reiterate Portelli's remarks on "the unique and precious element" of oral history, not just what his six subjects and a larger group of gay activists "did, but what they wanted to do, what they believed they were doing, what they now think they did." This suggestion has important implications for reading the allegedly complete, empirically grounded, and historically contextualized account of the riots *Stonewall* promises. Though the events themselves are recounted in substantial detail, it is ultimately Duberman's narrators and his written account of their stories that construct the events surrounding Stonewall as "facts" by locating those specific events in larger webs of socially mediated individual and collective meaning. As Joan Scott explains, experience occurs within discourse rather than in "a realm of reality outside discourse" and, because of the shared nature of discourse, "experience is collective as well as individual."[6] Such is the case not only with *Stonewall* the text but also with the text of Stonewall, "the symbolic 'Stonewall'" that Duberman seeks to ground and contextualize. These discourse-defined textualizations, in other words, are both interpretations and something to be interpreted.

In ways consistent with Scott's notion of agency – one in which subjects "are not unified, autonomous individuals exercising free will, but rather subjects whose agency is created through situations and statuses conferred on them" (p. 409) – Duberman's account shows how his subjects' sense of the (potential) significance of the riots worked differentially to construct those events as "facts" depending on the locations from which their choices were enabled, though his own narrative, in Scott's words, "reif[ies] agency as an inherent attribute of individuals" (p. 399). Moreover, Duberman's subjects' subsequent narration of events, and their roles in them, occurred only after the significant interval of nearly twenty-five years in which the riots have become legendary, invested with political significance, and as Duberman himself acknowledges "transmogrified into . . . myth" (p. xv).

Possessing a hard-to-come-by political savvy, both Craig Rodwell and Jim Fouratt, two of Duberman's narrators, immediately sought to expand the impact of the riot beyond a brief encounter with and resistance to the police. Rodwell, a white radical member of the New York Mattachine Society and owner of the Oscar Wilde Memorial Bookstore, "[e]ver conscious of the need for publicity – for visibility —" ran to a pay phone close by to alert New York's three dailies "that 'a major news story was breaking'" (p. 198). Jim Fouratt, a white former priest, an actor, and "a major spokesperson for the countercultural Yippie movement" (p. xx), "also dashed to the phones – to call his straight radical-left friends, to tell them 'people were fighting the cops – it was just like Newark,'" though he was unsuccessful in getting them to "lend their support" to his cause (p. 198). On the day following the raid, while Sylvia Rivera, a Puerto Rican hustler and founder of Street Transvestite Action Revolutionaries, walked about "setting garbage cans on fire, venting her anger" (p. 202), Rodwell "channeled [his excitement] according to his own temperament – by jump-starting some organizational work" (p. 203). In contrast to Rivera's frustration and racial and class disenfranchisement, Rodwell's sophisticated ability to articulate himself and his political and business experience, as well as his racially linked upward class mobility and his charismatic leadership skills, might well have provided both the vision and sense of entitlement that allowed him to see that "[w]hat was needed . . . was a leaflet, *some crystallizing statement* of what had happened and why, complete with a set of demands for the future" (p. 203, emphasis added). Though his immediate plans for such a statement were overtaken by the party-like atmosphere in the street in front of the Stonewall Inn that evening, Rodwell ultimately did act on the question he posed to himself at the time: "Didn't the events at Stonewall themselves require commemoration?" (p. 211), a rhetorical question that anticipates the symbolization that has constructed those events as emblematic "in modern lesbian and gay history."

In the same street scene in front of the bar that distracted Rodwell (including a media, police, and gay presence), Duberman writes, "'stars' from the previous night's confrontation reappeared to pose campily for photographs" (p. 203). Yet, this notion of "stars" posing to be photographed belies the ostensibly unmediated "truth" of mass media's photographic representation of the "news" and raises questions about who was photographed: who wanted to be photographed, who could "afford" such possible publicity, whom did the photographers target as suitable or "representative" subjects, what was their role in or relationship to the riots? Furthermore, it was not until Sunday that word of the riots reached Karla Jay, one of Duberman's two female narrators (neither of whom was part of the Stonewall crowd). Jay "tried [unsuccessfully] to get Redstockings [a New York-based radical feminist group] to issue some sort of sympathetic statement" (p. 207), an effort towards articulating a coalition politics that was dependent on Jay's analysis and interpretation of the events.[7] Jay's coalition-oriented political desires are echoed in her subsequent interest in the formation of "a Gay Liberation Front – men *and* women working together to produce broad social change" which developed out of what she initially saw as "'the little penny-ante thing' going on at Stonewall" (p. 219).

Departing from the threads loosened in my reading of Duberman's project in *Stonewall*, the remainder of this chapter focuses on racial, gender, and political difference in relation to the emblematic and the symbolic dimensions of Stonewall in post-Stonewall lesbian and gay political cultures.

Race matters

Despite its invisibility in the naming of the problematic subjects of lesbian and gay studies, cultures, and communities, race has been a central organizing principle in and across all of these overlapping domains. To whatever extent that queer identity exerts a centripetal force drawing "us" together towards some fictive or imagined center, it does so only against, even necessarily in tandem with, the centrifugal force of racial formations that ceaselessly pull "us" apart, moving us outward and away from each other towards other locations that mark our complexly racially divided societies. Yet, these forces must not be seen in mutually exclusive terms, as contradictory opposites, but rather as conceptual fictions that frame, inform, and overlap each other. In representations and analyses of Stonewall, race matters – the race of the rioters, the location of the riots at the tail-end of a decade defined by racial struggles, the complex racial makeup of New York City, the ways the police and the press dealt with the riots, the view of the riots as a point of rupture, and the organizations that quickly emerged after the riots – have received only minimal critical attention. But precisely because race matters, these racial dynamics bear importantly on how we understand the riots.

The week following the riots, *The Village Voice* published two front-page stories covering them: Lucian Truscott IV's "view from outside" and Howard Smith's "view from inside."[8] Accompanying these news accounts were two photographs of the post-riot scene taken by *Voice* photographer Fred McDarrah, the one of "some graffiti" in block letters reading "gay prohibition corrupt$ cop$, feed$ mafia," the other a nighttime shot of thirteen young men in front of the boarded-up, graffiti-covered bar, its caption reading simply "in front of the Stonewall." Though obviously staged for the camera rather than a "live-action" shot, the latter photograph provides the closest approximation of an on-the-scene visual image of the riots, its campily posed subjects continuing to garner anonymous fame with recent republications of the picture.[9] While it is perhaps difficult to use this visual text to ascertain "who was there," we can productively juxtapose it to the verbal texts on the riots. Such a juxtaposition reveals a pronounced disjunction between what the photograph shows us and what the written accounts tell us, even suggesting some of the different ways the two kinds of texts, verbal and visual, are mediated by and read through framing conventions.

Although this photograph shows a racially mixed group of young men (only one of whom is in drag), the print media accounts of the riots are (virtually) silent on the question of race. The literal visibility of men of color and the harmonious racial integration suggested by the camaraderie in McDarrah's photograph are paralleled by the unreadability in the written texts of these two ways that race matters. In contrast to the press coverage of the (admittedly much larger) "race" riots of a few years earlier (e.g. Watts, Chicago) in which the ("Negro") race of the participants is remarked in almost every paragraph and the uncontained "spread" of violence to "white areas" as "youths run wild" informs the journalistic analysis, the written text accounts of the Stonewall riots suggest, perhaps not without *some* reason, that they were racially neutral.[10] In a sense, the *Voice*'s headline "Gay Power Comes to Sheridan Square" reflects/constructs the social dynamics at play, something which is even revealed in the *New York Times*'s much more coded "4 Policemen Hurt in 'Village' Raid" and "Police Again Rout 'Village' Youths," where Greenwich Village is understood not purely as a way to pinpoint the location of the specific crime (allegedly operating a bar without a liquor license) within metropolitan New York but also as a metaphor for deviant sexuality.[11] Whereas Watts and Chicago's South Side have been racially defined (meaning black) in media representa-

tions, Greenwich Village has been sexually defined throughout the twentieth century.[12] This apparent racial neutrality of the riots, however, might
also be regarded as the absence of racial analysis in recountings of them,
an analysis in which racial and sexual dynamics are addressed simultaneously. This absence is, in other words, a veil which obscures racial differences and racial *meanings* under the unifying category of homosexuality.

The differences in the legibility of "race" in the two media representations suggest ways in which what Duberman calls Stonewall's resonance
"with *images* of insurgency and self-realization" (p. xv, emphasis added)
might begin to look (to retain his mixed metaphor) more like dissonance.
As a visual reminder of a particular moment in gay politics, a documentary
image of "*the* emblematic event in modern lesbian and gay history,"
McDarrah's photograph is also an enigma, an anomaly which only tem-
porarily disrupts the connection between pre- and post-Stonewall photographic representations of gay and lesbian political activism. On this
enigmatic rather than emblematic reading, McDarrah's *Voice* photograph
provokes consideration of, on the one hand, how narratives of queer
history are racialized and, on the other, how critical attention to racial
specificity and (feigned) racial neutrality erodes under the weight of "gay
identity" politics or emerges in light of complex current concerns.
Although photographs from the homophile era of the mid-1960s and those
from the Gay Liberation era of the early 1970s reveal that activists dressed,
embraced, and presented themselves in markedly different ways, they just
as clearly reveal a continuity across that emblematic/enigmatic point of
rupture – the overwhelming, not to say exclusive, whiteness of the groups.[13]
Indeed, however stunning the discontinuities between the earlier and later
styles of gay and lesbian self-representations in contexts specifically
intended as *political* appear to be, these differences are remarkable in part
because of the constricted range of what – more precisely, *who* – is visible
within the documentary photographic field.

Interestingly, except for Duberman's passing reference to "'stars' from
the previous night's confrontation [who] reappeared to pose campily for
photographs" (p. 203), McDarrah's visual text is conspicuously absent
from the secondary literature's discussions of the riots. Their slighting of
this valuable text, however, is puzzling, even acutely problematic, since it is
this one image which provides the most – indeed, the *only* – compelling
documentary evidence for their claims regarding the racial makeup of the
bar's clientele and the rioters. Relying exclusively on the *New York Times*,
the *Village Voice*, and the New York Mattachine Society *Newsletter*, for
instance, John D'Emilio and Lillian Faderman make statements about the
patrons and rioters which can only be (speculatively) supported by this sin-

gular photograph or by unacknowledged extra-textual information such as interviews, written eye-witness accounts, or hearsay.

In his groundbreaking *Sexual Politics, Sexual Communities*, D'Emilio writes:

> Patrons of the Stonewall tended to be young and nonwhite . . . Rioting continued far into the night, with Puerto Rican transvestites and young street people leading charges against rows of uniformed police officers and then withdrawing to regroup in Village alleys and side streets.[14]

For its part, Faderman's brief discussion of the riots in her survey of US lesbian history states:

> The two hundred working-class patrons – drag queens, third world gay men, and a handful of butch lesbians – congregated in front of the Stonewall and . . . commenced to stage a riot.[15]

Even more thorough secondary accounts – such as Duberman's book which relies extensively on oral sources and a larger number of published texts – barely corroborate D'Emilio's and Faderman's "hunches" that the Stonewall Inn's clientele and the rioters themselves were "nonwhite," "Puerto Rican," and "third world gay men." Other secondary literature mentions only "street queens," "drag queens, dykes, street people, and bar boys," "dykes, straights, kids, hippies, leather queens," "drag queens" and "sequined gays," "'dope-smokers,' 'acid heads,' or 'speed-freaks,'" "flamboyant homosexual cross dressers," and "a particularly unconventional group of homosexuals," "blatant queens – in full drag," and "transvestites." Race is not a factor in any of these descriptions of the rioters.[16] (It is, at any rate, notoriously difficult to ascertain racial proportions from impressionistic accounts; while not utterly unreliable, such estimates are likely to be inflated or deflated by individual racial biases, anxieties, projections, feelings of invisibility, or desires for racial harmony.)

Writing around Stonewall's twentieth anniversary, Mark Haile reminds us that "[i]n the retelling of the tale [of the riots], history has become myth and desperation is remembered as romance." He points to the larger context of (official) American historical representations in which "[c]hanges and omissions, whether accidental or intentional, are nothing new . . . when it concerns people of color, gays, or women" to frame his revised "truth about Stonewall." In this revision, Haile specifically identifies "drag queens, hustlers, jailbait juveniles, and gay men and lesbians of color" as "the key players who started it all."[17] What I am interested in remarking here, however, pertains less to positivist notions of a singular "truth" of these assertions than to how various *truths* about the riots circulate among "us"

in (de)racialized forms. For, despite Haile's perceptive and crucial observation regarding historical changes and omissions, the Stonewall riots have in
fact *become* uniquely racialized in queer fictions of the past: while the first
decade's reporting, commentary, and analysis ignored questions of race,
over the course of the 1980s (at least since the publication of D'Emilio's
book in 1983) people of color have been written into accounts of the riots,
perhaps rightly recentering them in narratives of an event which they
started and sustained.

Regardless of the veracity of claims that the clientele of the bar "tended
to be . . . nonwhite" and that the rioters were "third world gay men,"
however, it remains of equal (greater?) moment that other aspects of gay
and lesbian political history – that is, those that are regarded as pertaining
to all of "us" – have been left substantially unmarked in racial terms. Where
D'Emilio and Faderman, for instance, remark the race(s) of gay and
lesbian activists, they do so principally to draw attention to separate
organizations of people of color.[18] Unlike such groups as Gay American
Indians, Third World Gay Revolution, UNIDOS, and Asian Lesbians of
the East Coast, both such pre-Stonewall homophile groups as the
Daughters of Bilitis and the Society for Individual Rights and such post-
Stonewall gay organizations as the Gay Liberation Front and the Gay
Activists Alliance were racially unmarked, ostensibly racially neutral, in
principle perhaps even racially integrated. In fact, however, precisely like
American society as a whole, racial segregation was (and has been) the
norm defining the composition of such "open," "general," "non-sepa-
ratist," and "racially unmarked" activities.

It is here, I would like to suggest, that we might begin better to understand how race matters to Stonewall's troubling importance as an emblem
for gay and lesbian communities. Whether historically accurate or not,
those recountings of the riots which have placed Puerto Ricans, blacks, and
other people of color at the very center of "*the* emblematic event in modern
lesbian and gay history" render Stonewall's ability to signify "us" fairly
remarkable. To put it somewhat differently, just as the riots were a response
to the urgent crisis in political representation facing gays and lesbians at the
time, these racially marked queer fictions of Stonewall are emblems of the
crisis in historical representation attendant on gay and lesbian identity-
based politics, for their placement of race matters directly in the middle of
narratives of the past disrupts comic readings of unity across difference.
The cultural history of the riots, the multiple ways they were seized upon,
and their continued transformations as a symbol in the decades that
followed, in other words, necessarily make a substantially different sort of
sense when the abiding racial dissonance in queer contexts is held in focus.

I want to return to McDarrah's photograph – that uniquely valuable and enigmatic visual text of the riots – to address (briefly and somewhat polemically) the particular question of how men of color function in resolving these crises in political and historical representation. From one perspective, the apparent integration and harmony of this image might seem to portend a reconciliation of the tensions of racial differences, suggesting their ultimate dissolution as significant and meaningful aspects of queer identity. In a sense, this singular photograph provides an alternate picture of what gay identity politics might, and did, look like. Regarding the image this way inscribes gay and lesbian history – or at least its "emblematic event" – with a vivid instance of multiculturalism that could itself serve as a model for community.

As much as it posits an alternative to racial segregation, however, this vision also helps sustain a false sense of racial cooperation and simply displaces critical reflections on race matters. By (falsely) grounding the ostensible origins of contemporary queer politics in an already present resolution of racial differences, tensions, and segregation, the previous and subsequent white-dominated political organizations can be regarded – even criticized – as unauthentic, as merely historical aberrations for their failure to reconcile queer differences. It is, on this reading, not Stonewall – or the posed photographic image of the post-riot scene – that is an enigma visually challenging segregated racial representations in gay and lesbian political history; rather, it is that very history itself that is enigmatic. In addition to the false sense of racial cooperation that promises the security of an untroubled "us," (re)populating the riots with "racial minorities" disturbingly parallels the expendability of men of color evidenced in other violent conflicts staged for "the general good," such as the (undeclared) war in Vietnam which was concurrent with Stonewall.

At any rate, this provocatively problematic visual text of *"the* emblematic event in modern lesbian and gay history" consists of thirteen men and no women.

Gender trouble: "Were there lesbians at Stonewall?"[19]

As much as the Stonewall Inn meticulously described by Duberman was an "oasis" in an indifferent, uninviting, even hostile world (p. 182), so too were the atmosphere and clientele of this oasis decidedly male: "[v]ery few women ever appeared in Stonewall" (p. 190). One lesbian quoted by Duberman who occasionally went to the Stonewall in the company of gay male friends "recalls that she 'felt like a visitor.'" On her assessment, "[t]here didn't seem to be hostility" between the predominantly gay male

crowd and the few lesbians at the bar, "but there didn't seem to be camaraderie" either (p. 190). In contrast to this unnamed woman's account of
the gender dynamics at the bar as a relative indifference between the many
male patrons and the few female "visitors," Richard Savin, an "eyewitness"
to the riots profiled in a recent article in the *Advocate*, insists that most of
the lesbians at the bar on the night of the raid were helping the police. "The
women were used to keeping us in line" as bouncers at the door, he explains,
"and they didn't see this riot as a political statement. To them it was just a
barroom brawl, and they were just doing their jobs."[20] Possibly distorted by
his poorly concealed misogyny, Savin's claim appears to be of dubious
accuracy or validity when read against Duberman's account in which all the
bouncers are male: Ed Murphy, "Bobby Shades," Frank Esselourne (p.
187), and "Sascha L., who in 1969 briefly worked the door at the Stonewall
alongside Murphy" (p. 182). Just past the door, "the [all male] Junior
Achievement Mafia Team" (p. 187) staffed a table where one paid to get into
the bar itself. (One woman, Dawn Hampton, did work the hatcheck [p.
181].)

As reported in Duberman's oral history, however, Karla Jay's initial attitude towards "the 'little penny-ante thing' going on at the Stonewall" partially reflects Savin's understanding of how lesbians viewed the "barroom
brawl." To Jay, Duberman writes, the rioting "was just another all-male
squabble with the prize nothing more than the right to lead an unhampered
bar life . . . She had never been taken with the bar crowd, gay or lesbian,
and this unsavory bunch seemed to [her] to have *stumbled* into rebellion"
(pp. 219, 208). Although certain that the *real* revolution was nearing, Jay
nonetheless doubted whether "the Stonewall riots represented its imminent
arrival" (p. 208). She did, however, revise her assessment of the riots on
hearing of the plans to form a Gay Liberation Front. Jay's change of heart
both gives cause to ponder precisely how queer heterosocial relations have
constructed Stonewall as emblematic in *gay and lesbian* history and anticipates the differences and (mis)alliances "across" gender that are marked
and masked by such understandings of Stonewall's significance.

Over the same twenty-five years that the presence of black and Puerto
Rican gay men has been alternately evacuated from or located centrally
within queer fictions of Stonewall, a process of historical revision has also
sought to reconstruct Stonewall as an event equally populated by and
relevant to gay men *and* lesbians. A decade and a half ago, on the eve of the
tenth anniversary of the riots, Maida Tilchen recognized this reconstruction as a "mythology." Was Stonewall, Tilchen asked in 1979, "the beginning of gay liberation for both men and women, or is it just another case

of women being carried along in historical reports despite what they did or didn't do?"[21] One popular, though disputed, version of the riots locates *the* incendiary moment in the actions of a single lesbian. This particular queer fiction of Stonewall is so momentous that Elizabeth Kennedy and Madeline Davis make explicit reference to it in *Boots of Leather, Slippers of Gold*, an oral history-based study of butch and femme identities in the working-class lesbian community in Buffalo, New York, from the mid-1930s to the 1960s.

> In *lesbian and gay* mythology the first person to take a swing at the police in the Stonewall Riots, thereby igniting the street battle, was a lesbian. Assigning a rough and tough lesbian a primary role in the launching of gay liberation is completely in keeping with her character. Her fighting back would not be the isolated act of an angry individual but would have been an integral part of her culture.[22]

This "lesbian theory," as Maria De La O points out, reaches as far back as the *Village Voice* coverage of the riots which identifies "a dyke" as the first person to "put up a struggle."[23] Although doubts persist about whether a lesbian "started" the riot, De La O maintains, "there is no doubt that women were fighting alongside their 'gay brothers' on that hot summer night in 1969."[24] A striking commonality in these speculative, contested, even normative reconstructions of the riots recognizing lesbians' "involvement" in them, however, is still the preponderance of men: the Stonewall riots were as decidedly male as the bar itself.

In the same issue of the Boston-based *Gay Community News* as Tilchen's article, the staff of the collectively run weekly paper also recognized the "inadequacies" of existing representations of the past and editorialized the need for a co-gendered revision of queer fictions of Stonewall in order to enable future politics:

> We have a romantic vision and see ourselves fighting together towards common goals . . . Stonewall *must come to mean* lesbians and gay men fighting back against oppression, passionately and *together*.[25]

This imperative to invest Stonewall with a spirit of gay and lesbian cooperation articulates an explicitly figurative understanding of the riots as a symbol that draws on then-current emergent political practices. Prior to 1979, the editorial suggests, Stonewall did not yet resonate with such a spirit of cooperation, although it could – even should – do so. The future-oriented posture of this assertion is at least a partial call to move away from the highly separate gay male and lesbian movements that characterized the 1970s at a time when each of these movements was equally challenged by the powerful emergence of the New Right's explicit homophobia and to revitalize the immediate post-Stonewall activity that appealed to Karla Jay

– "men *and* women working together to produce broad social change."
While the *Gay Community News* editorial is perhaps overly ambitious in its
belief in the malleability of history in order to meet current or future needs,
it does remark the close configuration between knowledge and interest.

Revitalizing the Stonewall riots along an axis that connects the past to the
future through the "interests" of the present, however, begs the question
posed by Tilchen: "is [Stonewall] just another case of women being carried
along in historical reports despite what they did or didn't do?" The point is
more complex than a face-value reading of De La O's claim that there is no
"doubt that women took up Stonewall as a rallying cry for a more activist-
oriented fight for gay and lesbian liberation."[26] Indeed, lesbians have consistently noted their ambivalence towards the significance of Stonewall, as
is suggested by Victoria Brownsworth's critique of Stonewall 25, the series
of events held in New York City to commemorate the riots' twenty-fifth
anniversary.

The celebration of Stonewall is, for many lesbians, somewhat bittersweet because it
is symbolic of the real divergence between lesbians and gay men in the struggle for
queer civil rights . . . The simple fact that we, as a queer community, date our struggle for civil rights from the night of the riots at the Stonewall Inn in Greenwich
Village is indicative of [the] exclusion [of lesbians from both the pre-Stonewall
"gay" world and the post-Stonewall world of queer politics].[27]

Although in speaking of "a queer community" in the singular
Brownsworth displaces a central aspect of the problem she articulates ("the
real divergence between lesbians and gay men"), her critical observation
nonetheless enables us to reframe the literal and figurative relationship
between lesbians and Stonewall – between doubts about the literal presence
of lesbians at Stonewall and the figurative force of queer fictions of
Stonewall to pull lesbians into accounts of a past from which they might
very well have been absent.

Important documents of the gay liberation and lesbian-feminist movements not only demonstrate the divergence between them but also raise
fundamental questions about the relevance of Stonewall to the textual
articulation of lesbian-feminism, especially in the years immediately after
the riots. While most, if not all, gay male texts from this period refer to,
invoke, or analyze the riots (at least briefly), as a whole lesbian-feminist
texts are much less attentive to them. Several of the earliest post-Stonewall
lesbian-liberationist texts, however, did position the riots as transformative
for lesbians. In *Sappho Was a Right-On Woman*, Sidney Abbott and
Barbara Love wrote in 1972, "[t]he effects [of the riots] were far-reaching

and permanent *for Lesbians as for their gay brothers.*[28] Two years later, Dolores Klaich suggested in *Woman+Woman* that for lesbians in the gay liberation and women's movement "[n]othing has been the same since" Stonewall.[29] Yet, a far larger number of lesbian-feminist texts throughout the 1970s are silent on the issue; "Stonewall" is conspicuous principally by its absence from the majority of lesbian-feminist writings from the period. Although texts such as *Sappho Was a Right-On Woman*, *Woman+Woman*, and the lesbian contributions to co-gendered gay liberationist volumes such as Karla Jay and Allen Young's anthology *Out of the Closets* do consider Stonewall, they reiterate the split between the gay and lesbian-feminist movements as effectively as they suture across it. When they were not developing an explicitly autonomous discourse and politics, lesbian-feminist texts of the period were much more in dialogue or argument with the women's movement than they were with the gay liberation and later gay rights movements of the 1970s, including the significance of Stonewall.[30]

Even quite recent attempts to retain and specify the uncomfortable positioning of lesbians in relation to both the women's and the gay liberation movements, however, have (inadvertently) reiterated Stonewall's significance. Questioning whether "the gay/lesbian bar" is "a theoretical joint," Teresa de Lauretis returns to textual and historical differences between gay men and lesbians to resist the elision of differences effected "by the discursive coupling of th[e] two terms in the politically correct phrase 'lesbian and gay.'"[31] Her temporal marker of a key aspect of these differences, however, is rather telling, for it hypostatizes the events of Stonewall, whose "history" it should be interrogating. "Since the late 60s, *practically since Stonewall*," de Lauretis argues, "North American lesbians have been more or less painfully divided between an allegiance to the women's movement . . . and an allegiance to the gay liberation movement" (pp. vii–viii, emphasis added). Yet, because the riots occurred with only six months left in the decade, there is no *literal* difference between the phrases "since the late 60s" and "practically since Stonewall." Rather, the difference between them is figurative. While the former phrase references a specific point in time and, perhaps, a general sense of revolutionary political possibility, the precision of the latter phrasing is not temporal but rhetorical. The second phrase's purchase in current contexts is afforded by Stonewall's wealth of cultural capital and takes for granted, rather than decenters, Stonewall's emblematic status in the construction of a "queer common sense" that resonates across unresolved lines of social differentiation.

The construction of such a common sense is anticipated and called for by the *Gay Community News* editorial on Stonewall's tenth anniversary. Consistently emphatic and hortatory, the editorial is both reflective ("we must examine our culture") and prescriptive ("Stonewall must come to mean lesbians and gay men fighting back . . . together"). These reflective and prescriptive strains of the editorial, however, are framed by a rhetorical construction of Stonewall as a point of condensation, even an originary moment, for gay and lesbian resistance: "Stonewall," the editorial states in its opening sentence, "means fighting back," something that "gay people have begun" doing "[i]n the past ten years." Besides being historically myopic, these rhetorical positionings of Stonewall as both a unifying and originary historical moment from which the present logically and coherently followed have implications for how the past is reinterpreted for the future.

Although it acknowledges in general the varieties of who "we" are ("a nation across lines of gender and color and language and class"), the editorial's un-selfcritical use of the first person plural nonetheless constructs an undifferentiated "us" who "have a romantic vision and see ourselves fighting together toward common goals." Not only the references to then-immediate political crises – the successful effort in Dade County, Florida, to overturn civil rights protections based on sexual orientation; the unsuccessful Briggs Initiative, which sought to prevent gay men and lesbians from teaching in California's public schools; and the mockery of justice in the trial of Dan White, who assassinated San Francisco Supervisor Harvey Milk and Mayor George Moscone – but also the explicit call for a re-visioning of the Stonewall riots, seek to position "us" in relation to (unspecified longer-term) "common goals." This loosely pluralist identity-based political positioning, however, was not new in 1979. Precedents for it appeared throughout the 1970s at rallies and other political events and formed one of the core projects – and principal tensions – of the homophile organizations during the 1950s and 1960s.

Queer fictions of Stonewall create various versions of "us" by defining and refining the past. The powerful "common-sense" fiction that "we" share at least some common goals – goals that are symbolically represented by the resistance during the riots – is one centrally problematic way Stonewall erases and creates historical memory, in regard to relations between gay men and lesbians as well as racial and political differences. The period right after the riots – that period of men and women working together that interested Karla Jay – is especially salient in such reinscriptions. De La O, for instance, reflects favorably on "the cooperation among men and women at the riot and in the next couple of years of the GLF."[32] But this fabled cooperation in the early 1970s, though not non-existent, was far from complete. Part of the project of regarding "Stonewall" must continually return to this point, particularly as a lens to focus on the ostensible cooperation and community among lesbians and gay men in the present. The point is not that queer heterosociality does not include or enable cooperative interactions across difference. Rather, these cooperative moments are (often) limited, partial, and tense, and it is precisely *in* those limitations and tensions that queer heterosociality consists.

Stonewall was a riot

"To remember Stonewall," J. E. Freeman writes in a vaguely poetic reminiscence on the riots published on the eve of their twenty-fifth anniversary,

one must remember its context. Its moment in time. It was a time of politics. A time of demonstrations, awareness and idealism. It was a time to march on Washington. On the Pentagon. On the convention in Chicago.[33]

Urban disturbances of this sort were apparently so ordinary during this time of politics that when asked by her out-of-town companions what was going on as they neared Sheridan Square across from the Stonewall Inn on the first night of the riots, Martha Shelley, an increasingly radical officer of the New York chapter of the Daughters of Bilitis and soon-to-be gay liberationist, answered matter-of-factly, "Oh, it's a riot. These things happen in New York all the time."[34] Seeking to disabuse his readers of the notion that the first night's rioting was "a spontaneous outpouring of anger that changed the course of history," John D'Emilio also insists on the importance of the circumstances surrounding Stonewall, of "its moorings in time and place." "Yes," he acknowledges, "the riot was unplanned, impulsive, and unrehearsed – three common meanings of 'spontaneous' – but it was also rooted in a specific context that shaped the experience and consciousness of the participants."[35]

By the same token, however familiar these practices might have been to the bar's patrons, the Stonewall riots were tame in relation to the scope of protests, riots, and police brutality that would also have been familiar from elsewhere. Indeed, compared to attacks on civil rights activists, the Tlatelolco massacre in Mexico City, the events at the Sorbonne in May 1968, and the Columbia University strike, the level of violence surrounding the events at the Stonewall was low. "Yet," as Paul Berman points out in a review essay of several recent works in gay and lesbian historiography, "those June and July '69 crowds in Greenwich Village were furious even so. And their fury had an odd quality: *it didn't fade.*"[36] Though perhaps the fury did not fade, gay and lesbian liberation organizations were unable to sustain their original impulse and energy. In the less hospitable environment of the 1970s, as D'Emilio observes, radical gay liberation groups, "were being replaced by other kinds of gay and lesbian organizations," ones that were not only more narrowly focused but were also increasingly defined by the sharp divisions between men and women during the course of "the gendered seventies."[37]

Because both the specific modes of gay and lesbian politics and the larger context in which they were situated changed so quickly, and have continued to change in the nearly thirty years since the riots, it is difficult to construe the multiple meanings Stonewall still holds for gay men and lesbians simply in terms of the radicalism in which the riots were situated. Without either mourning the loss of such "a time of politics" or waxing nostalgic on the idealism of the times, it is important to ponder why "Stonewall" is still what Duberman calls "*the* emblematic event in modern lesbian and gay history." What is the "meaning" of a late-1960s riot in relation to current gay and lesbian contexts? The beginning of an answer to this question is suggested by the legacy of the gay liberation movement.

While Gay Liberation Fronts and similar groups clearly failed to sustain their radical activism beyond the early to mid-1970s, to focus on this "failure" is both to neglect the achievements those often loose-knit organizations did make and to construe politics – even radical politics – rather narrowly. Gay liberation's legacy includes a vast revisioning of the place and meaning of homosexuality in American society, with important implications for queer historical subjects, popular culture, and various state apparatuses. In particular, post-Stonewall activists created a new language of gay pride and a huge array of political, social, and cultural institutions that effectively brought people together and helped make the movement and the urban communities they were based in.

Central to this revisioning was the transformation of the meaning of "coming out" wrought by gay liberationists. "Before Stonewall," D'Emilio writes,

the phrase had signified the acknowledgment of one's sexuality to others in the gay world; after Stonewall, it meant the public affirmation of homosexual identity. This revised form of coming out became . . . the quintessential expression of sixties cultural radicalism. It was "doing your own thing" with a vengeance; it embodied the insight that "The personal is political" as no other single act could.[38]

By thus "flesh[ing] out the implications of the riot," gay liberationists "ensured [that Stonewall] would become the symbol of a new militance" (p. 245). Accordingly, on D'Emilio's reading, it is through "the magic of coming out" (p. 248) that the Stonewall riots have maintained – even achieved – their emblematic status in gay and lesbian history. This connection between the riots and the transformed meaning of coming out (both of which have dangerous and exhilarating aspects) explains why, as Duberman puts it, "[t]oday the word [Stonewall] resonates with images of insurgency *and self-realization* and occupies a central place in the iconography of lesbian and gay *awareness.*"[39] Although the earlier militance is still present in the form of "images of insurgency," Duberman points as well to how contemporary understandings of Stonewall have worked their alchemy on individuals, effecting a curious kind of self-knowledge that is also a knowledge of a collectivity. "The 1969 riots," Duberman states, "are now generally taken to mark . . . that moment in time when gays and lesbians recognized all at once their mistreatment *and* their solidarity" (p. xv, emphasis added).

Contesting the distinctions between the personal and the political has been the central tenet of gay and lesbian identity politics since Stonewall. Yet, as Diana Fuss cogently argues in the chapter on lesbian and gay theory in her book *Essentially Speaking*, the equation of the personal with the political is doubly damaging. While Fuss cautions us against "los[ing] sight of the historical importance of a slogan which galvanized and energized an entire political movement," she pointedly remarks that "attributing political significance to every personal action" quickly voids the political "of any meaning or specificity at all, and . . . paradoxically depersonalize[s]" the personal. Fuss states her position more emphatically a few lines later: "simply *being* gay or lesbian is not sufficient to constitute political activism."[40] Fuss's polemical point also resonates with D'Emilio's assessment of the historically important process. "Only later, as the movement matured," D'Emilio writes, "would it become clear that coming out was a first step only. An openly gay banker is still a banker."[41] Both Fuss's criticism of conflating the political with the personal and D'Emilio's observation on the limited political efficacy of coming out direct us to the equivocal "meaning" of the political at the nexus of several persistent modes of self-representation in lesbian and gay communities; from several of these perspectives, the politics of being gay or lesbian might be actively participating in a movement for liberation or reform, having an identity-based personal politics, or living a certain lifestyle. Less about the events themselves or "the actual story of the upheaval" that Duberman seeks to recount than about the meanings attributed to the riots, the disputes about Stonewall are reiterated in the ambiguity of the "political" in lesbian and gay movements, communities, and cultures.

In the postwar period, bars have been important meeting places, community institutions, and sites of resistance that have helped to forge public and collective (albeit problematic and tension-fraught) gay and lesbian identities.[42] This public and collective identity was clearly an important part of the context framing the Stonewall riots. As Duberman remarks, although it had its critics, including his narrators Craig Rodwell and Jim Fouratt, the Stonewall Inn was "the most popular gay bar in Greenwich Village" when the riots occurred.

Many saw it as an oasis, a safe retreat from the harassment of everyday life, a place less susceptible to police raids than other gay bars and one that drew a magical mix of patrons ranging from tweedy East Siders to street queens. It was also the only gay male bar in New York where dancing was permitted.[43]

Yet the attention to the public and collective aspects of gay bar life deflects attention away from the bar's location within the "private" sphere of the marketplace based on economic self-interest and commodity culture (and in the case of the Stonewall Inn, the collusion of the mafia and the police). More importantly, to the extent that they help to contain gay life in commercial enterprises, bars problematically reprivatize gay identities within what one commentator has called "the colossal closet."[44]

The commercial gay subculture of the 1970s, much vaster than its lesbian counterpart and less politicized than many other aspects of lesbian-feminist subcultures, is replete with consumerist, reprivatizing, and depoliticizing impulses. Yet the growth of this commercial scene during the 1970s had a positive impact on the lives of many gay men, providing them opportunities to escape the pervasive homophobia and heterosexism they experienced outside the gay ghettos. There has also been an important relationship between the proliferation of commercial venues and the growth of a political movement. As Dennis Altman puts it:

the victories of the movement help provide a climate in which bars and suchlike can flourish, while the growth of a commercial world can provide the beginnings of a sense of community that the movement can in turn mobilise.[45]

D'Emilio identifies this dialectical relationship more sharply. "[T]he absence of overt politicization" in the gay male subculture of the 1970s, he argues, "can be attributed in part to the success, in its own narrow terms, of reformist politics. Since the sexual subculture had been the location where gay men most acutely experienced both their gayness and their vulnerability," the reform movement's success in reducing harassment by the police "seemed incontrovertible evidence that they were free." Once gay men "could be open about their 'lifestyle' on the streets of the burgeoning gay neighborhoods suddenly visible in large American cities after the mid-1970s," the concerns of activists "seemed like the ravings of grim politicos who just didn't know how to have fun." In an unexplicit reference to the future that echoes Altman's assessment of the political potential of the commercial world, D'Emilio contends that "though it was not apparent at the time, the commercialized subculture was . . . the seedbed for a consciousness that would be susceptible to political mobilization."[46]

On this somewhat generous reading of it, the commercialized gay sub-culture is much like the post-Stonewall conception of coming out. Rather than purely public or political in their own right, both the disclosure made by coming out and the commercial gay subculture function as gateways or interfaces between private and public worlds, between the personal and the political.[47] More than suggesting merely a permeable or unfixed boundary between them, however, gay and lesbian identity politics rooted in and ani-mated by subcultural expressions are part of the larger process of democ-ratization that has begun to unsettle the public–private distinction and to politicize social relations.

Thus, not only has the political context changed since Stonewall, but there has also occurred a change in the nature and meaning of politics itself as a result of the politicization of social relations. By displacing the demarcation between the private and the public, as Ernesto Laclau and Chantal Mouffe argue in their influential book *Hegemony and Socialist Strategy*, this politicization "has . . . exploded . . . the idea and the reality itself of a unique space of constitution of the political."[48] For this reason, to identify Stonewall's "moment in time" as "a time of politics" reifies the political – as if the meanings, goals, and processes of "politics" were stagnant, universal, always the same – and evacuates the political from present contexts. In order to avoid reified, obfuscating, and ultimately dis-empowering conceptions of the political, therefore, we need to historicize "politics." As Fuss cautions, however, such a project "should not lead us on a quest to locate the 'true' identity of politics." Politics, she continues, "is irreducibly cast in the plural. That politics linguistically connotes difference . . . immeasurably frustrates our attempts to locate and anatomize the iden-tity of politics."[49]

Part of Fuss's own interest in theorizing politics is to resist conflating the personal and the political so that "[s]exual desire [does not become] invested with macropolitical significance." Retaining the distinction between the personal and the political, Fuss argues, serves to prevent "a telescoping of goals, a limiting of revolutionary activity to the project of self-discovery and personal transformation." Yet despite the rhetorical clarity of her distinction between the personal and the political, Fuss's argument slips on the equation of the "social" with the political. "Initially," she writes, "'the personal is political' operated as a gravitational point for attracting attention to minority group concerns" that originated in "con-crete social oppression." At some subsequent time (presumably "now," given the shift in verb tense), however, "'[t]he personal is political' re-pri-vatizes *social* experience" (p. 101, emphasis added). In Fuss's argument "the social" can (even, must) occupy only one location in the dichotomy between the public and the private. Against this understanding, which itself does nothing to frustrate our search for the identity of politics, Laclau and Mouffe's recognition of the social as the third term that destabilizes the hegemonic distinction between the personal and the political offers a more promising, and complex, way to approach queer transformations of the public sphere. What Fuss's position does allow, however, is an historicizing approach to identity politics that would, for instance, recognize the no longer novel, though perhaps still personally transforming, aspects of coming out, of taking what D'Emilio calls "a first step only."

The tensions between these two perspectives on the social are reflected in the precarious balance between gay and lesbian subcultures and gay and lesbian movements, between the resilient redefinitions of politics located in the politicization of the social itself and the relatively passive sense of the political in a "politics" of mere visibility. As D'Emilio stresses, however, this precarious balance is central rather than incidental to the articulation of the political in gay and lesbian contexts.

The history of lesbian and gay politics is as much the history of the creation and elaboration of a self-conscious community and culture as it is the story of a social movement . . . The structure of the community marks the terrain on which the movement can operate, and the actions of the movement are continually reshaping the life of the community.[50]

To say, however, as one observer rather glibly pronounced in anticipation of Stonewall 25, "[t]his is the gay gift: politics as party,"[51] might be a catchy one-line quip about gay people's unique contribution to the politicization of social relations, but its failure to distinguish between "politics" and "party" naively treats a point of abiding significance to considerations of political organizing, the analysis of social movements, and an under-standing of cultural politics. The steady growth and continued strength of the lesbian and gay movement through the 1980s and 1990s while other movements on "the left" have experienced, in D'Emilio's words, "a wide-spread sense of retrenchment, of losing ground, of being under siege" cannot be understood simply in terms of a conflation of social change with socializing, of reducing gay politics to a party.[52] Nonetheless, there exists a need to reconsider the vitality of the gay and lesbian movement, particu-larly in terms of the social terrain on which the movement operates.

Regarding the latter point, I want to pause briefly to echo a certain degree of critical skepticism towards the recent Stonewall 25 events in New York City. Anticipating that it would be yet "another weekend lost," Mary Breslauer wrote in the *Advocate*, "Stonewall 25 will be a massive reaffirmation of who we are. But it also graphically symbolizes our inability to organize en masse for anything but a party."⁵³ While on the one hand Breslauer's pessimism reiterates the naive, historically inaccurate, and ultimately homophobic reading of "the gay gift" that conflates lesbian and gay politics with an endless party, it does on the other hand point to the need to be wary of uncritically accepting huge public gatherings of gay men and lesbians as effective, viable forms of political activism simply because they make "us" "visible" to those who need to see "us" and make "us" feel good about who "we" "are." At the very least, one might wonder how one million people and the hundreds of millions of dollars they collectively spent to be in New York might have been put to use differently in this age of a socially constructed scarcity of resources.

Of course, part of the "queer money" spent during that long weekend was "reinvested" in the "community," either through purchases made at gay- and/or lesbian-owned businesses or through the donation to charity of the proceeds raised at various of the parties and so forth celebrating Stonewall. Consider the following, for instance. The cover of the Stonewall 25 and Gay Games "special supplement to *Out* magazine," by far the most successful of several relatively new slick "lifestyle" gay and lesbian publications to appear in the last several years, beckoned its readers with attractive and alluring promises of a chic and fulfilling fantasy vacation during what the attached advance-ticket order form proudly boasted would be an "historical week of events."

This June 18–26, come to New York City for Stonewall 25, Gay Games IV, and the events of Out in New York '94. See stars and celebrities! Dive into parties and concerts. Help raise $$ for AIDS.

Although all proceeds from the dozen and a half "Out in New York '94"-sponsored events benefitted "AIDS organizations nationwide," the cynic might read the promotional materials themselves as identifying this distribution of the profits as an incidental or serendipitous, rather than integral and planned, outcome. In addition, labelling a series of cocktail parties, concerts, and balls – even if they are fundraisers for important organizations – an "historical week of events" is itself a naive assessment that reflects both a failure to grasp the extent to which such social events are already institutionalized in gay and lesbian urban subcultures throughout the USA and an inability to differentiate between a busy week of attending expensive social gatherings and three days of rioting in the face of a large and hostile police presence.

As the most salient reminders of this emblematic event in gay and lesbian history, the annual parades, celebrations, and marches commemorating Stonewall locate the riots at the center of a collective, albeit temporary and partial, post-Stonewall gay-and-lesbian identity. Paradoxically, however, gay and lesbian freedom day parades also make visible myriad queer differences, ranging from relatively benign lifestyle choices to much more entrenched, overdetermined, and poignant differences having to do with historically constructed inequalities in social relations. As Richard Herrell observes in regard to the Chicago parade:

the gay and lesbian parade today uses a society-wide system of heterogeneity in religion, politics, sports teams, musical organizations, and other interests to claim an essential similarity. It says to Chicago, "We as gay people are fundamentally different among ourselves and that's why – and how – we're just like you."[54]

On this analysis, differences between and among queer historical subjects become visible in proportion to the degree that various gay and lesbian individuals, communities, and organizations participate in these annual commemorations. And, the more fully visible those differences become, the more completely gay and lesbian people can show ourselves to be just like heterosexuals.

In terms of Herrell's assessment of this paradoxical spectacle of identity and difference, the multiple differences between and among queer historical subjects are rendered equivalent, reduced to no more significance than their share of the whole. In other words, as simply mirroring "a society-wide heterogeneity" in which all differences are seen as "interests," the mere act of making queer heterosocial differences visible becomes sufficient, being itself a minimalist sort of participatory democratic practice. By conflating all differences to an essential similarity, however, this understanding equates categories of differences such as race and gender with a hobby, one's favorite bar, or the college one might have attended. In such a reading of the multiple differences among queer historical subjects, challenges to racism, sexism, and particular kinds of political practice are robbed of their ability to make critical interventions into specific historical relations and concrete social circumstances. Since every one of us is "different" according to this framework, certain, any, or all differences no longer matter because the specificity of differences that reflect social and historical processes of privilege, subordination, allegiances, alienation, resistance, and so forth is evacuated, leaving these differences undifferentiated from merely personal preferences and individual character traits.

This liberal-pluralist model invests visibility with a deep significance, ironically "transcending" the very differences it attempts to make visible. The multiplication of differences among queer historical subjects, which has made important inroads against the persistent fiction of a unified and stable gay and lesbian community, has turned towards the increased visibility of various categories of differences as the one political goal shared by all groups. Thus, as Martha Gever has pointed out in commenting on the divergent strategies in cinematic representations of lesbian history, "[v]isibility itself now constitutes the basis for a sense of interests shared across groups that have little in common otherwise."[55] Such efforts towards making visible multiple differences can be seen as reviving and revising the post-Stonewall meaning of coming out. In so doing, visibility itself becomes a new, if slippery and decentered, queer common sense indirectly framed in terms of the symbolic dimensions of Stonewall, using the annual celebrations of the riots and their legacies as staging grounds for the many differences among queer historical subjects. The reduction of advocacy in the public realm to (the not always so simple) task of achieving visibility, however, is ultimately a deeply unsatisfactory understanding of Stonewall as an emblem. By rendering all differences equivalent, the politics of visibility betrays the deep significance of queer historical practices that reread, reframe, and refuse various constructions of the present moment. Not only does its strategy of equating queer historical subjects with heterosexual subjects retreat from the very necessary processes of historicizing the social constructions of sexual differences, but it also implicitly articulates a consensus model of American society in which social, political, and historical struggles are recontained and curtailed.

Coda

Finally, I want to suggest that one of the primary meanings attached to the riots – perhaps *the* queer fiction of Stonewall – is the structuring of those events in a way that reiterates a larger tale of triumph over adversity and the reconciliation of differences and, thus, echoes the themes of a comic mode of emplotment in literary and dramatic works.[56] Such a comic plot structure, for instance, underlies Duberman's historical account of the riots. In spite of the conflicts, challenges, and disappointments written into *Stonewall*'s "actual story of the upheaval," the book ends with the commemorative marches in New York and Los Angeles on the first anniversary of the riots, festive occasions reconciling differences and promising a new secular order. Duberman's six subjects, we read in the book's final paragraph,

were all, in their own ways, euphoric, just as, in their own ways, they had all somehow come through, had managed to arrive at this unimaginable coming together, this testimony to a difficult past surmounted and a potentially better future in view.[57]

Although Duberman is careful not to evoke an image of "[t]he decades preceding Stonewall . . . as some vast neolithic wasteland" (p. xv), his decision to end the book when and how he does provides a particular kind of meaning to or interpretation of the Stonewall riots. Through a comic emplotment, *Stonewall* explains those events as crucial moments in a narrative of gay redemption and restates the mythic importance of the riots as "*the* emblematic event in modern lesbian and gay history."

   The undeniable significance of the riots and their annual commemoration notwithstanding, however, there are also compelling reasons to regard Stonewall differently, to tell or interpret the story in a different mode. While understanding the Stonewall riots through a comic emplotment allows us to read them as a story of progress that promises a harmonious resolution of gay differences and the problems gay people face in a heterosexist society, an alternative emplotment of Stonewall – for instance, one identifiable as archetypically "tragic" – might allow us to explore more fully the loss of "our unity for the rest of our lives," as Duberman's narrator Sylvia Rivera thought it might be (p. 246). Such a tragic emplotment would suggest that festive occasions of triumph and reconciliation are false or illusory ones and would indicate much deeper divisions among "us" than previously imagined. Certainly, "the unimaginable coming together" of the first year's anniversary march is only one way of reading the political differences between the Gay Liberation Front and the Gay Activists Alliance, the tensions between gay men and lesbians, and the still underexplored relationships among white and Third World activists, to mention only several of these divisions.[58]

   Because post-Stonewall gay and lesbian movements have been organized around the teleological premise of progress and liberation, pursuing a narrative of emancipation, of coming out, perhaps they can only make sense in a comic mode. In a sense, because there was a gay liberation movement which – in its new, militant, and unapologetic form – followed directly on the heels of the riots, the story of Stonewall had to be emplotted as a comedy (though not from a homophobic or reactionary perspective). But, however inevitable or necessary a comic emplotment of the riots and their aftermath might seem, I want to propose rethinking that premise, particularly in light of the multiple critiques of identity politics and movements organized around identity whose emphasis on difference, antagonism, and social inequality upset the possibility that, even in "triumphant" moments, some collective "we" have surmounted "the same" difficult past. Within the logic of such comic emplotments, commemorations of Stonewall offer a sense of stability, resolution, and narrative closure that masks crucial instabilities, dissolutions, and ruptures in gay and lesbian social, cultural, and political practices. While annual public celebrations of the riots and various institutional structures claiming Stonewall's legacy for themselves help to assert the queer nation of the late twentieth century, the highly salient points of social rupture in gay and lesbian political practices that disappear in comic readings of Stonewall persist nearly three decades after the riots. For this reason, we would do better to look at how these differences inform the multiple contests for meaning invoked and evoked in representations of and claims to the Stonewall riots.

Because the significance queer historical subjects find in the riots is always informed by the fact that most of us have no literal connection to them, the questions of identity, difference, and representation raised by the symbolic and figurative dimensions of Stonewall concern the ability to imagine communities, to see individuals and collectivities in relation to each other. Despite – one could say because of – their partiality, queer fictions of Stonewall allow us to reconsider the collective queer heterosocial differences among gay men and lesbians as problematic subjects in history. Indeed, it is the particularly public nature of the annual parades commemorating Stonewall that makes them especially well suited to the task of reforming the world. Furthermore, the unresolved debates about the meaning of the riots are themselves concerned with the public sphere, including the question of equal access to public spaces and those spaces defined as queer. In this way, these debates are fundamentally about the articulation and possibility of community across multiple differences. Finally, then, although they indicate a lack of consensus on who or what gay and lesbian people are and even highlight the anti-community aspects of the differences between and among queer historical subjects, queer fictions of Stonewall are also important social/cultural texts in the reconstruction and reiteration of the sexual differences of lesbian and gay sexualities from normative heterosexuality.

6

Re/writing queer histories

Necesitamos teorías that will rewrite history using race, class, gender, and ethnicity as categories of analysis, theories that cross borders, that blur boundaries – new kinds of theories with new theorizing methods.

(Gloria Anzaldúa)[1]

The postmodern enterprise is one that traverses the boundaries of theory and practice, often implicating one in and by the other, and history is often the site of this problematization.   (Linda Hutcheon)[2]

Now not only could I read and see and hear the past, discovering new relevance, significance unimagined, but I could also, in turn, speak to this past, and thus re-animate and re-shape it, define it anew.

(Marlon T. Riggs)[3]

Chapter 1's critique of modernism and gay identity drew on several strands of epistemological skepticism that began with an "incredulity towards metanarratives," included a rejection of the humanist conceptions of identity and subjectivity as unified and stable, and doubted our ability to know the past as it "really" happened. Reconceived and reanimated by post-modern theories and practices, these various forms of skepticism underlie the project of queer cultural studies of history that I have been developing in this book. Signaling a shift away from understanding lesbian and gay historical representations as literal or descriptive accounts of the past towards reading those representations as performative sites where meanings are invented, these queer cultural studies of history propose a new approach to thinking about the relationship between the past and the present, and they investigate queer fictions of the past as interventions into the material present. Such "postmodern" *reading* practices, however, are also motivated by the critical approaches to historical representation pursued by challenging new queer *writing* practices. These approaches are especially evident in a number of recent hybrid texts produced by lesbians and gay men of color that weave autobiography, poetry, documentary material, feminist theory, personal narratives of desire, critical analyses of the structures of social domination, (science) fiction, and at times visual images into complex representations of queer historical subjects.

These hybrid texts not only combine, and cross the boundaries between, generic writing strategies to reconfigure individual and collective historical identities and narratives, but as I point out presently, they also invite problems for their readers as embodied subjects with their own particular histories.

At the cusp of the queer 1990s, when I first began writing about lesbian and gay historical imaginations as social/cultural texts that construct and contest identities, differences, communities, and politics, I argued that gay men and lesbians should not take whatever we want from the past and call it a part of "our" history. To do so, I reasoned, would not only be a profound failure to understand the specificities of the social formation of queer historical subjects but it would, in fact, also reiterate one of the principal excesses of the modernism that I was critiquing. In that instance, I was in ironic agreement with neo-conservative critic Daniel Bell's assessment of modern culture, which, he argues, "is defined by [an] extraordinary freedom to ransack the world storehouse and to engorge any and every style it comes upon."⁴ In particular, I singled out as culturally and politically problematic the persistent efforts to claim various aspects of the Native American *berdache* phenomenon "as 'a traditional gay role'" and to incorporate them into gay and lesbian history.⁵

Prompted by Will Roscoe's letter to the editor responding to my article and the larger question of Native American representation, I wonder at this point what it means to say that something from the past is not "ours," especially in a project that regards historical narratives as performative rather than descriptive and seeks to investigate the power historical narratives have to construct boundaries of inclusion and exclusion, of identity and difference. How do "we" know which history is "ours"? Who are "we," and to whom does something that is "ours" – or *not* "ours" – belong? As Roscoe points out in his letter, "the recovery of the berdache tradition since the 1970's has been led . . . by gay and lesbian Indians themselves."⁶ So by what authority can I reject such projects as culturally and politically problematic? That is, specifically, who am *I*? Who are the "we" I had in mind at the time? Where was/am I in the problematic queer heterosocial fiction of the past I was imagining? How did I "know" that these specific queer fictions of the past were culturally and politically problematic? Where were Native Americans, on my insistent and presumptive analysis? At any rate, because I am white and *not* Native American, my own (actual? feigned? resistant?) distance from such recoveries of *berdache* traditions says something about me, my racialized self, and my ability to acknowledge different or conflicting historical imaginations, while also projecting *my* story on to (once again silenced) Native Americans. If, as Stuart Hall puts it, who "we" are has to do with "the different ways we are positioned by, and position ourselves within, the narratives of the past," then the question posed by Ramón Gutiérrez in an essay critical of efforts to identify gay models in Native American *berdaches* – "Must we deracinate Indians to find gay roots?" – implies a limited "we" who are not Indian that also makes no allowance for Native Americans themselves to identify themselves as gay.

Indeed, I do still want to maintain that certain "recuperations" of *berdache* traditions *will* remain problematic under certain conditions, in certain contexts, and for certain arguments. But "certain" does not mean *all*. Critiques of specific claims to a *berdache*-inflected queer history need to address questions of positionality, of racial formation, of national identity, of the systems through which social power is accorded and withheld and not merely to reiterate constructionist notions of historical discontinuity, paradigm shifts, and ultimately an "essential" difference between types of "sexuality." Powerful, historically embedded national histories, racial structures, and systems of representation continue to reproduce a sense of non-Indian entitlement to Native American real, personal, and intellectual properties for personal spiritual or financial gain. From this perspective, non-Indian claims to *berdache* and other third gender traditions are more than minimally racially problematic appropriations of Native American cultures that simply reflect a relative indifference to otherwise still-salient racial categories and national histories. But, as tempting and important as it is to draw out the implications of these power-laden practices of (mis)appropriation, such criticisms deflect attention from the lives, histories, and texts of Native Americans by constantly returning to an alleged "center" of cultural, social, and political meaning in "American" life and thus reiterating the imperial gestures of US history and historiography that posit an uncontested, originary, essential conception of "America" – a national concern that is also variously implied, invoked, reworked, and rejected in many gay and lesbian historical practices.[8]

The queer fiction of the present that "we" are "now" a "community" with a shared history, however, is very deeply troubled by queer fictions of the past that powerfully refract the historically embedded, highly consequential differences among us, rightly making any attempt to theorize or write the histories of queer heterosociality a problematic, uncomfortable, and disturbing endeavor. This differential – indeed, oppositional – reading of history is remarked in Paula Gunn Allen's "How the West Was Really Won," an essay that rewrites and demythologizes the allegedly heroic conquering, settling, and taming of "the Wild West" by "neo-Americans."[9] Refusing to acquiesce to the white lie of "manifest destiny" while duly recognizing its multiple consequences across space and time, Allen insists on the distinctiveness of Native American histories and cosmologies from those of other races. It is these distinct histories and cosmologies that are brought into play in the recovery of *berdache* and other traditional gender roles by Native American lesbians and gay men to propose specific differences and to reshape current social relations. "Gay and lesbian American Indians today," Randy Burns explains in the preface to an anthology of Native American writings,

are living the spirit of our gay Indian ancestors. Much has changed in American Indian life, but we are still here, a part of our communities, struggling to face the realities of contemporary life.[10]

As political acts situated in the material present that retain and revise highly charged aspects of Native American homosexuality, these projects suggest and develop non-static alternative ways of conceptualizing sexuality, gender, history, and identity in the "paradox of old and new."[11]

Despite their use of the terms gay and lesbian, however, these queer fictions of the past do not simply transpose modern(ist) conceptions of gay and lesbian identity on to the cultural practices and social arrangements of irretrievable precolonial Native societies; nor do these practices entail the "rediscovery" of a suppressed identity in a nostalgic longing to return to a mythologized, ahistorical pure Indian moment that existed prior to European contact. Rather, they involve the production of new identities that also contest and reimagine contemporary possibilities for sexual and racial politics within a larger context of social transformation that includes the continuing presence of Native Americans in a colonial environment. In this respect, the reclamation and reinterpretation of third gender roles by Native Americans provide more than a weak thread suturing the past to the present, and are certainly not deracinating misreadings of cultural histories. Furthermore, when understood as performative instead of literal retellings of history that are premised, as Allen writes, on not "know[ing]/about what was so longago,"[12] these reinterpretations can be read as rich forms of cultural articulation and critique that remark, insist on, and explore the centrality of racial and national categories and the social relations in which they are given meaning *within* queer fictions of the past.

I offer this reconsideration of my earlier position – but still wish to retain a critical stance towards (mis)appropriations and decontextualizations of Native American practices, cosmologies, and properties – as a point of entry into a larger discussion of my own location in the politics of race and, in particular, my relationship to reading and writing about queer fictions of the past that inscribe, and are inscribed in, difference from my own subject position. Given the significance of historical, material, and embodied social differences, is any attempt on my part to read across difference merely a presumptive excursion into textual spaces that are not my own, an example of what Caren Kaplan calls "theoretical tourism . . . where the margin becomes a linguistic or critical vacation, a new poetics of the exotic"?[13] Certainly, the question of such a colonialist holiday matters here, now, as I get ready not only to argue that lesbians and gay men of color have been producing queer fictions of the past that disrupt stable conceptions of identity and refigure historical representation but also to draw from those analyses certain conclusions that bear on queer historical subjects, cultural studies of history, and the promise of difference. While seriously grappling with the collective differences entailed by the particular notion of queer heterosociality grounding this book's argument might further the possibility of reconstructing the public sphere and personal relations within it, these various but specific differences also have material consequences in the heterogeneous and uneven social field in which queer historical subjects are actors.

In the preface, where I first broached these concerns about the problematic collective differences of queer heterosociality and my own investment in undertaking such a dialogical project, I proclaimed a desire to avoid a kind of autobiographical writing – not, however, because my own story does not matter but, rather, because it is insufficient. Yet, although I was gesturing there towards a project that would address concerns larger than a narcissistic or solipsistic focus on myself which, I felt, would reiterate a narrow conception of what counts as queer historical subjectivity where white men would be at the center of discourse, history, and politics and difference would be virtually evacuated, I also mentioned the paradoxical reemergence of the autobiographical as a fundamental reason for wanting to develop the argument of this book. I was then, and am now, interested in historical narratives, accounts of the past, stories about the world that would make a difference in the ways "we" conceive of – theorize – social relations *in order to transform them.* My reason for avoiding the autobiographical, however, was twofold; in one sense, it was "political," in another sense, "personal." On the one hand, the previously unexpressed private reason for avoiding the autobiographical reflects a desire to protect myself from the vulnerability and self-exposure concomitant with writing about oneself personally that is further reflected by my opting for the distancing, even defensive, strategy of "objective" scholarly prose that I have been using throughout this project to analyze and survey a variety of queer historical self-representations. On the other hand, my already stated political reasons for writing something other than autobiography ostensibly concern a desire to transgress the limitations such a project would have placed on my ability to discuss the complex social relations informing queer historical subjectivity and the interested knowledges of queer fictions of the past. I say these concerns *ostensibly* grew out of a wish to get beyond myself because reading knowledge and interest as closely configured makes such a move rather suspect; moreover, as evidenced by the compelling texts I look at below, writing about oneself can generate quite remarkable transformative power, giving us "theories that cross boundaries" in a "postmodern enterprise" that aims to "re-animate and re-shape" history.

Indeed, this political desire emerged, in part, from conflating writing about myself with a racial and gender exclusivity. In making that conflation, I implied that although my sexuality is – or could be – a site of inquiry, problematization, and flexibility, my race and gender – collapsed into a singular identity – are somehow permanent and stable, so that when I spoke, I would be speaking as a white man (which is true) in such a way as to replicate existing discourses that concretize race and gender categories as seemingly authentic, inflexible, restrictive, and self-contained signifiers of cultural identity (an invalid assumption). In thus stabilizing my own race and gender, I also inadvertently stabilized race and gender as social formations and categories of analysis and effectively reconstructed self/other dichotomies as unbridgeable and permanent. Understanding the self differently – not as the site of authenticity, rigidity, and permanent closure but as the necessary starting point for an embodied intersubjective dialogue – makes writing about the self a viable and powerful mode of transforming social relations. Such a transformative dialogue, however, rests on the problematic necessity of crossing "difference" so that we can speak with – but not for – each other using language that at once affirms and disavows particular individual and collective identities. By seriously engaging the close configuration between knowledge and interest, the texts discussed below authorize and depend on new forms of communication without denying the specific differences or complex oppressions of variously situated subjects.

It is also the case, however, that within queer heterosocial conversations, analyses of race, racial formation, and racism have been more fully developed and more consistently engaged by lesbians and gay men of color – reinscribing race matters as unilaterally of historical urgency for people of color, ministering to white people's needs for the lazy and false security of our own racial (in)difference, and undermining the full range of possibilities for cultural, social, and political change that queer heterosocial relations promise.

Recently, Jackie Goldsby has forcefully reminded us of the importance of racial analysis to gay and lesbian political, theoretical, and historical work, suggesting that race not only matters as a particularly salient category of experience to people of color but also as an organizing principle for lesbian and gay communities and civil rights struggles. In a passage at once admonitory and uneasy, Goldsby offers a necessarily distrustful assessment of the much-celebrated recent developments in lesbian and gay communities:

As the gay community counters its marginalization by institutionalizing itself, I'm concerned about the erasure of *race* from gay political culture; that is, I worry that the subjective voice of people of color is being excluded from the crosstalk of culture and politics that's regenerating the gay community.[14]

From Goldsby's perspective, this queer cultural renaissance in the absence of a discussion of race and especially the sexual politics of people of color is damaged by its exclusionary development; nor is such a development necessarily new in regard to questions of racial difference, geographic and institutional segregation, and cultural privilege.

Following Goldsby's critical warning, I seek in the following pages to do (some) of the hard work of listening to the subjective voices of people of color that have been speaking past histories to transform the queer heterosocial present. Whereas chapter 4 looked at the gender-inscribed imagined cultural geography of ancient Greece as a powerful social/cultural text in the construction of whiteness and white racial (in)difference, suggesting how even in its absence race is everywhere present, the remainder of this chapter considers three problematically crucial queer historical sites – the community, the nation, and the body – as points of condensation and articulation for racial meanings, discourses on queer heterosociality, and theorizing social transformation.

Two autobiographical queer fictions of the past that compellingly challenge white racial indifference *and* proper historical representation – Audre Lorde's *Zami* and Samuel Delany's *The Motion of Light in Water* – re/write the history of gay life in Greenwich Village during the 1950s as complex narratives of desire, difference, and discourse.[15] Each of these black-authored texts' "decentered" or "eccentric" positions relative to white racial (in)difference is instructive for rethinking the modernist illusion of a reified "gay identity" uniting people across race, sex, and class, and they are equally instructive for reconsidering modernist queer theories of history.

As modernist social histories of gay identity anticipate, the promise of the city (ironically the same "village" in each case) figures centrally in both of these texts and provided the space where Lorde and Delany could be gay. Yet, in "making sense" of gay urban spaces, modernist models do not account for the interaction of the changing social structures of race with those of sexuality.[16] Such accounts cannot tell us, for instance, how the invisibility of black women in Greenwich Village informed Lorde's experience and how such invisibility affected individual and collective notions of identity and community. Nor can these narratives explore the meaning of the "more or less indifferent silence" in which Delany, "light-skinned enough so that four out of five people who met [him], of whatever race, assumed [he] was white," made the twice-daily "journey of near ballistic violence" across "110th Street – Harlem's southern boundary" in order to get to and from school.[17]

In the context of the Greenwich Village gay bar scene, Lorde writes, "it was hard for me to believe that my being an outsider had anything to do with being a lesbian." "But," she continues,

when I, a Black woman, saw no reflection in any of the faces there week after week, I knew perfectly well that being an outsider in the Bagatelle had everything to do with being Black.[18]

The complex intersections of race, gender, class, and sexuality brought into powerful focus in *Zami* present a city that is not only full of promise and possibility but that is also a multivalent, unstable, and conflicted set of spaces. "For some of us," Lorde explains, "there was no particular place, and we grabbed whatever we could from wherever we found space . . . Each of us had our own needs and pursuits, and many different alliances" (p. 226). Wherever she went – from the Bagatelle, a lesbian bar in the Village, to Hunter College where she was a student, from her mother's home in Harlem to the library where she worked – "there was a piece of [her] bound in each place" (p. 226) but never her whole self. Though crucial to the text, the meaning of lesbianism – the place of an individual and collective "gay identity" in movements premised on the notion that the personal is polit-ical – is significantly decentered in *Zami*. "Self-preservation," Lorde observes, "warned some of us that we could not afford to settle for one easy definition, one narrow individuation of self" (p. 226). This historically specific decentering of lesbianism complicates and challenges notions of a single common or shared identity as sufficient for transforming public space, politics, and culture.

Set in roughly the same time and place as *Zami*, Delany's memoir also upsets stable historical representations of the "making" of gay identity. While the Mattachine Society, the Daughters of Bilitis, and One, Inc. were "creating" their constituency in urban America, Delany was discovering "that there was a population of millions of gay men, and that *history had, actively and already*, created for us whole galleries of institutions, good and bad, to accommodate our sex (p. 174, emphasis added). He distinguishes between, on the one hand, the dominant "fifties model of homosexuality" as "a solitary perversion" and even "'gay bar society,'" both of which required "[t]he abandonment of sex," and, on the other hand, "the exodus from the trucks" and "the orgy at the baths" (p. 174). For Delany, gay identity – gay community – was found in or constructed through sex with other men, not the social scene of the gay bars or the respectable homophile organizations.

Yet, because "[o]nly the coyest and the most indirect articulations could occasionally indicate the boundaries of a phenomenon whose centers could not be spoken or written of, even figuratively," Delany maintains, "there is no way to gain from it a clear, accurate, and extensive picture of extant public institutions" (p. 176). Earlier in his book, Delany meditates on a performance of Allan Kaprow's *Eighteen Happenings in Six Parts*, which left him with "the disappointment of that late romantic sensibility we call modernism presented with the postmodern condition" (p. 116). The performance piece's "subversion of expectations about the 'proper' aesthetic employment of time, space, presence, absence, wholeness, and fragmentation, as well as the general locatability of 'what happens . . .'" (p. 115) serves as a metaphor for Delany's subsequent discussion of New York's gay male subculture which "while [it] accommodated sex, cut it . . . up into tiny portions . . . *No one ever got to see it whole*" (p. 174, emphasis added). Delany's view of gay community – specifically informal male sexual institutions – is remarkably fluid, fragmented, and finally a phenomenon "all but impossible" to apprehend in its totality (p. 174).

In part, of course, John D'Emilio's research is an attempt to elucidate the impersonal, unspecified, but active "history" named by Delany as the subject that created this array of sexual institutions for gay men. When read together, however, striking gaps emerge between *The Motion of Light in Water*, and *Zami*, on the one hand, and on the other hand, *Sexual Politics, Sexual Communities*' overview of the formation of a gay minority popula-

tion in the United States and its discussion of the early homophile movement's central place in that process of articulation. For instance, like
Delany, D'Emilio also distinguishes gay sexual institutions such as public
cruising from gay bars; unlike Delany, however, D'Emilio regards the latter
as having accomplished what the former cannot, namely as having "fostered an identity that was both public and collective."[19]

> The bars offered an all-gay environment where patrons dropped the pretension of
> heterosexuality, socializing with friends as well as searching for a sexual partner.
> When *trouble* struck, as it often did in the form of a police raid, the crowd suffered
> *as a group*, enduring the penalties together. The bars were a seedbed for a *collective
> consciousness* that might one day flower politically.   (p. 33, emphasis added)

Delany also writes about his visits to gay (or "mixed" gay–straight) bars
and includes mention of the "irregular intervals" of a policeman's visit "to
check the place out" (p. 149). D'Emilio's evaluation of the bars as the social
institutions "contain[ing] the greatest potential for reshaping the
consciousness of homosexuals and lesbians" (p. 32), however, displaces
Delany's identity-building sexual experiences (and those of "millions of
[other] gay men") to the margins of gay history. This displacement is
especially intriguing in light of Delany's suggestion that it was *only* the
boundaries – and not the center – of gay male sexual institutions that could
be represented.

   Furthermore, Lorde's experiences as a black woman in the Greenwich
Village gay scene serves as a powerful reminder of the severe limits to a
public and collective gay identity. Though she too socialized in the bars,
Lorde's assessment of them is ambivalent: not only did she continue to see
the pretensions of heterosexuality mirrored in butch-femme role-playing
(see especially, p. 221), but the possibility of "collective consciousness" was
constrained, even mired, by the bars' racial dynamics. Some bars, such as
Laurel's, "had a family feeling" (p. 222) or were generally a "place to refuel
and check your flaps" (p. 225), while "Black lesbians in the Bagatelle faced
a world *only slightly* less hostile than the outer world which we had to deal
with every day" (p. 225, emphasis added). In Lorde's biomythography,
racism – whether the subtle racism of the white racial indifference that left
her invisible as a black woman or, conversely, the more overt racism that
made her visible for precisely the same reason – unambiguously dis-
integrates the stabilizing, collectivizing effects posited by modernist
conceptions of gay identity.

   Delany's use of *Eighteen Happenings in Six Parts* as a metaphor for the
fragmentation of the gay male sexual subculture in pre-Stonewall New
York provides a productive way for critiquing modernist social histories of

gay identity. While these projects' historicizing approaches attempt to represent the "whole" history of that identity, albeit in abstract and general form, Delany's metaphor questions the possibility of ever making such a representation and suggests instead that only certain parts of that history can be made visible. In D'Emilio's interpretation of gay bars, the focus on the development of a "collective consciousness" expressly marks out, without fully describing, an important "center" – some essential quality – of 1950s gay life that represents or symbolizes a quality shared by all the other parts as well as by the "whole" of gay life in the 1950s. This characteristic quality, this ostensible "center" of gay identity, however, is itself a queer fiction of the past and the present; it makes a circular argument between past and present so that what "we" already "know" about gay identity prefigures the past and offers the metaphysical principle for translating difference into similarity. Both Delany's and Lorde's texts, however, help us to rethink the particular and the general, abstract theory and detailed example, part and whole. A crucial aspect of them is their disruption of "proper" historical representation which confuses those categories by asking us to consider the frame(s) of reference of gay and lesbian historical imaginations.

Both texts are autobiographies, and therefore directly engaged in "subjective" writing. Yet they both also illuminate the constructed nature of all representations of the past, however ostensibly "real" they might be. In contrast to D'Emilio's project of developing "a new, more accurate theory of gay history" severed from the mythologies of the gay liberation era that attempts to transcend the role of the imagination in writing about the past,[20] Lorde's *Zami* not only explicitly acknowledges itself as a fiction but indirectly calls attention to the imagination's intervention into all accounts of the real world. Her neologism "biomythography," which she uses to describe her text, places myth directly in between life (=bio) and writing (=graphy), both interrupting realist writing about life and seamlessly connecting life to writing through myth. Delany's memoir is also self-consciously framed in terms of the fictions of memory.

From the outset of his memoir Delany not only writes of himself as the central subject of the discourse, but he also recognizes his subjective, perspectival grasp of the events narrated. We see this dual subjectivity in the first pages of the introduction, when Delany recounts the time of his father's death (pp. ix–xi). Delany quickly points out, however, that the account just read contains a fair number of errors of fact (p. xii). Although, in pointing out these factual inaccuracies, Delany concedes a certain susceptibility to persuasion through "document and deduction," his willingness to admit to a "disjunction in memory . . . strong enough to make [him], now and again, even argue the facts" (p. xvii) recenters the production of narratives of the past in subjective memory and experience, in the realm that Popular Memory Group calls the past–present relation. For Delany, his

> inaccurate statement, "My father died when I was seventeen in 1958 . . ." is an emblem of the displacements and elisions committed upon that more objective narrative . . . [a] bare and untextured chronology . . . for the year and a half that straddled [his] nineteenth birthday.   (pp. xvi, xii)

Despite his contention that there was "a time in which, objectively, [his father's death] occurred," the brief chronology Delany provides "is not the story [*he*] remembers from that time" (pp. xvii, xvi).

> While all the incidents listed are, in my own mind, associated with vivid moments, rich details, complexes of sensations, deep feelings, and the texture of the real (*so indistinguishable from that of a dream*), their places on the list are wholly a product of research.   (p. xvi)

Summing up his highly qualifying prefatory comments, Delany makes a similar point, but this time he expressly acknowledges the fictive character of the many, frequently discordant representations of history that can be articulated:

> I hope . . . to sketch, as honestly and effectively as I can, something I can recognize as my own, aware as I do so that even as I work after honesty and accuracy, memory will make this only *one possible fiction among the myriad* – many in open conflict – anyone might write of any of us, as convinced as any other that what he or she wrote was the truth.   (p. xviii, emphasis added)

As with Lorde's neologism, Delany's ready acknowledgement of the partiality of his particular historical fiction challenges us to regard the meaning it imposes on us and the past as provisional. In light of their self-consciousness of this imposition, I want to suggest that Delany's and Lorde's autobiographical texts not only disqualify claims to an innocent or neutral historical representation of queer identities but are themselves inventions of new ways of writing past histories. Not only do these conflicting fictions demand that we look at their locations in socially inscribed relations of power, but they also do the work of critical interventions into the (con)text of lesbian and gay pasts.

While Lorde's and Delany's specific re/writings of gay life in Greenwich Village in the 1950s problematize the stability, coherence, and meaning of the community, its institutions, and the collective consciousness those institutions fostered, a number of queer fictions of the past have worked to disrupt the larger-scale cultural and political discourses that regard and construct national borders as primary, logical, and necessary. Although they also continue to recognize that the particular historical differences of national contexts matter, these social/cultural texts question the appropriateness and logic of using national boundaries to limit the study of culture and history, and recognize the inadequacies of any national focus for understanding subject formation. Against such nation-defined practices, which intentionally or inadvertently reify geopolitical entities, these texts recognize the nation as a residual product and project of modernity. Accordingly, they recode national identities as partial, self-privileging, political discourses of cultural authenticity, and respond to, as well as help to articulate, the transnational identifications of the late twentieth century that are rooted in histories of imperialism, colonialism, slavery, capitalism, migration, and displacement. Multiple and scattered, these transnational queer identifications occur at various and dynamic intersections of history, politics, economics, and culture that do not condense at one particular point or funnel themselves unilaterally towards a fixed and unified singular present.

These kinds of specific yet transnational recodings are pivotal thematic concerns in the films and videos of Pratibha Parmar and Isaac Julien. Independent artists working in England since the mid-1980s, both Parmar and Julien have been at the forefront of a movement of queer image-making that sutures together and cuts across history and the present to raise and explore questions of race and sexuality, appropriating and reworking images, texts, and ideologies to redefine culture and identity. Many of their projects have been supported by Channel 4 television, Britain's commercial broadcast channel which was founded in 1979 to provide funding and programming opportunities for innovative televisual projects and which more recently includes the gay and lesbian series *Out on Tuesday*. Although they both work in the specific context of Britain (including the way cultural production is funded there, the construction of English identity and nation that their work challenges, and the specific histories of marginalization and institutions of oppression that they resist), Parmar and Julien also participate in the articulation of (problematic) transnational collectivities and imagined communities. Addressing multiple, overlapping, and mutually constituting social and political issues of identity, difference, racism, homophobia, nationalism, aesthetics, and desire, their postmodern reinscriptions pose complex questions of and to history that make strange the notion of returning to an authentic national or cultural homeland while also retaining the salience of national, racial, and ethnic differences within particular historical contexts.

Much of Parmar's film and video work has concerned itself with the South Asian diaspora, and is linked autobiographically to her own family's forced migration to England in the 1960s; her feminist, anti-racist, and queer political activism; and her involvement in British cultural studies work on race and colonialism. Acknowledging the importance of these various autobiographical links, Parmar articulates her investments in addressing these concerns through her art in terms that are at once explicitly personal and connected to a series of overlapping community identifications. "In some ways," Parmar explains in a paraphrase of Toni Morrison,

the reason why I make the films and videos that I do is because they are . . . the kinds of films and videos I would like to see: films and videos that engage with the creation of images of ourselves as women, as people of color and as lesbians and gays; images that evoke passionate stirrings and that enable us to construct ourselves in our complexities.[21]

In such hybrid filmic texts as *Sari Red* (1988), *Memory Pictures* (1989), *Flesh and Paper* (1990), and *Khush* (1991), Parmar consistently and compellingly complicates national histories; discourses of desire; racial, sexual, and gender identities; and the ways those formations are named. The fragmentary, multilayered video *Memory Pictures*, for instance, uses its focus on the gay photographer Sunil Gupta, an Indian immigrant to Canada now working in London, to trace larger patterns of the connections between personal history, sexuality, diasporic experiences, and racism – connections that the video also ties into Parmar's own life and work through inclusion of scenes from her photo show "Wall of Images." Although formally closer to a conventional documentary than *Memory Pictures*, Parmar's more recent film *Khush* also mixes a number of representational strategies – talking heads, archival material, dramatic sequences, and dance – to create multiple, overlapping modes of address in the exploration of Indian homosexuality, both on the subcontinent and throughout the diaspora. As Parmar writes of these films and their articulation of individual and collective histories:

I interrogate Asian gay and lesbian identities in ways which point to the complexities that we occupy as lesbians and gays of color. I explore our histories of diaspora, the memories of migration and upheaval, the search for an integration of our many selves, and the celebration of "us," our differences, our eroticisms.   (p. 9)

Through their textual, thematic, and stylistic hybridity, these interrogations simultaneously disrupt specific discourses on the past – such as British imperialist representations of Asian women and hegemonic conceptions of a homogeneous English culture – and reconnect discussions of desire, aesthetics, race, and power to specific material, cultural, and social relations – including, as Parmar points out, the long history of homosexuality in India which problematizes both Indian homophobia and modernist paradigms of the history of sexuality (p. 6).

Disruptions and reconstructions of identity, nation, and diaspora are also central to the concern with history and "the black Atlantic" in Julien's films *Territories* (1984), *Looking for Langston: A Meditation* (1989), *Young Soul Rebels* (1991), *The Attendant* (1993), *A Darker Side of Black* (1994), and *Frantz Fanon: Black Skin, White Mask* (1995).[22] Interrogating the complex roles of popular culture (especially music), icons of community (Langston Hughes), the legacies of British and American slavery in the construction of cultural and sexual identities, and the various possibilities of and for black consciousness, these films explore what Julien views as "a 'sense of continuity' across the Atlantic, 'a Black Diasporan sense,' in which a shared sense of exile unites both [black British and black American] cultures."[23] Nor can these films be understood outside of the specific historical construction of such a transnational imagined community. As Kobena Mercer asks in a discussion of *Looking for Langston*, Julien's meditation on Langston Hughes which challenges heterosexist readings of Hughes's life, intervenes in ideologies of realist representation, and problematizes the relationship between past and present,

without the notion of a collective historical imagination, how could we understand why a black British filmmaker whose parents migrated to London from St. Lucia would choose to make a film about a black American writer from Kansas City?[24]

In the fictive space of such a transnational imagined community, Julien is able to rework globalized cultural formations in order to articulate the similarity-in-difference of black subjects' experience in anglophone societies.

By deliberately evoking the past as framed through contemporary discourse and locating the film "in mid-Atlantic," however, he also manages to name the constructed specificity of desire, race, and identity at particular historical moments in particular locations.[25] Like Parmar's intervention into multiple discourses on South Asian sexuality, Julien's project in *Looking for Langston* opens for reconsideration, as Mercer puts it, "what has been hidden from history, not only the fluidity of sexual identities within the black cultural expression of [the Harlem Renaissance], but the intertwining of black culture and European modernism," which has been erased from "official histories of modernism" (pp. 249–250).[26] This rewriting of history is evidenced differently, though just as strongly, in Julien's exploration of music as a transnational form of cultural politics, ranging from *A Darker Side of Black*'s investigation of homophobia in reggae and rap to *Young Soul Rebels'* thematization of the hybrid influences of soul to prefigure a reconstructed culture of difference where, in Julien's words, "histories do matter."[27]

Although many of their more experimental films have used a variety of languages of visual representation which subject both content and form to close scrutiny and occupy "third spaces" between and beyond the constructed differences of documentary and fantasy filmmaking, both Parmar and Julien have also recently made relatively more conventional or mainstream narrative films that speak to and provoke different sorts of audiences without compromising their interventionist strategies. As Julien points out, "narrative films can provide interest and meaning for audiences who have previously been disenfranchised from participating in those channels of desire and pleasure."[28] Utilizing the seductive pleasure of narrative to generate and maintain a diverse film audience's interest in their as yet untold or already forgotten stories, Parmar's short *Memsahib Rita* (1994) and Julien's feature *Young Soul Rebels* create multiple points of access to the complexities of subject formation in conjunction with specifically British, but nonetheless also transnational, racial formations (postcolonial subjects living in English society), gender constructs (representations of masculinity, interpersonal relations, and the gender-coding of streets and other public spaces), and political contexts (the National Front and the royalist pomp of Queen Elizabeth II's Silver Jubilee). In each of these films, the thematization of popular culture – both Indian and Hollywood film on the one hand, and dance music on the other – provides a powerful metaphor for articulating both the problematics of the status quo and modes of reconstructing the social.

Understood in relation to their involvement in developing what Parmar calls "a whole new language of visual representation," Julien's and Parmar's narrative films also raise questions of visibility, audience, and effect in ways that recognize multiple, diverse, and conflicting publics with different identities, allegiances, structures of feeling, and relations to cultural consumption.[29] In a conversation with Parmar, Joy Chamberlain and Stuart Marshall, Julien points out that his use of a conventional narrative form in *Young Soul Rebels* is directly, albeit problematically, concerned with his larger avant-garde filmmaking practice, which he sees as a kind of political intervention into cultural spaces:

behind [the decision to make a work that is more of a narrative] there's a political imperative, which is that I want to make work which gets seen by more people and which questions more people. In all the work that we've done to date in Sankofa [a London-based, black, filmmaking collective] we were talking to a converted audience. That began to worry me, especially after *Looking for Langston*.[30]

In particular, because he has been interested in "engaging with a black audience as well as a gay audience," Julien has had "to think in different film vocabularies or film languages" (p. 42). For Julien, "the problem of genre is how you can best articulate the points you want to address" (p. 42) – how, in other words, "to make your own kind of political statements and at the same time not totally pull the mat from underneath the feet of the audiences who are watching" (p. 44). In this sense, narrative filmmaking that engenders significant discussion of complex issues and attempts to speak to fragmented, diverse audiences rather than to an imagined homogeneous consuming public can be understood as a crucial part of an engaged cultural politics of postmodernism that multiplies available representations in the public sphere, including how those representations construct particular versions of reality.

By investigating the social, cultural, and material conditions that overdetermine subjective experiences in the historical present across fictive but powerful borders of differentiation, the recombinant qualities of Parmar's and Julien's film and video projects suggest alternative possibilities and provide us with what Julien calls "an image of the future. And of now."[31] Because they also recall and draw out specific histories, however, their projects cannot be recuperated as safe or familiar. Rather, they move discussions of subjectivity beyond either static essentialisms or ceaselessly fractured conceptions that evacuate the specific histories of racialized, sexualized, and gendered oppression and resistance as well as cultural creation and affirmation. Finally, the particular archaeological practices of their films not only move historical investigation away from the search for an unequivocal resolution or understanding of what happened in the past, but they also direct us towards a consideration of historical representation as a way of struggling over and addressing current social problems.

At this point, I want to return to my proposal to imagine the historical subjects of lesbian and gay studies, politics, and communities as part of a problematic and tenuous social formation that I have termed queer heterosociality. When I introduced this term in the preface and sketched my own interest in cultivating its realization as a way of reconstructing the public sphere, I briefly considered Jewelle Gomez's powerful observation on the particular collective political associations across social differences that queer historical subjects have sought – and needed – to develop. Her essay "Out of the Past," which appeared in the companion volume to the

US public television series *A Question of Equality*, displays a remarkable ability to remain generously, albeit cautiously, optimistic about lesbians' and gay men's potential to transform social relations through the unique connections afforded by queer subjectivity.[32] Yet in making this assessment, Gomez finds it both impossible and unnecessary to overlook or diminish the significance of the recurrent varieties of racism and sexism that have continued to mar such a transformation. Picking up on this concern as explicitly articulated in her historical essay, I want to consider Gomez's novel *The Gilda Stories*, a science-fiction work that contemplates the past but also moves into the future, as an imaginative attempt to re/write the hybrid complexity of queer histories in terms that are as critical as they are hopeful.[33]

From its beginning in Louisiana in 1850 to its ending in the Land of Enchantment 200 years later, this vampire novel spins a speculative fiction that rearticulates the blood/histories of queer bodies as powerful sites for constructing embodied, intersubjective, connected meanings. The provocative way that *The Gilda Stories* locates queer heterosocial relations within webbed networks of the abiding but irretrievable presence of the past disrupts the search for pure, uncomplicated origins and proposes instead a genealogical method that itself vexes genealogy by playing with the meaning of hybridity. Situated in a back-and-forth, mutually constituting relationship between dream and reality, *The Gilda Stories'* opening pages invoke both the specific material racism of the American South's plantation culture and "a picture of the Fulani past – a natural rhythm of life without bondage" (p. 10). The ostensible geographic, temporal, and ontological distances between these two historical contexts are bridged by "the stories that the Girl's mother, now dead, had pieced together from many different languages to describe the journey to this land" (p. 10). Through this constructed polyglot historical memory, the novel identifies the Middle Passage as the inaugural instance of hybridity within its project of reinscribing the past which urgently reminds us that "blood . . . is a shared thing. Something we must all learn to share or simply spill onto battlefields" (p. 44).

In a graphic instantiation of this hybridity as made literal through the sexual/racial terror of antebellum slave society, the book opens with the Girl – a runaway female slave – stabbing a white man while he tries to rape her and thus reversing the phallic power of penetration within this particular kind of asymmetrical relationship that existed under patriarchal racial slavery.

His center was bright and blinding as he placed his arms – one on each side of the Girl's head – and lowered himself. She closed her eyes. He rubbed his body against her brown skin and imagined the closing of her eyes was a need for him and his power. He started to enter her, but before his hand finished pulling her open, while it still tingled with the softness of her insides, she entered him with her heart which was now a wood-handled knife.   (p. 11)

At once an act of desperate violence and "a cleansing" (p. 12), this particular blood-letting – "signalling the death of a beast and [the Girl's] continued life" (p. 12) – is one extremity of the complex field of commingled blood/histories that mark the novel's racially heterogeneous characters, and it reiterates the centrality of racialized violence to Euro-American modernity.

After the murder, the Girl is found by Gilda, a white woman whom she mistakes for a man but who is really "*a woman as no other you have known*" (p. 16). Having reassured her "under the persuasive power of her thoughts" that she would be safe with her (p. 13), Gilda takes the Girl to recuperate at Woodard's, Gilda's bordello on the outskirts of New Orleans. In the midst of this primarily white world where "she could no longer hide from the plantation owners and the bounty hunters," the Girl's sudden appearance had to be explained as the transfer of property between white women in order to avoid suspicion. Gilda tells her:

You just listen and remember when anyone asks: You're new in the house. My sister sent you over here to me as a present. You've been living in Mississippi. Now you live here and work for me. Nothing else, do you understand?   (p. 17)

But it is here as well that the Girl begins to be exposed to the various worlds that had been closed to her as a young field slave. She learns to read the Bible and newspapers and "struggle[s] to see a white world through words on a page" (p. 21); listens to Bird, Gilda's lover, tell stories of her Lakota childhood which would surely have contradicted the dominant, binarized racial narratives of white over black while also complementing and extending the slaves' counternarratives, such as her mother's stories, with which the Girl was already familiar; overhears intimations of an impending war over slavery; observes the hypocritical color-stratified social system among free blacks, mulattos, and quadroons in New Orleans; and, finally, is initiated into the world of the vampires who "draw life into [them]selves, yet . . . give life as well" (p. 45). By the end of the first story, exhausted by 300 years of false utopian beliefs that "taking a stand, fighting a war would bring the solution to the demons that [haunt] us" (p. 45), Gilda gives her final blood to the Girl, whose subsequent rebirth as Gilda is ultimately only enabled by Bird, who must "complete the circle" of the familial blood exchange (p. 47).

This circular exchange propels the novel forward, opening (the new)

Gilda's future to movement and travel through the gift of "time that's not really time" (p. 44) and restates the centrality of hybridity – miscegenation – to the book's historical re/vision. With the first Gilda's quietus assured by her death, Bird leaves Woodard's in order to return to her family. Ten years later, Gilda also departs on a two-year journey to the east and north before heading westward towards Yerba Buena – San Francisco – where she arrives in 1890 to stay with Sorel, a fellow member of the blood circle of intimates who populate the novel. This resituation further establishes the principal thematic concerns that lend *The Gilda Stories* such promise as a queer fiction of the past.

Gomez's interest in the specific collective difference of gay men and lesbians recurs throughout the novel. The vibrant materiality of queer heterosociality, however, is most insistently depicted in the scenes that take place in the decidedly public space of Sorel's salon. Although it is never explicitly (and anachronistically) identified as a queer bar, both textual references and extratextual evidence support reading it as queer – among the latter, Gomez's other (autobiographical) writings.[34] This fictive but not implausible social space contains and condenses many of the differences and contradictions that mark queer subjectivity: as in the lesbian bar in Audre Lorde's *Zami* and the gay bar in Isaac Julien's *Looking for Langston*, the co-gendered queer bar in *The Gilda Stories* is a site of troubled hetero-sociality. Far from a utopian space, the bar is riddled with the tensions of identification and differentiation, suggesting the ambivalence and dis-comfort that reside in partially shared public spheres and partially shared collective identities. Despite its imperfections, however, "to those like [Gilda] it was a home of sorts. They came late in the evening to gather in the back rooms and bar, talking, laughing, mixing with the townspeople as if there were no difference between them" (p. 56). But there *are* differences. Within the physical space of Sorel's salon, the clientele are divided along gender lines in a way that puzzles Gilda, who "hesitated inside the door deciding whether to sit on one of the brightly striped settees, as all of the women seemed to have done, or to follow her impulse and stand at the bar with the men" (p. 58). While gender differences account for much of the dynamics of sharing space within the bar, Gilda senses an equally shared dynamic that complicates this gendering. As (perhaps) the only (visibly) black person in the salon, Gilda is acutely aware of the collective (un)con-scious of the white clientele's racism which unites them across gender; she senses both the obvious stares of several people and "pick[s] up the thoughts of patrons around her" that "revealed disapproval of both her well-traveled clothes and her dark skin" (p. 59).

The pretense of the five or so people who "were absolutely unable to accept [Gilda's] presence" but who "resolved to sit a while longer so that there would be no chance that Sorel would interpret their departure as an insult to one he had named as his family" (p. 60) suggests that the bar might be understood as something other than solely a queer space, that it is perhaps more like one of the mixed gay–straight venues that Samuel Delany briefly describes in *The Motion of Light in Water*, a place where sexual difference creates two separate groups existing side-by-side within the same location. I want to resist such a reading, however, not only because it is not readily supported by the text but also because it too easily inscribes some kind of queer nation as a site of already and thoroughly resolved histories of difference over and against a still deeply flawed monolithic straight society unable to deal with, comprehend, or transcend differences. Although the text distinguishes between "those like [Gilda]" and "the townspeople" (p. 56), which might appear to reiterate this sexual division that gives queer historical subjects the benefit of the doubt and heaps all responsibility for racial injustice on to heterosexuals, Gilda's strong impression on first entering the salon that "few, if any, of those gathered here were as she was, but they looked unlike any people she had seen before" (p. 58) hints at a more ambiguous, and ambitious, sense of identity within queer heterosociality. This reading is bolstered by Gomez's work elsewhere, particularly her efforts to label, map, and critique the historical dimensions of racism within post-Stonewall gay and lesbian movement-based practices. Moreover, the particularly fictive quality of such a queer heterosocial identity is reinforced by the fact that of all the bar's patrons, only the vampires, a co-gendered racially and ethnically mixed group of literally unreal beings who exist nowhere but in our imaginations, have learned that "[b]etraying our shared life, our shared humanity makes one unworthy of sharing, unworthy of life" (p. 62). By thus locating a fully realized social transformation in the unreal hybrid bodies of the vampires, Gomez is able to introduce critical commentary on certain queer social practices without either polarizing the community along false and unchanging divisions between "good" and "bad" subjects or proposing that specific, identifiable subjects constitute the vanguard in an inevitable, if orthodox, movement for social change.

Nonetheless, as suggested by the critique of queer nationalism that its attention to racism within the salon points to and the possibility for social transformation that the vampires' hybridity prefigures, the novel's vision of queer heterosociality is framed by two (related) projects of theorizing race, identity, and the body, each of which maintains connections to the specificities of history and historical differences. Although the flow of blood during the exchanges literalizes the recurrent metaphor of connection, sharing, and hybridity (which is, at any rate, not simply a metaphor) and calls into question the desire to be centered in a stable, hermetic body, the novel also maintains a strong sense of embodied subjectivity where the past continues to matter and recognizes racial categories as unstable and fictive but historically meaningful. As Gilda explains to Anthony, Sorel's lover, while she is still in Yerba Buena in the late nineteenth century, the significance of race abides: "although the institution of enslavement [is] no longer sanctioned, our world ha[s] not become a more hospitable place for me or my people" (p. 82). Later, in 1971, some five score and eight years after the Emancipation Proclamation was to become effective, we learn how memories of the past, including the horrors of slavery, the racial terror of the post-Reconstruction American South, and the centrality of race to the political economy of housework, animate Gilda's particular way of being in the world.

Life was indeed interminable. The inattention of her contemporaries to some mortal questions, like race, didn't suit her. She didn't believe a past could, or should, be so easily discarded. Her connection to the daylight world came from her blackness. The memories of her master's lash as well as her mother's face, legends of the Middle Passage, lynchings she had not been able to prevent, images of black women bent over scouring brushes – all fueled her ambition. She had been attacked more than once by men determined that she die, but of course she had not. She felt their hatred as personally as any mortal. The energy of the struggles of those times sustained her, somehow.   (p. 180)

Even as *The Gilda Stories* focuses centrally on racial differences, including projecting the cynical staying-power of *de facto* Jim Crow segregation into the future at least until the year 2020, when "[c]itizens [in Iowa] are still trying to figure out if brown people and white people should eat sitting at the same table" despite the fact that "there ain't that much food to speak of" (p. 225), its vision of the blood/histories of embodied subjectivity rejects both white racist and black nationalist discourses on literal or figurative racial purity (pp. 168–170). Suggesting that race – and by extension, other kinds of social identification and differentiation – is not "essentially" blood-based, the novel proposes instead a metaphoric anti-essentialist corporeality that cuts across gender and other differences inscribed on to the body without evacuating the specificities of those inscriptions. The Girl's question posed early in the novel – "Why white people feel they got to mark us?" (p. 23) – resonates throughout the text, resurfacing towards the end of the book with Gilda's reflection on the "extraordinary gift – this variety of textures and hues" of human flesh and her "fail[ure] to understand how it instilled such fear and horror in others" (p. 208).

Like Audre Lorde's, Samuel Delany's, Pratibha Parmar's, and Isaac

Julien's re/writings of the queer past, *The Gilda Stories* also undertakes an historiographic project that meditates on the consequences and possibilities of history, memory, and the meanings attached to them. While the novel's various interwoven stories take place against a social and cultural background of chronologically ordered events, both the narrative itself and the text's internal commentary disrupt "episodic" representations of the past where events occur at discrete moments and then disappear without a trace. Through this metahistorical project, *The Gilda Stories* creates a paradoxical conceptual space for regarding the relationship between the past, as both a lived event and a lasting social/cultural text with multiple orders of meaning, and the present. On the one hand, as Gilda explains to her uncomprehending mortal lover in Rosebud, Missouri, in 1921, "[t]he past does not lie down and decay like some dead animal, Aurelia. It awaits you to find it again and again" (p. 126). On the other hand, however, the book explicitly reminds us that there is always something "that loom[s] there in our past entreating us cruelly because there is no way to ever go back" (p. 43), that the past is "distant, unreal" (p. 39) and consists of "intangibles that make [it] so alluring" (p. 43). Framed and motivated by this insistent paradox, Gomez's novel distinguishes and draws out several specific processes of historical loss and the persistence of memory as mediated by social relations of power to designate the past variously and simultaneously as a site of difference, resistance, pain, and human connectedness.

Early in the novel, when the Girl is still under her tutelage, "Bird wonder[s] what creatures, as invisible as she and the Girl [are], [do] with their pasts" (p. 21), knowing full well that they abide somewhere. Bird's curiosity anticipates the book's central and recurrent thematic concern with the constructed forms of obscurity, distortion, and silence that are not only integral to "official" histories but also form a mode of survival in response to related practices of domination and upheaval within specific historical relations, such as the ever-present possibility of being regarded as "just another slave, likely to be sold away" (p. 179) and "the terrible campaign that had been waged against the Lakota to the north of Louisiana in the years before the end of the war between the states" (p. 54). While for the Girl the pain of historical loss creates a desire "to leave the past alone for a while" (p. 21), for the first and much older Gilda history's cruel entreaty forces a deliberate turning away from the past (p. 17). By the latter part of the novel, these meditations on the paradoxical combination of historical loss and the persistence of memory culminate in the ironic reiteration of the inescapability of – indeed the necessity of remembering – the past even, or especially, when looking forward to create the future.

Directed against the nihilistic impulses of an intentionally amnesiac present that "[has] conspired to forget [its] past" and "plow[s] ahead at top speed to some mythical future as if the wild west existed in the stars" (p. 220), Gilda's decision to write romances drawing on the many stories of her long existence underscores the novel's claim against the imagined irrelevance of history. Yet this choice of genres, identified as "one of the few forms of written literature the populace still followed" early in the twenty-first century (p. 219), also displaces a concern with expert knowledges on the past and focuses instead on the wider range of historical discourses that emerge within the multiple, heterogeneous, and conflicted public spheres of popular culture. Moreover, by deliberately calling attention to popular fiction as a valuable and necessary form of constructing historical knowledge, the writer-within-the-text strategy of *The Gilda Stories* self-consciously points to Gomez's own role in the articulation of the past as a repository of possible meanings – particularly ones that are contradictory or troubling. Finally, Gomez's deliberate implication of the constructed, provisional, unsettled, and paradoxical nature of the meanings fiction imposes on and pulls from the past suggests a way of rethinking the myriad projects that queer historical subjects have developed in conspiring, not to forget, but rather to remember our histories.

In re/writing queer histories, the above texts echo the concern with the past that runs through a wide variety of lesbian and gay cultural practices, some of which I have looked at in earlier chapters, including historiography and the continued resonance of various events, locations, and people in gay and lesbian historical imaginations. Like John D'Emilio and Donna Penn, who in their quite different projects argue that an understanding of the past is vital to contemporary practice and future possibilities, Audre Lorde, Samuel Delany, Pratibha Parmar, Isaac Julien, and Jewelle Gomez also maintain a strong interest in history as a contested site for constructing current and prospective meanings. Additionally, they display commitments to reworking the past that at least partially reflect the imaginative appropriations of ancient Greece and Stonewall as social/cultural texts discussed in chapters 4 and 5. In important ways, however, Lorde, Delany, Parmar, Julien, and Gomez also modify some of the implications of those gay and lesbian historical practices.

On one level, their postmodern queer historical texts' mappings of the cultural, social, and political contours of race complicate those discussions of queer subjectivity from which race matters have been absent, and they insist on the necessity of naming the specific differences that exist among queer historical subjects. Against the failure to name difference, which amounts to an *in*difference that increases the gaps between variously situated historical subjects, these texts show what some of those differences are and articulate how and why those differences matter to queer movement-based knowledges. Pointing out the uncertainty of alliances *and* the transformative possibilities of connections across differences, these projects look to how culturally marked bodies – not despite but precisely because of the ways they are inscribed in specific histories – can provide alternative ways of knowing in which knowledge claims are understood as mediated, partial, and interested.

But, although these texts are significant for their "social content," they also need to be read and analyzed for their formal and theoretical innovations in historical representation.[35] Specifically, these authors' strategies for summoning up the past deliberately fail to adhere to the orthodox narrative structures and codes of realist representation that mark historiographical practices. Self-consciously performative rather than descriptive historical accounts, their texts cross boundaries and pursue new approaches to historical representation that enable them to reanimate the past as an active presence and to problematize the distinction between literal and figurative meanings in popular memory, social practice, and collective debates on identity and difference. The dialogues between past and present that they initiate and develop not only articulate very queer oppositions to the multiple, and connected, regimes of the normal, but they also offer equally queer suggestions for possible futures with an eye to the here and now. I would, finally, like to suggest that it is in that speculation that these works so radically change not only *what* we think about queer histories but also *how* we think about them.

PART III

In/conclusion

7

Queer fictions for the future

> History should be a hammock for swinging and a game for playing, the
> way cats play. Claw it, chew it, rearrange it and at bedtime it's still a ball
> of string full of knots.   (Jeanette Winterson)[1]

As I turn to write the closing chapter of this book, I realize that an attempt
to offer a final or decisive statement about the meaning(s) of history for
queer historical subjects would be inconsistent with the interest in the
past–present relation that has permeated my approach to gay and lesbian
historical imaginations in the previous chapters. A genuine "conclusion"
would stabilize arguments about queer fictions of the past that themselves
need to be historicized and debated. Indeed, because this approach refuses
both a notion of total history and a singular interpretation of any particular event, period, or historical narrative, undertaking a project of queer
cultural studies of history as I have done throughout this book invites,
anticipates, and necessitates such further discussions, and I hope the preceding pages will enable those kinds of ongoing conversations. I do,
however, want to offer a few summary remarks as a way to tie together
several strands of my argument and to draw out several implicit points.

Concerned though it is with written accounts of the gay and lesbian past,
with the writing of queer histories, this book has focused substantially
more on *readings* of gay and lesbian historical representations as a way of
investigating how some of those representations – *fictions* – of the past
operate in the construction of queer presents. Obviously, I have not undertaken an archival or oral history project that further defines lesbian and gay
historiography as an empirical field of study. Rather, I have sought to
develop a critical–theoretical project of queer cultural studies of history
which looks at the uses of the past in queer discourses in order to interrogate what – and how – history means for gay men and lesbians as

historical subjects. In formulating a notion of gay and lesbian historical imaginations that takes seriously the insistent engagement with history in a wide range of queer discursive practices, I have read these queer fictions of the past along two primary lines of analysis.

On the one hand, by reframing compelling initial questions of identity, history, community, and politics in terms of multiple socially constituted differences, I have sought to investigate the always already problematic collective difference of queer heterosociality. By retaining the irreducible differences among gay men and lesbians, this notion of queer heterosociality allows us both to consider the unique possibilities for transformative social relations among queer historical subjects and to resist the totalizing aspects of certain queer fictions of the past in which those differences are (a)voided. On the other hand, I have taken advantage of the deep but promising crises in historical studies to rethink queer history as a field of interested knowledge. In my reappraisals of the trope of the making of the modern homosexual, the imagined cultural geography of ancient Greece in white queers' historical fictions, and the Stonewall riots as the emblematic event in lesbian and gay history, I have attempted to open up specific historical representations to critical analyses. By thus troubling these particular accounts of the past, I have sought not merely to indicate that historical narratives lack a stable and decisive meaning but also to evoke some of the various possible meanings that those narratives render. Against stability and decisiveness in historical representation, I have considered queer fictions of the past as important mechanisms – as vital social/cultural texts – for investigating and understanding as well as articulating and enabling complex differences and the relationships among them as hybrid and syncretic formations. Even the most impressive or obvious queer historical narratives – such as the comic story of Stonewall which seemingly offers its sense of redemptive closure as an inevitable consequence of that moment of rupture – can be opened to readings that refuse the singular meaning implied by their particular resolutions of the past. I would also like to suggest, however, that it is precisely such differences, multiplicities, refusals, and contradictions that continue to make queer historical studies so compelling, as indeed I hope to have indicated in looking at the differences in history articulated by the rich re/writings of the queer past that I considered in chapter 6.

In developing this argument about queer fictions of the past, I have directed much of my critical reading at some of the most provocative and consequential work in gay and lesbian historiography. My engagement with these varied texts' ideas and arguments, however, reflects rather than diminishes the importance of their contributions to gay and lesbian politics and theory. Although it also needs to develop its own set of arguments, critique – even pointed criticism – is ultimately not very interesting, useful, or worthwhile if the work under analysis is itself not very interesting, useful, or worthwhile. Yet I also want to caution against misreadings of the two principal axes of this project. I want to stress now, at the end of this book, that I am not suggesting that gay and lesbian historians – or anyone else, for that matter – should abandon efforts to write historical accounts that are more inclusive or ones that challenge the censorious, self-certain histories that have repeatedly denied lesbians and gay men a past – and a present. The varieties and specificities of lesbian and gay experiences, however, demand a mode of writing history that is contingent, mutable, and ultimately partial – or, rather, one that is self-conscious of its partiality, for, as I have insisted throughout this study, all history writing is already and inescapably partial, perspectival, and interested. An integral part of such work must be to offer critical histories of the ways we – and queer historical subjects who have come before us – have accounted for and sought to construct identity, community, and politics in relation to our deviant sexualities and our multiple differences and to explore those specific histories' legacies for various futures.

It is, as the recent generation of historical scholarship surveyed in chapter 3 has begun to show, not only possible but also necessary to examine gay and lesbian communities, subcultures, and sites of resistance in complex, localized, and specific contexts, and to do so in relation to other kinds of social phenomena which mediate *all* sexualities: gender gaps and privileges, age and generational differences, racism and racial formations, political and national ideologies, the division of labor and class relations, to name just a few. Its contingency and particularity make such an approach suited to a historiography that is at once much more inclusive of differences and critical of the social construction of those differences. As part of a practice of interested knowledge, however, we also need to explore the historical development of gay and lesbian political movements, organizations, agendas, and strategies. Such a research program requires coming to terms much more fully with the abiding presence of a social order in which the distribution of cultural and material resources has been and remains exceedingly inequitable as well as acknowledging the many differing conceptions of "the political" that traverse and motivate those movements. However noble they might seem, gestures towards simply writing previously absent people "into" lesbian and gay history are insufficient and misdirected. As Allan Bérubé's research on the Marine Cooks and Stewards Union suggests, it is also necessary to address social, economic, historical, and political relations of power in order to understand how and why individuals and groups have been written out of lesbian and gay movements and the histories "we" write of them.

In addition to the pursuit of these modes of specific and local historical analysis, however, we also need to continue to reassess the meaning of "history" in lesbian and gay studies and communities. A consistent problem in gay and lesbian historical imaginations – whether "properly" historiographical or theories of history or self-consciously invented traditions or complex moments of public celebration or something else altogether – is the possibility of reifying "history" in several different ways. Most regularly, the "hidden from history" approach to understanding and representing lesbian and gay pasts has suggested that "history" itself can ultimately become an omniscient subject and that a politics of visibility is an adequate and self-explanatory form of resistance to the very processes that construct the "invisibility" these projects aim to counter. Furthermore, I want to caution against reifying history as either "the past," which is therefore distinct from "the present," or exclusively a mode of inquiry that uses specific disciplinary techniques to produce historical understanding. As I discussed in chapter 2, Popular Memory Group's insistence on the dialectical relationship between the social processes through which the past shapes us and those through which we reshape the past both warns of and disables these various reifications. Their expansion of "the idea of historical production . . . to include *all* the ways in which a sense of the past is constructed" retains the democratic history that has countered multiple practices of exclusion and sanctioned ignorance *and* promotes a historical democracy that challenges professional historiography's self-authorizing constructions of power/knowledge in relation to the past.[2]

Under the critical lens of queer cultural studies of history that investigate the retellings of history as vehicles for mobilizing new social subjects, contesting hegemonic social definitions, and creating new cultural possibilities both in the present and for the future, this book has tried to make the questions raised and the answers provided by reflection on gay and lesbian pasts substantially more problematic and problematically more substantial. As I hope to have demonstrated in the previous pages, pushing the limits of what counts as history for lesbian and gay studies elucidates the concerns of identity, difference, community, and politics – what Martin Duberman, Martha Vicinus, and George Chauncey recognize as "some of the most important issues facing, agitating, and sometimes dividing [gay and lesbian communities] today" – in productive new ways.[3] This move towards engaging new conceptions of queer fictions of the past also reinflects the powerful queer theory strands of lesbian and gay studies that have incorporated and contributed to a range of discourses problematizing subjectivity and have opened up the possibility, if not always the actuality, of regarding multiple differences between and among queer historical subjects.

One of the principal concerns guiding this project, and the reason I undertook it, is the belief that the production of historical knowledges takes place in many sites, on many levels, and through many forms. Although historiography continues to matter to how lesbians and gay men represent ourselves, queer historical subjects' imaginative appropriations of the past on a larger scale have also been crucial to queer cultural politics, including arguments about identities and differences, struggles over community definitions, and reconstructions of the public sphere. For this reason, we need to stretch rather than reinforce the boundaries that define queer history and its academic study, to think outside the historically specific formations that distinguish absolutely between the literal and the figurative, the real and the imaginary – between, in other words, "fact" and "fiction." In the end, the ultimate point at issue is what these diverse and plural social/cultural texts so directly concerned with the past tell us about the constitution of queer cultures and the possibilities of queer cultural politics in transforming social relations, even if those projects of transformation are never fully realized and remain incomplete as still newer challenges emerge that exceed our previous expectations. As Jewelle Gomez reminds us through the words of her character Gilda, "the real dream is to make a world," although "you can't really know, no one can, until it's done" what that world will look like. "The reality of [such a revolution] can never be as one imagines."[4] Nonetheless, we continue to imagine new futures from the diverse perspectives of the present, and gay and lesbian historical imaginations are central to those musings. In this sense, queer fictions of the past are equally visions for the future, making provisional statements about conditional, undecided, perhaps alternative worlds which we might someday inhabit.

Notes

1 Metanarrative and gay identity

1 Susan K. Cahn, "Sexual Histories, Sexual Politics," *Feminist Studies*, 18.3 (fall 1992), p. 637.
2 Stuart Hall, "Cultural Identity and Diaspora," in *Colonial Discourse and Post-Colonial Theory: A Reader*, ed. Patrick Williams and Laura Chrisman (New York: Columbia University Press, 1994), p. 394.
3 Jean-François Lyotard, *The Postmodern Condition: A Report on Knowledge*, trans. Geoff Bennington and Brian Massumi (Minneapolis: University of Minnesota Press, 1984), pp. xxiv, xxv.
4 On ancient Greece and Stonewall, see chapters 4 and 5; on biographical reclamations, see Terry Boughner, *Out of All Time* (Boston: Alyson Publications, 1988) and Thomas Cowan, *Gay Men and Women Who Enriched the World* (New Canaan, CT: Mulvey Books, 1988); on *berdaches*, see Will Roscoe (ed.), *Living the Spirit: A Gay American Indian Anthology* (New York: St. Martin's Press, 1988); on the Harlem Renaissance, see note 17 below; on butch-femme, see Joan Nestle, "Butch-Femme Relationships: Sexual Courage in the 1950s," in her *A Restricted Country* (Ithaca, NY: Firebrand Books, 1987), pp. 100–109 and Karen Everett's 1992 film, *Framing Lesbian Fashion*; on pink and black triangles, see Stuart Marshall, "The Contemporary Political Use of Gay History: The Third Reich," in *How Do I Look?: Queer Film and Video*, ed. Bad Object-Choices (Seattle: Bay Press, 1991), pp. 65–101.
5 Martin Bauml Duberman, Martha Vicinus, and George Chauncey, Jr., "Introduction," in *Hidden from History: Reclaiming the Gay and Lesbian Past*, ed. Martin Bauml Duberman, Martha Vicinus, and George Chauncey, Jr. (New York: New American Library, 1989), p. 11.
6 The phrase in quotation marks comes from Kenneth Plummer (ed.), *The Making of the Modern Homosexual* (London: Hutchinson, 1981). For a general discussion, see Steven Connor, *Postmodernist Culture: An Introduction to Theories of the Contemporary* (Oxford: Basil Blackwell, 1989).
7 See Barry Adam, "Structural Foundations of the Gay World," *Comparative*

Studies in Society and History, 27.4 (1985), pp. 658–671; John D'Emilio, "Capitalism and Gay Identity," in *Powers of Desire: The Politics of Sexuality,* ed. Ann Snitow, Christine Stansell, and Sharon Thompson (New York: Monthly Review Press, 1983), pp. 100–113; Lillian Faderman, "The Morbidification of Love Between Women by 19th-Century Sexologists," *Journal of Homosexuality,* 4.1 (fall 1978), pp. 73–90; Ann Ferguson, "Patriarchy, Sexual Identity, and the Sexual Revolution," in *Feminist Theory: A Critique of Ideology,* ed. Nannerl O. Keohane, Michelle Z. Rosaldo, and Barbara C. Gelpi (Chicago: University of Chicago Press, 1982), pp. 147–161; Michel Foucault, *The History of Sexuality: Volume One, An Introduction,* trans. Robert Hurley (New York: Vintage, 1979); Estelle B. Freedman, "The Historical Construction of Homosexuality," *Socialist Review,* 25.1 (January–March, 1995), pp. 31–46; Jonathan Ned Katz, *Gay/Lesbian Almanac: A New Documentary* (New York: Harper and Row, 1983), pp. 137–174; Mary McIntosh, "The Homosexual Role," *Social Problems,* 16.2 (fall 1968), pp. 182–192; and Jeffrey Weeks, *Coming Out: Homosexual Politics in Britain from the Nineteenth Century to the Present* (London: Quartet, 1977).

8 John D'Emilio, "Gay History: A New Field of Study," in his *Making Trouble: Essays on Gay History, Politics, and the University* (New York: Routledge, 1992), p. 103.

9 Marshall Berman, *All That Is Solid Melts into Air: The Experience of Modernity* (New York: Penguin Books, 1988), p. 15.

10 Judith Butler, "Imitation and Gender Insubordination," in *The Lesbian and Gay Studies Reader,* ed. Henry Abelove, Michèlle Aina Barale, and David M. Halperin (New York: Routledge, 1993), pp. 309–320; Diana Fuss, *Essentially Speaking: Feminism, Nature, and Difference* (New York: Routledge, 1989), esp. pp. 99–100; Eve Kosofsky Sedgwick, *Epistemology of the Closet* (Berkeley: University of California Press, 1990), pp. 67–90.

11 Weeks, *Coming Out,* p. ix.

12 Sedgwick, *Epistemology of the Closet,* p. 45.

13 Foucault, *History of Sexuality: Vol. I,* p. 101.

14 Jeffrey Escoffier, "Sexual Revolution and the Politics of Gay Identity," *Socialist Review,* 82/83 (July–October, 1985), p. 147.

15 Monique Wittig, "The Mark of Gender," in *The Poetics of Gender,* ed. Nancy K. Miller (New York: Columbia University Press, 1986), pp. 63–73.

16 Martha Vicinus, "'They Wonder to Which Sex I Belong': The Historical Roots of the Modern Lesbian Identity," in *Which Homosexuality?: Essays from the International Scientific Conference on Lesbian and Gay Studies,* ed. Dennis Altman et al. (London: Gay Men's Press, 1989), p. 176.

17 See Amatai F. Avi-Ram, "The Unreadable Black Body: 'Conventional' Poetic Form in the Harlem Renaissance," *Genders,* 7 (spring 1990), pp. 32–45; George Chauncey, Jr., *Gay New York: Gender, Urban Culture, and the Making of the Gay Male World, 1890–1940* (New York: Basic Books, 1994), pp. 244–266; Eric Garber's three articles, "T'aint Nobody's Bizness: Homosexuality in 1920s Harlem," in *Black Men/White Men: A Gay Anthology,* ed. Michael J. Smith (San

Francisco: Gay Sunshine Press, 1983), pp. 7–16, "Gladys Bentley: Bulldagger Who Sang the Blues," *Outlook: National Lesbian and Gay Quarterly,* 1 (spring 1988), pp. 52–61, and "A Spectacle in Color: The Lesbian and Gay Subculture in Jazz Age Harlem," in *Hidden from History: Reclaiming the Gay and Lesbian Past,* ed. Martin Bauml Duberman, Martha Vicinus, and George Chauncey, Jr. (New York: New American Library, 1989), pp. 318–331; Gloria T. Hull, "'Lines She Did Not Dare': Angela Weld Grimké, Harlem Renaissance Poet," in *The Lesbian and Gay Studies Reader,* ed. Henry Abelove, Michèlle Aina Barale, and David M. Halperin (New York: Routledge, 1993), pp. 453–466; Alden Reimonencq, "Countee Cullen's Uranian 'Soul Windows,'" in *Critical Essays: Gay and Lesbian Writers of Color,* ed. Emmanuel S. Nelson (New York: Harrington Park Press, 1993), pp. 143–165; Charles Michael Smith, "Bruce Nugent: Bohemian of the Harlem Renaissance," in *In the Life: A Black Gay Anthology,* ed. Joseph Beam (Boston: Alyson Publications, 1986), pp. 209–220; and Gregory Woods, "Gay Rereadings of the Harlem Renaissance Poets," in *Critical Essays: Gay and Lesbian Writers of Color,* ed. Emmanuel S. Nelson (New York: Harrington Park Press, 1993), pp. 127–142. On the Harlem Renaissance, see Nathan Irvin Huggins, *Harlem Renaissance* (New York: Oxford University Press, 1971); Nathan Irvin Huggins (ed.), *Voices of the Harlem Renaissance* (New York: Oxford University Press, 1976); David Levering Lewis, *When Harlem Was in Vogue* (New York: Alfred Knopf, 1981); Alain Locke (ed.), *The New Negro: An Introduction,* reprint edn. (New York: Atheneum, 1968).

18 For a useful discussion of the relationship between anomalies and paradigms, see Thomas S. Kuhn, *The Structure of Scientific Revolutions,* 2nd edn. (Chicago: University of Chicago Press, 1970).

19 Lisa Duggan recognizes some of these same problems but does not consider them to be embedded in the narrative logic of social constructionist accounts of gay identity formation. See her "History's Gay Ghetto: Contradictions of Growth in Lesbian and Gay History," in *Presenting the Past: Essays on History and the Public,* ed. Susan Porter Benson, Stephen Brier, and Roy Rosenzweig (Philadelphia: Temple University Press, 1986), p. 285. For some additional critique, see also Tracy Morgan, "Pages of Whiteness: Race, Physique Magazines, and the Emergence of Gay Public Culture, 1955–1960," *Found Object,* 4 (fall 1994), pp. 108–126.

2 Queer historical subjects

1 Jane Gallop, *The Daughter's Seduction: Feminism and Psychoanalysis* (Ithaca, NY: Cornell University Press, 1982), p. xii.

2 Jeffrey Weeks, "Against Nature," in *Which Homosexuality?: Essays from the International Scientific Conference on Lesbian and Gay Studies,* ed. Dennis Altman et al. (London: Gay Men's Press, 1989), p. 210.

3 Monique Wittig, "The Mark of Gender," in *The Poetics of Gender,* ed. Nancy K. Miller (New York: Columbia University Press, 1986), pp. 63–73.

4 Eve Kosofsky Sedgwick, *Epistemology of the Closet* (Berkeley: University of California Press, 1990), p. 32.

5 Judith Butler, *Gender Trouble: Feminism and the Subversion of Identity* (New York: Routledge, 1990), p. 6.

6 Specifically excluded from the referent of Sedgwick's "we" here are those anti-homophobic readers and writers who *are* used to asking these kinds of questions. See, for example, Tomás Almaguer, "Chicano Men: A Cartography of Homosexual Identity and Behavior," *differences: A Journal of Feminist Cultural Studies,* 3.2 (summer 1991), pp. 75–100; Katie King, "Audre Lorde's Lacquered Layerings: The Lesbian Bar as a Site of Literary Production," *Cultural Studies,* 2.3 (October, 1988), pp. 321–342; Audre Lorde, *Sister Outsider* (Trumansburg, NY: The Crossing Press, 1985); Cherríe Moraga, "A Long Line of Vendidas," in *Loving in the War Years: Lo que nunca pasó por sus labios* (Boston: South End Press, 1983), pp. 90–144; Minnie Bruce Pratt, "Identity: Skin, Blood, Heart," in Elly Bulkin, Minnie Bruce Pratt, and Barbara Smith, *Yours in Struggle: Three Feminist Perspectives on Anti-Semitism and Racism* (Ithaca, NY: Firebrand Press, 1988), pp. 9–63; and Marlon Riggs, "Black Macho Revisited: Reflections of a SNAP! Queen," in *Brother to Brother: New Writings by Black Gay Men,* ed. Essex Hemphill (Boston: Alyson Publications, 1991), pp. 253–257.

7 Diana Fuss, "Lesbian and Gay Theory: The Question of Identity Politics," in *Essentially Speaking: Feminism, Nature, and Difference* (New York: Routledge, 1989), pp. 97–112.

8 The title of Fuss's more recent edited volume *Inside/Out: Lesbian Theories, Gay Theories* (New York: Routledge, 1991) retains the mark of gender and pluralizes each of these gender-separatist categories of theoretical inquiry. Jacquelyn Zita rightly contests Fuss's claim that lesbian theorists have tended to be more "essentialist" than gay male theorists; see her "Gay and Lesbian Studies: Yet Another Unhappy Marriage?" in *Tilting the Tower: Lesbians Teaching Queer Subjects,* ed. Linda Garber (New York: Routledge, 1994), esp. pp. 263–265.

9 John D'Emilio, "After Stonewall," in *Making Trouble: Essays on Gay History, Politics, and the University* (New York: Routledge, 1992) pp. 246–256.

10 The quotations are from Teresa de Lauretis, "Queer Theory: Lesbian and Gay Sexualities, an Introduction," *differences: A Journal of Feminist Cultural Studies,* 3.2 (summer 1991), p. iv; Sue-Ellen Case, "Tracking the Vampire," *differences: A Journal of Feminist Cultural Studies,* 3.2 (summer 1991), p. 2; and Allan Bérubé and Jeffrey Escoffier, "Queer/Nation," *Outlook: National Lesbian and Gay Quarterly,* 11 (winter 1991), p. 12. See also, Bad Object-Choices (eds.), *How Do I Look?: Queer Film and Video* (Seattle: Bay Press, 1991); Alexander Doty, *Making Things Perfectly Queer: Interpreting Mass Culture* (Minneapolis: University of Minnesota Press, 1993); Lisa Duggan, "Making It Perfectly Queer," *Socialist Review,* 22.1 (January–March, 1992), pp. 11–31; Arlene Stein, "Sisters and Queers: The Decentering of Lesbian Feminism," *Socialist Review,* 22.1 (January–March, 1992), pp. 33–55; David J. Thomas, "The 'Q' Word," *Socialist Review,* 25.1 (January–March, 1995), pp. 69–93; and Michael Warner

(ed.), *Fear of a Queer Planet: Queer Politics and Social Theory* (Minneapolis: University of Minnesota Press, 1993).

11 See Barbara Christian, "The Race for Theory," *Cultural Critique*, 6 (spring 1987), pp. 51–63.

12 Case, "Tracking the Vampire," p. 2.

13 Jewelle Gomez, "Out of the Past," in *The Question of Equality: Lesbian and Gay Politics in America since Stonewall*, ed. David Deitcher (New York: Scribner, 1995), p. 39.

14 This material is taken from an edited transcript of Hall's presentation at the symposium "Fantasy/Identity/Politics" which took place at the Institute of Contemporary Arts, London, February 16, 1989. See Victor Burgin, "Stuart Hall on Imaginary Identification and Politics," *Center for Cultural Studies Newsletter* (University of California, Santa Cruz) (winter 1991), n.p.; Benedict Anderson, *Imagined Communities: Reflections on the Origin and Spread of Nationalism* (London: Verso, 1983).

15 For examples of this latter work, see Joshua Gamson, "Must Identity Movements Self Destruct?: A Queer Dilemma," *Social Problems,* 42.3 (August, 1995), pp. 390–407; Steven Seidman, "Identity and Politics in a 'Postmodern' Gay Culture: Some Historical and Conceptual Notes," in *Fear of a Queer Planet: Queer Politics and Social Theory*, ed. Michael Warner (Minneapolis: University of Minnesota Press, 1993), pp. 105–142; and Stein, "Sisters and Queers."

16 Paul Veyne, *Writing History: Essay on Epistemology*, trans. Mina Moore-Rinvolucri (Middletown, CT: Wesleyan University Press, 1984), p. ix.

17 Stefan Dudink, "Sinds 1978," *Homologie: Tweemaandelijks Lesbo/Homoblad,* 15.3 (May–June, 1993), p. 2, my translation.

18 Michel Foucault, *The History of Sexuality: Volume One: An Introduction*, trans. Robert Hurley (New York: Vintage, 1979), p. 101.

19 Donna Penn, "Queer: Theorizing Politics and History," *Radical History Review,* 62 (spring 1995), p. 36; see in the same volume, Martha M. Umphrey, "The Trouble with Harry Thaw," pp. 8–23 and Henry Abelove, "The Queering of Lesbian/Gay History," pp. 44–57. See also Lisa Duggan, "The Discipline Problem," *GLQ: A Journal of Lesbian and Gay Studies,* 2.3 (August, 1995), pp. 179–191 and Joan Scott, "The Evidence of Experience," in *The Lesbian and Gay Studies Reader*, ed. Henry Abelove, Michèlle Aina Barale, and David M. Halperin (New York: Routledge, 1993), pp. 397–415.

20 Hayden White, "Droysen's *Historik*: Historical Writing as a Bourgeois Science," in *The Content of the Form: Narrative Discourse and Historical Representation* (Baltimore: Johns Hopkins University Press, 1987), pp. 83–103.

21 Michael Warner, "Introduction," in *Fear of a Queer Planet: Queer Politics and Social Theory*, ed. Michael Warner, p. xxvi, emphasis added. In note 19, Penn quotes this passage in abbreviated form, omitting the (crucial) last eight words.

22 Penn, "Queer," p. 40.

23 John D'Emilio, "Capitalism and Gay Identity," in *Powers of Desire: The Politics of Sexuality*, ed. Ann Snitow, Christine Stansell, and Sharon Thompson (New York: Monthly Review Press, 1983), p. 101.

24 Hayden White, "Historical Pluralism," *Critical Inquiry,* 12.3 (spring 1986), p. 487.

25 See Derek Attridge, Geoff Bennington, and Robert Young (eds.), *Post-Structuralism and the Question of History* (Cambridge: Cambridge University Press, 1987); Michel de Certeau, "History: Science and Fiction," in *Heterologies: Discourse on the Other,* trans. Brian Massumi (Minneapolis: University of Minnesota Press, 1986), pp. 199–221 and *The Writing of History,* trans. Tom Conley (New York: Columbia University Press, 1988); Linda Hutcheon, *A Poetics of Postmodernism: History, Theory, Fiction* (New York: Routledge, 1988); Fredric Jameson, *The Political Unconscious: Narrative as a Socially Symbolic Act* (Ithaca, NY: Cornell University Press, 1981); Dominick LaCapra, *History and Criticism* (Ithaca, NY: Cornell University Press, 1985); Louis O. Mink, *Historical Understanding,* ed. Brian Fay, Eugene O. Golob, and Richard T. Vann (Ithaca, NY: Cornell University Press, 1987); Paul Ricoeur, *The Reality of the Historical Past* (Milwaukee, WI: Marquette University Press, 1984); Veyne, *Writing History;* Hayden White, *The Tropics of Discourse: Essays in Cultural Criticism* (Baltimore: Johns Hopkins University Press, 1978), *Metahistory: The Historical Imagination in Nineteenth-Century Europe* (Baltimore: Johns Hopkins University Press, 1973), and *The Content of the Form.*

26 White, *Tropics of Discourse,* p. 121.

27 de Certeau, "History: Science and Fiction," p. 208, emphasis added.

28 Hutcheon, *A Poetics of Postmodernism,* p. 8.

29 Popular Memory Group, "Popular Memory: Theory, Politics, Method," in *Making Histories: Studies in History-Writing and Politics,* ed. Richard Johnson, Gregor McLennan, Bill Schwarz, and David Sutton (London: Hutchinson, 1982), p. 206.

30 See Marita Sturken, "Conversations with the Dead: Bearing Witness in the AIDS Memorial Quilt," *Socialist Review,* 22.2 (April–June, 1992), pp. 65–95.

31 For some discussion of this point, see my "Invented Traditions: Take One on the Lesbian and Gay Past," *NWSA Journal,* 3.1 (winter 1991), pp. 81–92.

32 Jameson, *The Political Unconscious,* p. 35.

33 White, *The Content of the Form,* p. 14.

34 de Certeau, *The Writing of History,* p. 85, original emphasis.

35 Dana Polan, *Power and Paranoia* (New York: Columbia University Press, 1986), p. 10.

36 See Stanley Aronowitz, "Postmodernism and Politics," in *Universal Abandon?: The Politics of Postmodernism,* ed. Andrew Ross (Minneapolis: University of Minnesota Press, 1988), pp. 46–62, esp. p. 51.

3 Reading queer history

1 George Chauncey, Jr., *Gay New York: Gender, Urban Culture, and the Making of the Gay Male World, 1890–1940* (New York: Basic Books, 1994); Lillian Faderman, *Odd Girls and Twilight Lovers: A History of Lesbian Life in*

Twentieth-Century America (New York: Columbia University Press, 1991); Elizabeth Lapovsky Kennedy and Madeline D. Davis, *Boots of Leather, Slippers of Gold: The History of a Lesbian Community* (New York: Routledge, 1993); and Esther Newton, *Cherry Grove, Fire Island: Sixty Years in America's First Gay and Lesbian Town* (Boston: Beacon Press, 1993).

2 Among the feminist criticisms of gay historiography are Teresa de Lauretis, *Technologies of Gender: Essays on Theory, Film, and Fiction* (Bloomington: Indiana University Press, 1987), pp. 1–30 and Diana Fuss, *Essentially Speaking: Feminism, Nature, and Difference* (New York: Routledge, 1989), pp. 110–111.

3 Allan Bérubé, "'Fitting In': Expanding Queer Studies beyond Gay Identity and Coming Out," paper presented at Pleasure/Politics: Fourth Annual Lesbian, Bisexual, and Gay Studies Conference, Harvard University, October 26–28, 1990; "Intellectual Desire," *GLQ: A Journal of Lesbian and Gay Studies,* 3.1 (February, 1996), pp. 139–157; "'Dignity for All': The Role of Homosexuality in the Marine Cooks and Stewards Union, 1930s–1950s," paper presented at the Annual Meeting of the American Historical Association, San Francisco, January 6–9, 1994 (see also the abstract of this paper which was printed in the *Committee on Lesbian and Gay History Newsletter* [January, 1994], p. 6); guest lecture, April 19, 1994, Community Studies 80F, University of California, Santa Cruz.

4 Bérubé, "'Dignity for All,'" abstract, p. 6.

5 See for instance, Carl Boggs, *Social Movements and Political Power: Emerging Forms of Radicalism in the West* (Philadelphia: Temple University Press, 1986); Bert Klandermans and Sidney Tarrow, "Mobilization into Social Movements: Synthesizing European and American Approaches," in *From Structures to Action: Comparing Social Movement Research across Cultures* (London: JAI Press, 1988), pp. 1–38; Ernesto Laclau and Chantal Mouffe, *Hegemony and Socialist Strategy: Towards a Radical Democratic Politics* (London: Verso, 1985); Scott Lash and John Urry, *The End of Organized Capitalism* (Madison, WI: University of Wisconsin Press, 1987); Alberto Melucci, *Nomads of the Present: Social Movements and Individual Needs in Contemporary Society* (Philadelphia: Temple University Press, 1989); Claus Offe, "New Social Movements: Challenging the Boundaries of Institutional Politics," *Social Research,* 52.4 (winter 1985), pp. 817–868; Alain Touraine, *The Voice and the Eye: An Analysis of Social Movements,* trans. Alan Duff (New York: Cambridge University Press, 1981); and Thomas Weisskopf, "The Current Economic Crisis in Historical Perspective," *Socialist Review,* 57 (May–June, 1981), pp. 9–53.

6 John D'Emilio, *Sexual Politics, Sexual Communities: The Making of a Homosexual Minority in the United States, 1940–1970* (Chicago: University of Chicago Press, 1983), p. 5.

7 D'Emilio, *Sexual Politics, Sexual Communities,* ch. 5.

8 Chauncey, *Gay New York,* p. 286.

9 Katie King, "Audre Lorde's Lacquered Layerings: The Lesbian Bar as a Site of Literary Production," *Cultural Studies,* 2.3 (October, 1988), pp. 321–342; Stuart

Marshall, "The Contemporary Political Use of Gay History: The Third Reich," in *How Do I Look?: Queer Film and Video*, ed. Bad Object-Choices (Seattle: Bay Press, 1991), pp. 65–101; Martha Gever, "What Becomes a Legend Most?" *GLQ: A Journal of Lesbian and Gay Studies,* 1.2 (May, 1994), pp. 209–219.

10 Michel Foucault, *The History of Sexuality: Volume One, An Introduction*, trans. Robert Hurley (New York: Vintage, 1979), p. 101.

11 Certainly, Stonewall matters in (Western) Europe where the (almost) annual Europride celebrations have been held in late June in various major European cities since 1992. To judge by the title (though not the contents) of a recent book (Emma Healy and Angela Mason [eds.], *Stonewall 25: The Making of the Lesbian and Gay Community in Britain* [London: Virago Press, 1994]), the symbolic dimensions of the riots might have a particularly strong resonance in the United Kingdom. For its part, however, Dutch gay and lesbian politics and commentary, rooted in specific historical and social relations quite dissimilar to those of the USA, have been resistant to the "Americanization" of Stonewall as a "global" phenomenon (although the annual Roze Zaterdag [Pink Saturday] gay and lesbian celebrations in the Netherlands are also held in late June). For the Dutch case in general, see Jan Willem Duyvendak (ed.), *De Verzuiling van de Homobeweging* (Amsterdam: SUA, 1994); Irene Costera Meijer, Jan Willem Duyvendak, and Marty PN van Kerkhof (eds.), *Over Normaal Gesproken: Hedendaagse Homopolitiek* (Amsterdam: Schorer, 1991); A. X. van Naerssen (ed.), *Gay Life in Dutch Society* (New York: Harrington Park Press, 1987); Judith Schuyf, *Een Stilzwijgende Samenleving: Lesbische Vrouwen in Nederland, 1920–1970* (Amsterdam: Stichting Beheer, 1994); and Rob Tielman, *Homoseksualiteit in Nederland: Studie van een Emancipatie Beweging* (Meppel/Amsterdam: Boom, 1982). On Americanization, see Hans Warmerdam, "Een Kloon van Uncle Sam: De Amerikanisering van Homoseksueel Nederland," in *Tolerantie onder NAP: 20 Essays over Homoseksualiteit voor Rob Tielman* (Utrecht: Rijksuniversiteit Utrecht/Homostudies, 1992), pp. 217–239. On Stonewall in particular, see Hans Warmerdam, "Zelfbevestiging in Apartheid: De Opstelling Van het COC tegenover De Gay Pride Day 1969–1978," *Homologie: Tweemaandelijks Lesbo/Homoblad* 11.4 (July/August, 1989), pp. 10–13 and Rob Tielman, "Stonewall: Amerikanisering en Nederlands Nationalisme," *Homologie: Tweemaandelijks Lesbo/Homoblad,* 16.4 (July–August, 1994), pp. 8–11. The importance of the Stonewall riots as either a practical example or a symbolic text for gay and/or lesbian movements elsewhere – say Colombia, Thailand, and Bulgaria – is not something that has been critically addressed. Yet, even recognizing Stonewall's absence might construct this lack as merely another indication of the apparent "underdevelopment" of gay identity/politics in these locations when considered against modernist narratives of development, the liberal state, and a discourse of a civil rights. In a recent article ("In the Shadows of Stonewall: Examining Gay Transnational Politics and the Diasporic Dilemma," *GLQ: A Journal of Lesbian and Gay Studies* 2.4 [December, 1995], pp. 425–438), Martin F.

Manalasan IV considers the problem of the globalization of the gay movement and the transformation of the meaning of Stonewall by looking at Filipino "gay" men in the Philippines and New York City.

4 The lesbian and gay past: it's Greek to whom?

1 Hom made this comment at the outset of her talk at Flaunting It!: First National Graduate Student Conference on Lesbian and Gay Studies, University of Wisconsin, Milwaukee, April 18–20, 1991.

2 John Addington Symonds, *A Problem in Greek Ethics* (London: private edn., 1883).

3 John Addington Symonds, *A Problem in Modern Ethics* (London: private edn., 1896). Among the recent scholarship, see K. J. Dover, *Greek Homosexuality* (New York: Vintage, 1980); Michel Foucault, *The History of Sexuality: Volume Two, The Use of Pleasure,* trans. Robert Hurley (New York: Vintage, 1986); David Halperin, *One Hundred Years of Homosexuality and Other Essays on Greek Love* (New York: Routledge, 1990); and John J. Winkler, *The Constraints of Desire* (New York: Routledge, 1990).

4 See Louis Crompton, *Byron and Greek Love: Homophobia in 19th-Century England* (Berkeley: University of California Press, 1985) and Martin Bernal, *Black Athena: The Afroasiatic Roots of Classical Civilization, Volume I: The Fabrication of Ancient Greece 1785–1985* (New Brunswick, NJ: Rutgers University Press, 1987), passim.

5 Jeffrey Weeks, *Coming Out: Homosexual Politics in Britain from the Nineteenth Century to the Present* (London: Quartet, 1977), p. 52.

6 Others have made this argument before me; here I will provide two rather different examples. Byrne R. S. Fone devotes fully a quarter of his edited volume *Hidden Heritage: History and the Gay Imagination* (New York: Irvington Publishers, 1981) to "the Greek experience," arguing in his introductory note to the text that "[t]hough the factual evidence of history is sometimes at odds with what people have chosen to believe . . . [t]he homosexual imagination has chosen to create in the matter of Greece a paradigm for freedom" (p. 4). In "Lesbian Intertextuality," Elaine Marks argues that Sappho has been an explicit and implicit model for representations of women-loving women, whatever the gender or sexual orientation of the author (in *Homosexualities and French Literature,* ed. George Stambolian and Elaine Marks [Ithaca, NY: Cornell University Press, 1979], pp. 353–377). See also Robert Aldrich, *The Seduction of the Mediterranean: Writing, Art, and Homosexual Fantasy* (New York: Routledge, 1993), passim.

7 The idea of belonging and possession expressed by the term "ours" is most pointedly a reference to the constructions of British, French, and German Classicists, and not at all to modern Greek ones. See Michael Herzfeld, *Anthropology through the Looking-Glass: A Critical Ethnography in the Margins of Europe* (New York: Cambridge University Press, 1987) in which Herzfeld

argues that contemporary Greek scholars have deferred to outsiders' definitions and interpretations of classical Greek culture in order to discover what its meaning is to themselves.

8 Bernal, *Black Athena*, pp. 29, 1.

9 Linda Dowling, *Hellenism and Homosexuality in Victorian Oxford* (Ithaca, NY: Cornell University Press, 1994), p. xiv.

10 See Joan DeJean, *Fictions of Sappho, 1546–1937* (Chicago: University of Chicago Press, 1989), Jeffrey M. Duban, *Ancient and Modern Images of Sappho* (Lanham, MD: University Press of America, 1983), and André Lardinois, "Lesbian Sappho and Sappho of Lesbos," in *From Sappho to de Sade: Moments in the History of Sexuality*, ed. Jan Bremmer (New York: Routledge, 1989), pp. 15–35.

11 Carroll Smith-Rosenberg, "The Female World of Love and Ritual: Relations between Women in Nineteenth-Century America," in *Disorderly Conduct: Visions of Gender in Victorian America* (New York: Alfred A. Knopf, 1985), pp. 53–76.

12 Michael Bronski, *Culture Clash: The Making of Gay Sensibility* (Boston: South End Press, 1984), pp. 193, 194, emphasis added.

13 Judy Grahn, *The Highest Apple: Sappho and the Lesbian Poetic Tradition* (San Francisco: Spinsters, Ink, 1985), p. 83, emphasis added.

14 As part of the emergent reverse discourses on male homosexuality, a number of English writers, artists, and philosophers – including Carpenter, Symonds, and many less familiar men such as Baron Corvo, William Cory, Edward Lafroy, Renell Rodd, and Simeon Soloman – formed a loose-knit cultural movement whose purpose was, in part, to mitigate the effects of the extremely repressive atmosphere of late nineteenth-century English society in relation to male homosexuality. Deriving its name from Plato's *Symposium*, this "Uranian movement" helped to bring into a larger discourse the ideas of the sexologist Karl Heinrich Ulrichs who had argued that homosexuality was a congenital rather than an acquired condition. On the Uranian movement, see Brian Reade (ed.), *Sexual Heretics: Male Homosexuality in English Literature from 1850 to 1900* (London: Routledge and Kegan Paul, 1970) and Timothy d'Arch Smith, *Love in Earnest: Some Notes on the Lives and Writings of English "Uranian" Poets from 1889 to 1930* (London: Routledge and Kegan Paul, 1970).

15 Quoted in H. Montgomery Hyde, *Oscar Wilde: A Biography* (New York: Farrar, Straus, and Giroux, 1975), pp. 257–258, emphasis added. See also Ed Cohen, *Talk on the Wilde Side: Toward a Genealogy of a Discourse of Male Sexualities* (New York: Routledge, 1993).

16 On the Wolfenden Report, see Weeks, *Coming Out*, passim.

17 Edward Carpenter, *The Intermediate Sex* in *Selected Writings, Volume One: Sex* (London: GMP, 1984), p. 188; cf. p. 208.

18 Kevin Porter and Jeffrey Weeks (eds.), *Between the Acts: Lives of Homosexual Men, 1885–1967* (London: Routledge, 1991), p. 3.

19 The supposition that Carpenter, Ellis, and Symonds were significant to a

nascent gay male literary production can be supported further. Henry James received a copy of Symonds's *A Problem in Modern Ethics* from Edmund Gosse and, in his letter of acknowledgement to Gosse, referred to Symonds as a "great reformer" (Leon Edel [ed.], *Henry James Letters* [Cambridge, MA: Harvard University Press, 1984], Vol. III, p. 398). American literary critic F. O. Matthiessen also read Carpenter, Ellis, and Symonds; see *Rat and the Devil: Journal Letters of F. O. Matthiessen and Russell Cheney*, ed. Louis Hyde (Boston: Alyson Publications, 1988), pp. 26, 47.

20 Jonathan Katz, *Gay American History: Lesbians and Gay Men in the USA* (New York: Thomas Crowell, 1976), p. 343.

21 Jonathan Ned Katz, *Gay/Lesbian Almanac* (New York: Harper and Row, 1983), pp. 433–434.

22 Mention of the importance of visits to libraries for information on homosexuality is a recurrent theme in gay and lesbian coming-out stories. For just a few examples, see Judy Grahn, *Another Mother Tongue: Gay Words, Gay Worlds* (Boston: Beacon Press, 1984), p. xi; Ann Heron (ed.), *One Teenager in Ten: Writings by Gay and Lesbian Youth* (Boston: Alyson Publications, 1983), passim; Julia Penelope Stanley and Susan J. Wolfe (eds.), *The Coming Out Stories* (Watertown, MA: Persephone Press, 1980), passim. Donald Webster Cory's *The Homosexual in America: A Subjective Approach* (New York: Greenberg, 1951) includes a chapter called "On a Five-Foot Bookshelf," a "bibliography of technical literature" on homosexuality, and a "check list of literary works" (pp. 167–177, 293–295, 296–315). Cory points out that Van Wykes Brooks's *John Addington Symonds, a Biographical Study* (New York: Michael Kennerley, 1914) "omitted all mention of homosexuality, which was basic to Symonds's critique of the Greek poets and the Renaissance, but even omitted to mention, no less evaluate, several books Symonds had written" (p. 160); both *A Problem in Greek Ethics* and *A Problem in Modern Ethics* are included in Cory's list of references and sources.

23 On male appropriations of Sappho, see Jean-Pierre Jacques, *Les Malheurs de Sapho* (Paris: Graset, 1981), pp. 51–55. On how the predicament of representing female sexual subjectivity operated in the lyric poet's work, see Eva Stehle Stigers, "Sappho's Private World," in *Reflections of Women in Antiquity*, ed. Helene P. Foley (New York: Gordon and Breach Science Publishers, 1981), pp. 45–61. For a discussion of homophobia and misogyny in both ancient and modern responses to the poet's work, see Judith P. Hallet, "Sappho and her Social Context: Sense and Sensuality," *Signs: Journal of Women in Culture and Society*, 4.3 (spring 1979), pp. 447–471. On the lives of Clifford and Barney, see Elyse Blankley, "Return to Mytilène: Renée Vivien and the City of Women," in *Women Writers and the City: Essays in Feminist Literary Criticism*, ed. Susan Merrill Squier (Knoxville: University of Tennessee Press, 1984), pp. 45–67; Jean Chalon, *Portrait of a Seductress: The World of Natalie Barney*, trans. Carol Barko (New York: Crown Publishers, 1979); Karla Jay, *The Amazon and the Page: Natalie Clifford Barney and Renée Vivien* (Bloomington: University of Indiana Press, 1988); Dolores Klaich, *Woman+Woman* (New York: Simon and

Schuster, 1974), ch. 5; and George Wickes, *The Amazon of Letters: The Life and Loves of Natalie Barney* (New York: G. P. Putnam's Sons, 1976).

24 Renée Vivien (trans.), *Sapho* (Paris: Lemerre, 1909). Vivien's story "Bona Dea," for example, is a compilation of a number of Sappho's fragments (in *The Woman of the Wolf and Other Stories*, trans. Karla Jay and Yvonne M. Klein [New York: Gay Presses of New York, 1983], pp. 116–122).

25 Natalie Barney, *A Perilous Advantage: The Best of Natalie Clifford Barney*, trans. and ed. Anna Livia (Norwich, VT: New Victoria Publishers, 1992), p. 22.

26 Vivien wrote about their arrival on the island in her poem "En débarquant à Mytilène" ("Landing at Mytilène"); Barney discusses their trip in *A Perilous Advantage*, pp. 43–45.

27 Renée Vivien, "Psappha revit," trans. Karla Jay, quoted in Jay, *The Amazon and the Page: Natalie Clifford Barney and Renée Vivien* (Bloomington: University of Indiana Press, 1988), p. 66

28 Barney, *A Perilous Advantage*, p. 45; on Vivien's identification with/as Sappho, see her *A Woman Appeared to Me*, trans. Jeannette H. Foster (Reno, NV: The Naiad Press, 1976). George Wickes suggests that Barney "seems to be dedicating herself to reliving the life of [Sappho]" in the first of her pseudonymously published *Cinq petits dialogues grecs (antithèses et parallèles)* (Paris: Plume, 1902); Wickes, *The Amazon of Letters*, p. 59.

29 Jay, *The Amazon and the Page*, p. 67.

30 Vivien, *A Woman Appeared to Me*, p. 8. In Barney's unpublished play "Le Mystère de Psyché," Aphrodite dismisses Sappho's love for Phaon as "a legend, my child, a legend ... a man's legend." Quoted in Jay, *The Amazon and the Page*, p. 68.

31 Barney writes with reference to heterosexism: "The expression against nature has naturally fallen out of use, but we should recognize that nothing could be more unnatural than the uniformity we seek to achieve." *A Perilous Advantage*, p. 85.

32 Jay, *The Amazon and the Page*, p. 116.

33 Vivien, "Bona Dea," p. 117, emphasis added.

34 Gayle Rubin, "Introduction" to Renée Vivien, *A Woman Appeared to Me*, p. x.

35 Renée Vivien, "The Friendship of Women," in *The Woman of the Wolf and Other Stories*, p. 102

36 Barney, *A Perilous Advantage*, pp. 83, 89; on serial monogamy, see, for instance, Elizabeth Lapovsky Kennedy and Madeline D. Davis, *Boots of Leather, Slippers of Gold: The History of a Lesbian Community* (New York: Routledge, 1993), esp. pp. 231–277 and Carol S. Becker, *Unbroken Ties: Lesbian Ex-Lovers* (Boston: Alyson Publications, 1988), passim.

37 Jay, *The Amazon and the Page*, p. 114. The quotations, cited by Jay, are from Barney's manuscript "Her Legitimate Lover" and her book *Eparpillements*.

38 Dudley Fitts, "Foreword," in Mary Barnard (trans.), *Sappho: A New Translation* (Berkeley: University of California Press, 1958), pp. vii, viii.

39 Monique Wittig and Sande Zeig, *Lesbian Peoples: Materials for a Dictionary* (New York: Avon Books, 1979), p. 136.

40 Susan Gubar, "Sapphistries," *Signs: Journal of Women in Culture and Society,* 10.1 (fall 1984), pp. 46–47, emphasis added.

41 For example, Hieronymous K. (pseud.), "What Is His Country," *One,* 1.5 (May, 1953), pp. 14–17 discusses the "ambiguous attitudes of the ancients toward homosexuality;" *One's* occasional "Out of the Past Column" offered "reprints from the classics [and] biographies of famous homosexuals" and published extracts from Plato's *Symposium (One,* 3.10 [October, 1955], pp. 16–18); Mary-Faith Albert reviewed Peter Green's book about Sappho, *The Laughter of Aphrodite* in *One,* 14.4 (April–May, 1966), p. 27; the "Lesbiana" column made mention of Pierre Louÿs's works in *The Ladder,* 1.6 (March, 1957), p. 12 and 2.4 (January, 1958), p. 13; and see Jan Fraser's poem, "Sappho," in *The Ladder,* 4.6 (March, 1960), p. 14.

42 Del Martin and Phyllis Lyon, *Lesbian/Woman* (San Francisco: Glide Foundation, 1972), p. 219; Pierre Louÿs, *Les Chansons de Bilitis,* volume III of *Oeuvres complètes* (Geneva: Slatkine, 1973), pp. 1–174.

43 Valerie Taylor, *Stranger on Lesbos* (New York: Fawcett Crest, 1960) and *Return to Lesbos* (reprint edn., Tallahassee, FL: The Naiad Press, 1982); Richard Robertiello, *Voyage from Lesbos: Psychoanalysis of a Female Homosexual* (New York: Citadel Press, 1959).

44 Lindsay van Gelder and Pamela Robin Brandt, *Are You Two . . . Together?: A Gay and Lesbian Travel Guide to Europe* (New York: Random House, 1991), p. 277. See also Anthony Aspinall, "Greece: Ancient and Modern," *Gay Times* (London) (February, 1993), pp. 57–60; the bilingual Greek/English *Greek Gay Guide '94* (Athens: Kraximo, 1994); *Gaia's International Guide* (New York: Gaia's Guide, various years); *Spartacus International Gay Guide* (Berlin: Bruno Gmünder, various years); and *Women Going Places* (London: Women Going Places Productions, various years).

45 Ed Cohen, "Who Are 'We'? Gay 'Identity' as Political (E)motion (A Theoretical Rumination)," in *Inside/Out: Lesbian Theories, Gay Theories,* ed. Diana Fuss (New York: Routledge, 1991), pp. 71–92.

46 Ming-Yeung Lu, "Passion Tales: Allegories of Identity," *Lavender Godzilla* (spring 1992), p. 6; Bret Hinsch, *Passions of the Cut Sleeve: The Male Homosexual Tradition in China* (Berkeley: University of California Press, 1990).

47 Sidney Abbott and Barbara Love, *Sappho Was a Right-On Woman: A Liberated View of Lesbianism* (New York: Stein and Day, 1972).

48 See, for instance, Sucheng Chan, *Asian Americans: An Interpretive History* (Boston: Twayne Publishers, 1991) and Ronald Takaki, *Strangers from a Different Shore: A History of Asian Americans* (New York: Penguin, 1990).

49 Bonnie Zimmerman, *The Safe Sea of Women: Lesbian Fiction, 1969–1989* (Boston: Beacon Press, 1990), p. 124.

50 See Norma Alarcón, "The Theoretical Subject(s) of *This Bridge Called My Back* and Anglo-American Feminism," in *Making Face, Making Soul/Haciendo Caras: Creative and Critical Perspectives by Women of Color,* ed. Gloria Anzaldúa (San Francisco: Aunt Lute, 1990), pp. 356–369.

5 Queer fictions of Stonewall

1 Martin Duberman, *Stonewall* (New York: Dutton, 1993), p. xv.
2 Respectively, the first four quotations are taken from Chris Adams, "Birth of Defiance," review of Martin Duberman, *Stonewall*, in the *San Francisco Chronicle*, review section (June 20, 1993), p. 1; Diana Walsh, "250,000 Watch S.F. Gay March, a Parade of Firsts," *San Francisco Examiner* (July 1, 1991), p. A-10; an unnamed witness to the riot quoted in Donn Teal, *The Gay Militants* (New York: Stein and Day, 1971), p. 20; and [Dick Leitsch], "The Hairpin Drop Heard Round the World," supplemental leaflet to *New York Mattachine Newsletter* (July, 1969). The rather odd term "modern" to describe gay and lesbian history since Stonewall is used with such frequency that it would be impossible to list all of its occurrences, but see Duberman, *Stonewall*, p. xv.
3 Duberman, *Stonewall*, p. xv, emphasis added.
4 Duberman's style is also informed by the trope of the historian as visual artist engaged in portraiture, drawing, and painting (p. xvi). In other words, Duberman's *Stonewall* is informed by both a verbal style and a visual metaphor that draw on realist models of historical representation which purport merely to describe or to make visible the events of the past in small and precise detail and to offer them as literal, unmediated, and true "images" of what happened.
5 Alessandro Portelli, "The Peculiarities of Oral History," *History Workshop*, 12 (autumn 1981), pp. 98–99.
6 Joan W. Scott, "The Evidence of Experience," in *The Lesbian and Gay Studies Reader*, ed. Henry Abelove, Michèlle Aina Barale, and David M. Halperin (New York: Routledge, 1993), pp. 399, 407, 409
7 On Redstockings, see Alice Echols, *Daring to Be Bad: Radical Feminism in America, 1967–1975* (Minneapolis: University of Minnesota Press, 1989), pp. 139–158.
8 Howard Smith, "Full Moon over the Stonewall," *Village Voice* (July 3, 1969), pp. 1, 25, 29 and Lucian Truscott IV, "Gay Power Comes to Sheridan Square," *The Village Voice* (July 3, 1969), pp. 1, 18.
9 The photograph has recently been reprinted opposite Sara Hart, "Stonewall 25," *Ten Percent* (June, 1994), p. 47; in Fred W. McDarrah and Timothy S. McDarrah, *Gay Pride: Photographs from Stonewall to Today* (Chicago: A Capella, 1994), on the front cover and opposite p. 1; and in the *Village Voice* (November 14, 1995), p. 41 as part of their forty-year retrospective. An alternate image of this scene appears in *Gay Pride*, p. xxiii.
10 Exemplary, though not unique, are the following: "New Negro Riots Erupt on Coast; 3 Reported shot," *New York Times* (August 13, 1965), p. 1; "2,000 Troops Enter Los Angeles on Third Day of Negro Rioting; 4 Die as Fires and Looting Grow," *New York Times* (August 14, 1965), p. 1; and "2,000 Guardsmen on Chicago Alert," *New York Times* (August 15, 1965), p. 1.
11 "4 Policemen Hurt in 'Village' Raid," *New York Times* (June 29, 1969), p. 33; "Police Again Rout 'Village' Youths," *New York Times* (June 30, 1969), p. 22.

12 A more explicit marking of this racial–sexual dichotomy is reflected in a police officer's comment overheard by a New York Mattachine Society member: "I like nigger riots better because there's more action, but you can't beat up a fairy. They ain't mean like blacks; they're sick" (quoted in [Leitsch], "The Hairpin Drop Heard Round the World," p. 23). Jim Fouratt also argued along these lines, noting that "[n]ot one straight radical group showed up at Stonewall. *If* it had been a *black* demonstration they'd have been there" (quoted in Duberman, *Stonewall*, p. 211, emphasis added). On Greenwich Village, see George Chauncey, *Gay New York: Gender, Urban Culture, and the Making of the Gay Male World, 1890–1940* (New York: Basic Books, 1994), esp. pp. 228–244 and Ellen Kay Trimberger, "Feminism, Men, and Modern Love: Greenwich Village, 1900–1925," in *Powers of Desire: The Politics of Sexuality*, ed. Ann Snitow, Christine Stansell, and Sharon Thompson (New York: Monthly Review Press, 1983), pp. 131–152.

13 Consider, in particular, the following pictures reprinted in Duberman, *Stonewall*: the 1965 ECHO convention; the May 21, 1965, picket in front of the White House; and the Gay Liberation Front poster.

14 John D'Emilio, *Sexual Politics, Sexual Communities: The Making of a Homosexual Minority in the United States 1940–1970* (Chicago: University of Chicago Press, 1983), pp. 231, 232. In more recent writings, D'Emilio vacillates on the relative numbers of men of color involved in the riots and leaves white participants unmarked. Citing no sources in either instance he maintains, "[y]oung gay men of color as *many* of the [patrons of the Stonewall] were, they could not have been immune to the rhetoric and politics of groups such as the Black Panthers and the Young Lords" ("After Stonewall," pp. 240–241, emphasis added) and "*some* of [the rioters] were young men of color whose home communities were permeated by radical politics" (John D'Emilio, "Foreword," in *Out of the Closets: Voices of Gay Liberation*, ed. Karla Jay and Allen Young, reprint edition [New York: New York University Press, 1992], p. xix, emphasis added).

15 Lillian Faderman, *Odd Girls and Twilight Lovers: A History of Lesbian Life in Twentieth-Century America* (New York, Columbia University Press, 1991), p. 194.

16 Sidney Abbott and Barbara Love, *Sappho Was a Right-On Woman: A Liberated View of Lesbianism* (New York: Stein and Day, 1972), p. 159; Barry Adam, *The Rise of a Gay and Lesbian Movement* (Boston: Twayne, 1987), p. 75; Sam Binkley, "'I'm Sorry I Threw Bricks at Stonewall!': A Faghag's Historical Commentary: Excerpts from an Interview with Penny Arcade," *Found Object,* 4 (fall 1994), p. 127; Mike Long, "The Night the Girls Said No!" *San Francisco Sentinel* (June 22, 1989), p. 2; Toby Marotta, *The Politics of Homosexuality* (Boston: Houghton Mifflin Company, 1981), pp. 71, 74; Cindy Stein, "Stonewall Nation 69–79: What Really Happened, Anyhow?" *Gay Community News* (June 23, 1979), p. 9; Teal, *The Gay Militants*, p. 18; Allen Young, "Out of the Closets, Into the Streets," in *Out of the Closets*, p. 25.

17 Mark Haile, "The Truth about Stonewall," *BLK*, 7 (June, 1989), p. 8.

18 John D'Emilio, "After Stonewall," in *Making Trouble: Essays on Gay History, Politics, and the University* (New York: Routledge, 1992), p. 261; Faderman, *Odd Girls and Twilight Lovers*, pp. 284–288.

19 Maida Tilchen, "Mythologizing Stonewall," *Gay Community News* (June 23, 1979), p. 16.

20 Robert L. Pela, "Stonewall's Eyewitnesses," *The Advocate* (May 3, 1994), p. 52.

21 Tilchen, "Mythologizing Stonewall," p. 16.

22 Elizabeth Lapovsky Kennedy and Madeline D. Davis, *Boots of Leather, Slippers of Gold: The History of a Lesbian Community* (New York: Routledge, 1993), p. 378, emphasis added.

23 Truscott, "Gay Power Comes to Sheridan Square," p. 1.

24 Maria De La O, "Stonewall: The Queer Revolution Twenty Years Later," *Deneuve* (June, 1994), p. 30; see Duberman's discussion of the persistent doubts about whether a lesbian "started" the riots (*Stonewall*, pp. 196ff.).

25 Editorial, "A Stonewall Nation," *Gay Community News* (June 23, 1979), p. 4, emphasis added.

26 De La O, "Stonewall," p. 30; John D'Emilio argues that "Stonewall was the catalyst that allowed gay women and men to appropriate to themselves the example, insight, and inspiration of the radical movements of the 1960s – black power, the new left, the counterculture, *and, above all, feminism* – and take a huge step forward toward liberation" ("Dreams Deferred: The Birth and Betrayal of America's First Gay Liberation Movement," in *Making Trouble*, p. 54, emphasis added).

27 Victoria A. Brownsworth, "Stonewall 25: Not a Happy Anniversary for Lesbians," *Deneuve* (June, 1994), p. 38.

28 Abbott and Love, *Sappho Was a Right-On Woman*, p. 159, emphasis added.

29 Dolores Klaich, *Woman+Woman* (New York: Simon and Schuster, 1974), p. 219.

30 Abbott and Love, *Sappho Was a Right-On Woman*; Dennis Altman, *Homosexual: Oppression and Liberation* (New York: Outerbridge and Dienstfrey, 1971); Ti-Grace Atkinson, *Amazon Odyssey* (New York: Links, 1974); Jay and Young (eds.), *Out of the Closets*; Jill Johnston, *Lesbian Nation: The Feminist Solution* (New York: Simon and Schuster, 1973); Klaich, *Woman+Woman*; Del Martin and Phyllis Lyon, *Lesbian/Woman* (San Francisco: Glide Foundation, 1972); Nancy Myron and Charlotte Bunch (eds.), *Lesbians and the Women's Movement* (Baltimore, MD: Diana Press, 1975); Len Richmond and Gary Noguera (eds.), *The Gay Liberation Book* (San Francisco: Ramparts Press, 1972); Ruth Simpson, *From the Closets to the Courts* (New York: Viking, 1976); Teal, *The Gay Militants*.

31 Teresa de Lauretis, "Queer Theory: Lesbian and Gay Studies, an Introduction," *differences: A Journal of Feminist Cultural Studies* 3.2 (summer 1991), pp. iv, v.

32 De La O, "Stonewall," p. 31.

33 J. E. Freeman, "I Remember," *San Francisco Examiner Magazine* (June 19, 1994), p. 11.

34 Interview with Martha Shelley in Eric Marcus, *Making History: The Struggle for Gay and Lesbian Equal Rights, 1945–1990, an Oral History* (New York: HarperCollins, 1992), p. 180.

35 D'Emilio, "After Stonewall," p. 240.

36 Paul Berman, "Democracy and Homosexuality," *The New Republic* (December 20, 1993), p. 24, emphasis added.

37 D'Emilio, "After Stonewall," pp. 245, 246–256.

38 D'Emilio, "After Stonewall," p. 244.

39 Duberman, *Stonewall*, p. xv.

40 Diana Fuss, *Essentially Speaking: Feminism, Nature, and Difference* (New York: Routledge, 1989), p. 101.

41 D'Emilio, "After Stonewall," p. 249.

42 Abbott and Love, *Sappho Was a Right-On Woman*, ch. 3; Allan Bérubé, *Coming Out under Fire: The History of Gay Men and Women in World War Two* (New York: The Free Press, 1990), passim; Donald Webster Cory (pseud.), *The Homosexual in America: A Subjective Approach* (New York: Greenberg, 1951), ch. 11; D'Emilio, *Sexual Politics, Sexual Communities*, p. 32; Faderman, *Odd Girls and Twilight Lovers*, esp. pp. 161–167; Leslie Feinberg, *Stone Butch Blues* (Ithaca, NY: Firebrand Books, 1993), passim; Evelyn Hooker, "Male Homosexuals and their 'Worlds,'" in *Sexual Inversion*, ed. Judd Marmor (New York: Basic Books, 1965), pp. 83–107; Kennedy and Davis, *Boots of Leather, Slippers of Gold*, passim; Audre Lorde, *Zami: A New Spelling of My Name* (Trumansburg, NY: The Crossing Press, 1982), passim; Joan Nestle, "Butch-Femme Relationships: Sexual Courage in the 1950s," in *A Restricted Country* (Ithaca, NY: Firebrand Books, 1987), pp. 100–109; Kenneth E. Read, *Other Voices: The Style of a Male Homosexual Tavern* (Novato, CA: Chandler and Sharp, 1980); and Wayne Sage, "Inside the Colossal Closet," in *Gay Men: The Sociology of Male Homosexuality*, ed. Martin P. Levine (New York: Harper and Row, 1979), pp. 148–163.

43 Duberman, *Stonewall*, p. 182.

44 Sage, "Inside the Colossal Closet."

45 Dennis Altman, "What Changed in the Seventies?" in *Homosexuality: Power and Politics*, ed. Gay Left Collective (London: Allison and Busby, 1980), p. 57.

46 D'Emilio, "After Stonewall," p. 251.

47 This ambiguous status *vis-à-vis* the public is reflected in the transformation of the rallying cry of gay liberationists ten years after Stonewall on the night of the riots at San Francisco's City Hall in protest at the lenient sentence given to Dan White for assassinating Supervisor Harvey Milk and Mayor George Moscone. In recognition of the vastly transformed nature of the gay subculture and in a fairly explicit attempt to equate the closet of the late 1960s with the commercial subculture of the late 1970s, the earlier slogan "Out of the closets, into the streets" became "Out of the bars and into the streets." See Allen Young, "Out of the Closets, Into the Streets" and Randy Shilts, *The Mayor of Castro Street: The Life and Times of Harvey Milk* (New York: St. Martin's Press, 1982), p. 327.

48 Ernesto Laclau and Chantal Mouffe, *Hegemony and Socialist Strategy: Towards a Radical Democratic Politics* (London: Verso, 1985), p. 181.
49 Fuss, *Essentially Speaking*, p. 105.
50 D'Emilio, "After Stonewall," p. 237.
51 Paul Rudnick, "Gaytown, USA," *New York* (June 20, 1994), p. 38.
52 D'Emilio, "After Stonewall," p. 236.
53 Mary Breslauer, "Another Weekend Lost," *The Advocate* (February 22, 1994), p. 5.
54 Richard Herrell, "The Symbolic Strategies of Chicago's Gay and Lesbian Pride Day Parade," in *Gay Culture in America: Essays from the Field*, ed. Gilbert Herdt (Boston: Beacon Press, 1991), p. 245.
55 Martha Gever, "What Becomes a Legend Most?" *GLQ: A Journal of Lesbian and Gay Studies,* 1.2 (May, 1994), p. 210. Rosemary Hennessey has argued that "for those of us caught up in the circuits of late capitalist consumption, the visibility of sexual identity is often a matter of commodification, a process that invariably depends on the lives and labor of invisible others." See her "Queer Visibility in Commodity Culture," *Cultural Critique,* 29 (winter 1994–1995), pp. 31–76; the quotation is on p. 31.
56 On emplotment in general, see Northrop Frye, *The Anatomy of Criticism: Four Essays* (Princeton, NJ: Princeton University Press, 1957); on emplotment and historical explanation, see Hayden White, *Metahistory: The Historical Imagination in Nineteenth-Century Europe* (Baltimore: Johns Hopkins University Press, 1973), esp. pp. 7–11.
57 Duberman, *Stonewall*, p. 280.
58 Although the scope of inclusion is defined by the politics of gay liberation, the writings anthologized in Jay and Young (eds.), *Out of the Closets* suggest some of these acute differences. See also, Terrence Kissack, "Freaking Fag Revolutionaries: New York's Gay Liberation Front, 1969–1971," *Radical History Review* 62 (spring 1995), pp. 104–134.

6 Re/writing queer histories

1 Gloria Anzaldúa, "Haciendo caras, una entrada," in *Making Face, Making Soul/Haciendo Caras: Creative and Critical Perspectives by Women of Color,* ed. Gloria Anzaldúa (San Francisco: Aunt Lute, 1990), p. xxv.
2 Linda Hutcheon, *A Poetics of Postmodernism: History, Theory, Fiction* (New York: Routledge, 1988), p. 90.
3 Marlon T. Riggs, "Ruminations of a Snap Queen: What Time Is It?!" *Outlook: National Lesbian and Gay Quarterly,* 12 (spring 1991), p. 16.
4 Daniel Bell, *The Cultural Contradictions of Capitalism* (New York: Basic Books, 1976), p. 13.
5 See my "Telling (Hi)stories: Rethinking the Lesbian and Gay Historical Imagination," *Outlook: National Lesbian and Gay Quarterly,* 8 (spring 1990), p. 74. I was referring to Will Roscoe, "The Zuni Man-Woman," *Outlook: National*

Lesbian and Gay Quarterly, 2 (summer 1988), pp. 56–67 and Ramón A. Gutiérrez, "Must We Deracinate Indians to Find Gay Roots?," *Outlook: National Lesbian and Gay Quarterly,* 4 (winter 1989), pp. 61–67. The quotation is Roscoe's (p. 64).

6 Will Roscoe, "Who Speaks for Gay Native Americans?" letter to the editor, *Outlook: National Lesbian and Gay Quarterly,* 10 (fall 1990), p. 80.

7 Stuart Hall, "Cultural Identity and Diaspora," in *Colonial Discourse and Post-Colonial Theory: A Reader,* ed. Patrick Williams and Laura Chrisman (New York: Columbia University Press, 1994), p. 394; Gutiérrez, "Must We Deracinate Indian Roots?"; see also Benedict Anderson, *Imagined Communities: Reflections on the Origin and Spread of Nationalism* (London: Verso, 1983) and Eric Hobsbawm and Terence Ranger (eds.), *The Invention of Tradition* (Cambridge: Cambridge University Press, 1983).

8 For a good introduction to and overview of current scholarship, criticism, and politics, see the essays in M. Annette Jaimes (ed.), *The State of Native America: Genocide, Colonization, and Resistance* (Boston, MA: South End Press, 1992).

9 Paula Gunn Allen, "How the West Was Really Won," in *The Sacred Hoop: Recovering the Feminine in American Indian Traditions* (Boston: Beacon Press, 1986), pp. 194–208.

10 Randy Burns, "Preface," in *Living the Spirit: A Gay American Indian Anthology,* ed. Will Roscoe (New York: St. Martin's Press, 1988), p. 2. It is worth noting in this regard, however, the relationship between Native American cultural production and white scholars as supporters of this work. Roscoe's position as coordinating editor for this anthology "compiled by Gay American Indians" is something of a contemporary parallel to Lucullus Virgil McWhorter's complex role in the publication of Mourning Dove's *Cogewea: The Half Blood* (1927; reprint edn., Lincoln: University of Nebraska Press, 1981), one of the earliest novels by a Native American woman.

11 M. Owlfeather, "Children of Grandmother Moon," in *Living the Spirit,* ed. Will Roscoe, p. 99

12 Paula Gunn Allen, "Some Like Indians Endure," in *Living the Spirit,* ed. Will Roscoe , p. 9

13 Caren Kaplan, "Deterritorializations: The Rewriting of Home and Exile in Western Feminist Discourse," *Cultural Critique,* 6 (spring 1987), p. 191, special issue: "The Nature and Context of Minority Discourse," ed. Abdul R. JanMohamed and David Lloyd.

14 Jackie Goldsby, "What It Means to Be Colored Me," *Outlook: National Lesbian and Gay Quarterly,* 9 (summer 1990), p. 14.

15 Audre Lorde, *Zami: A New Spelling of My Name* (Trumansburg, NY: The Crossing Press, 1982) and Samuel R. Delany, *The Motion of Light in Water: Sex and Science Fiction Writing in the East Village, 1957–1965* (New York: New American Library, 1988).

16 For an analysis of the relationship between the structures of race and sexuality in the urban north, see Kevin Mumford, "Homosex Changes: Race, Cultural Geography, and the Emergence of the Gay," *American Quarterly,* 48.3 (September, 1996), pp. 395–414.

17 Delany, *The Motion of Light in Water*, pp. 10, 52.
18 Lorde, *Zami*, p. 220.
19 John D'Emilio, *Sexual Politics, Sexual Communities: The Making of a Homosexual Minority in the United States 1940–1970* (Chicago: University of Chicago Press, 1983), p. 32.
20 John D'Emilio, "Capitalism and Gay Identity," in *Powers of Desire: The Politics of Sexuality*, ed. Ann Snitow, Christine Stansell, and Sharon Thompson (New York: Monthly Review Press, 1983), p. 101.
21 Pratibha Parmar, "That Moment of Emergence," in *Queer Looks: Perspectives on Lesbian and Gay Film and Video*, ed. Martha Gever, John Greyson, and Pratibha Parmar (New York: Routledge, 1993), pp. 5–6.
22 The term "the black Atlantic" is Paul Gilroy's; see his *The Black Atlantic: Modernity and Double Consciousness* (Cambridge, MA: Harvard University Press, 1993).
23 Jim Marks, "Looking for Isaac," *Outweek* (October 1, 1989), p. 33.
24 Kobena Mercer, "Dark and Lovely Too: Black Gay Men in Independent Film," in *Queer Looks*, ed. Gever, Greyson, and Parmar, p. 248.
25 See Essex Hemphill, *"Looking for Langston*: An Interview with Isaac Julien," in *Brother to Brother: New Writings by Black Gay Men*, ed. Essex Hemphill, conceived by Joseph Beam (Boston: Alyson Publications, 1991), pp. 174–180, esp. p. 177.
26 See my "Isaac Julien's *Looking for Langston*: Hughes, Biography, and Queer(ed) History," *Cultural Studies*, 7.2 (May, 1993), pp. 311–323.
27 See Don Belton, "Young Soul Rebel: A Conversation with Isaac Julien," *Outlook: National Lesbian and Gay Quarterly*, 16 (spring 1992), pp. 15–19, esp. pp. 16–17. See also Isaac Julien and Kobena Mercer, "True Confessions: A Discourse on Images of Black Male Sexuality," in *Brother to Brother*, ed. Hemphill, pp. 172–173.
28 Belton, "Young Soul Rebel," p. 19. Elsewhere, Julien pinpoints a specific racialized funding logic that is imposed on black directors: "There was no doubt in our minds that what [Channel 4] really wanted from black film-makers were documentaries of a realist nature, although Sankofa and Black Audio Film Collective were allowed to make experimental films under their remit of innovation" (Isaac Julien, "Introduction," in Isaac Julien and Colin MacCabe, *Diary of a Young Soul Rebel*, with screenplay by Paul Hallam and Derrick Saldaan McClintock [London: British Film Institute, 1991], pp. 4–5).
29 Parmar, "That Moment of Emergence," p. 7.
30 "'Filling the Lack in Everyone Is Quite Hard Work, Really . . .,' A Roundtable Discussion with Joy Chamberlain, Isaac Julien, Stuart Marshall, and Pratibha Parmar," in *Queer Looks*, ed. Gever, Greyson, and Parmar, p. 42.
31 Belton, "Young Soul Rebel," p. 17.
32 Jewelle Gomez, "Out of the Past," in *The Question of Equality: Lesbian and Gay Politics in America since Stonewall*, ed. David Deitcher (New York: Scribner, 1995), pp. 18–65. The four-part television series was first aired in 1995.
33 Jewelle Gomez, *The Gilda Stories* (Ithaca, NY: Firebrand Books, 1991).

34 See especially, Jewelle Gomez, *Forty-Three Septembers* (Ithaca, NY: Firebrand Books, 1993). The historical possibility for such a queer space in San Francisco around the turn of the century is mentioned briefly in Susan Stryker and Jim Van Buskirk, *Gay By the Bay: A History of Queer Culture in the San Francisco Bay Area* (San Francisco: Chronicle Books, 1996), pp. 19, 24.
35 In several historiographical accounts, Audre Lorde's *Zami* has received attention as a primary source on lesbian life in the 1950s, without acknowledgment that "a biomythography" might need to be read somewhat differently, though no more or less critically, from other kinds of materials. See, for example, Martin Duberman, *Stonewall* (New York: Dutton, 1993), pp. 43, 90–91, 282 n.3, and Lillian Faderman, *Odd Girls and Twilight Lovers: A History of Lesbian Life in Twentieth-Century America* (New York: Columbia University Press, 1991), p. 144.

7 Queer fictions for the future

1 Jeanette Winterson, *Oranges Are Not the Only Fruit* (New York: Atlantic Monthly Press, 1987), p. 93.
2 Popular Memory Group, "Popular Memory: Theory, Politics, Method," in *Making Histories: Studies in History-Writing and Politics*, ed. Richard Johnson, Gregor McLennan, Bill Schwarz, and David Sutton (London: Hutchinson, 1982), p. 207.
3 Martin Bauml Duberman, Martha Vicinus, and George Chauncey, Jr., "Introduction," in *Hidden from History: Reclaiming the Gay and Lesbian Past*, ed. Martin Bauml Duberman, Martha Vicinus, and George Chauncey, Jr. (New York: New American Library, 1989), p. 11.
4 Jewelle Gomez, *The Gilda Stories* (Ithaca, NY: Firebrand Books, 1991), pp. 44, 191.

Select bibliography

Abbott, Sidney and Barbara Love, *Sappho Was a Right-On Woman: A Liberated View of Lesbianism* (New York: Stein and Day, 1972)

Abelove, Henry, "The Queering of Lesbian/Gay History," *Radical History Review*, 62 (spring 1995), pp. 44–57

Abelove, Henry, Michèlle Aina Barale, and David M. Halperin (eds.), *The Lesbian and Gay Studies Reader* (New York: Routledge, 1993)

Adam, Barry D., *The Rise of a Gay and Lesbian Movement* (Boston: Twayne Publishers, 1987)

"Structural Foundations of the Gay World," *Comparative Studies in Society and History*, 27.4 (1985), pp. 658–671

Aldrich, Robert, *The Seduction of the Mediterranean: Writing, Art, and Homosexual Fantasy* (London: Routledge, 1993)

Allen, Paula Gunn, *The Sacred Hoop: Recovering the Feminine in American Indian Traditions* (Boston: Beacon Press, 1986)

Almaguer, Tomás, "Chicano Men: A Cartography of Homosexual Identity and Behavior," *differences: A Journal of Feminist Cultural Studies*, 3.2 (summer 1991), special issue: "Queer Theory: Lesbian and Gay Sexualities," ed. Teresa de Lauretis, pp. 75–100

Altman, Dennis, *AIDS in the Mind of America: The Social, Political, and Psychological Impact of a New Epidemic* (Garden City, NY: Anchor Press/Doubleday, 1986)

Homosexual: Oppression and Liberation (New York: Outerbridge and Dienstfrey, 1971)

The Homosexualization of America, The Americanization of Homosexuality (New York: St. Martin's Press, 1982)

Altman, Dennis et al. (eds.), *Which Homosexuality?: Essays from the International Scientific Conference on Lesbian and Gay Studies* (London: Gay Men's Press, 1989)

Anderson, Benedict, *Imagined Communities: Reflections on the Origin and Spread of Nationalism* (London: Verso, 1983)

Anzaldúa, Gloria, *Borderlands/La Frontera* (San Francisco: Spinsters/Aunt Lute, 1987)

Anzaldúa, Gloria (ed.), *Making Face, Making Soul/Haciendo Caras: Creative and Critical Perspectives by Women of Color* (San Francisco: Aunt Lute, 1990)

Aronowitz, Stanley, "Postmodernism and Politics," in *Universal Abandon?: The Politics of Postmodernism*, ed. Andrew Ross, pp. 46–62

Aspinall, Anthony, "Greece: Ancient and Modern," *Gay Times* (London) (February, 1993), pp. 57–60

Atkinson, Ti-Grace, *Amazon Odyssey* (New York: Links, 1974)

Attridge, Derek, Geoff Bennington, and Robert Young (eds.), *Post-Structuralism and the Question of History* (Cambridge: Cambridge University Press, 1987)

Avi-Ram, Amatai F., "The Unreadable Black Body: 'Conventional' Poetic Form in the Harlem Renaissance," *Genders*, 7 (spring 1990), pp. 32–45

Bad Object-Choices (eds.), *How Do I Look?: Queer Film and Video* (Seattle: Bay Press, 1991)

Barnard, Mary, *Sappho: A New Translation* (Berkeley: University of California Press, 1958)

Barney, Natalie Clifford, *Cinq petits dialogues grecs (antithèses et parallèles)* (Paris: Plume, 1902)

  A Perilous Advantage: The Best of Natalie Clifford Barney, trans. and ed. Anna Livia (Norwich, VT: New Victoria Publishers, 1992)

Bayer, Ronald, *Homosexuality and American Psychiatry: The Politics of Diagnosis* (New York: Basic Books, 1981)

Beam, Joseph (ed.), *In the Life: A Black Gay Anthology* (Boston: Alyson Publications, 1986)

Beck, Evelyn Torton (ed.), *Nice Jewish Girls: A Lesbian Anthology* (Boston: Beacon Press, 1989)

Bell, Daniel, *The Cultural Contradictions of Capitalism* (New York: Basic Books, 1976)

Belton, Don, "Young Soul Rebel: A Conversation with Isaac Julien," *Outlook: National Lesbian and Gay Quarterly*, 16 (spring 1992), pp. 15–19

Benstock, Shari, *Women of the Left Bank, Paris, 1900–1940* (Austin: University of Texas Press, 1986)

Bergman, David, *Gaiety Transfigured: Gay Self-representation in American Literature* (Madison: University of Wisconsin Press, 1991)

Berman, Marshall, *All That Is Solid Melts into Air: The Experience of Modernity* (New York: Penguin, 1988)

Berman, Paul, "Democracy and Homosexuality," *The New Republic* (December 20, 1993), pp. 17–35

Bernal, Martin, *Black Athena: The Afroasiatic Roots of Classical Civilization, Volume I: The Fabrication of Ancient Greece 1785–1985* (New Brunswick, NJ: Rutgers University Press, 1987)

Bersani, Leo, *Homos* (Cambridge, MA: Harvard University Press, 1995)

Bérubé, Allan, *Coming Out under Fire: The History of Gay Men and Women in World War Two* (New York: The Free Press, 1990)

"Intellectual Desire," *GLQ: A Journal of Lesbian and Gay Studies,* 3.1 (February, 1996), pp. 139–157

Bérubé, Allan and Jeffrey Escoffier, "Queer/Nation," *Outlook: National Lesbian and Gay Quarterly,* 11 (winter 1991), pp. 12, 14

Bhabha, Homi K., "The Commitment to Theory," in *Questions of Third Cinema,* ed. Jim Pines and Paul Willeman (London: British Film Institute, 1989), pp. 111–131

Binkley, Sam, "'I'm Sorry I Threw Bricks at Stonewall': A Faghag's Historical Commentary: Excerpts from an Interview with Penny Arcade," *Found Object,* 4 (fall 1994), pp. 127–132

Birkby, Phyllis et al. (eds.), *Amazon Expedition: A Lesbian-Feminist Anthology* (Albion, CA: Times Change Press, 1973)

Blackwood, Evelyn, (ed.), *The Many Faces of Homosexuality: Anthropological Approaches to Homosexual Behavior* (New York: Harrington Park Press, 1986)

Blankley, Elyse, "Return to Mytilène: Renée Vivien and the City of Women," in *Women Writers and the City: Essays in Feminist Literary Criticism,* ed. Susan Merrill Squier (Knoxville: University of Tennessee Press, 1984), pp. 45–67

Blasius, Mark, *Gay and Lesbian Politics: Sexuality and the Emergence of a New Ethic* (Philadelphia: Temple University Press, 1994)

Boggs, Carl, *Social Movements and Political Power: Emerging Forms of Radicalism in the West* (Philadelphia: Temple University Press, 1986)

Boswell, John, *Christianity, Social Tolerance, and Homosexuality: Gay People in Western Europe from the Beginning of the Christian Era to the Fourteenth Century* (Chicago: University of Chicago Press, 1980)

Boughner, Terry, *Out of All Time* (Boston: Alyson Publications, 1988)

Bravmann, Scott, "Invented Traditions: Take One on the Lesbian and Gay Past," *National Women's Studies Association Journal,* 3.1 (winter 1991), pp. 81–92

"Isaac Julien's *Looking for Langston*: Hughes, Biography, and Queer (ed) History," *Cultural Studies,* 7.2 (May, 1993), pp. 311–323

Bray, Alan, *Homosexuality in Renaissance England* (London: Gay Men's Press, 1982)

Breslauer, Mary, "Another Weekend Lost," *The Advocate* (February 22, 1994), p. 5

Bronski, Michael, *Culture Clash: The Making of Gay Sensibility* (Boston: South End Press, 1984)

Brooks, Van Wykes, *John Addington Symonds, a Biographical Study* (New York: Michael Kennerley, 1914)

Brown, Judith C., *Immodest Acts: The Life of a Lesbian Nun in Renaissance Italy* (Oxford: Oxford University Press, 1986)

Brownsworth, Victoria A., "Stonewall 25: Not a Happy Anniversary for Lesbians," *Deneuve* (June, 1994), p. 38

Bullough, Vern L., *Homosexuality: A History* (New York: New American Library, 1979)

Sexual Variance in Society and History (Chicago: University of Chicago Press, 1976)

Bunch, Charlotte, *Passionate Politics: Feminist Theory in Action* (New York: St. Martin's Press, 1987)

Burgin, Victor, "Stuart Hall on Imaginary Identification and Politics," *Center for Cultural Studies Newsletter* (University of California, Santa Cruz) (winter 1991), n.p.

Butler, Judith, *Gender Trouble: Feminism and the Subversion of Identity* (New York: Routledge, 1990)

Cahn, Susan K., "Sexual Histories, Sexual Politics," *Feminist Studies*, 18.3 (fall 1992), pp. 629–647

Campbell, Jane, *Mythic Black Fiction: The Transformation of History* (Knoxville: University of Tennessee Press, 1986)

Cant, Bob and Susan Hemmings (eds.), *Radical Records: Thirty Years of Lesbian and Gay Liberation* (London: Routledge, 1988)

Caplan, Pat (ed.), *The Cultural Construction of Sexuality* (London: Tavistock, 1987)

Carpenter, Edward, *Selected Writings, Volume One: Sex* (London: GMP Publishers, 1984)

Casselaer, Catherine van, *Lot's Wife: Lesbian Paris, 1890–1914* (Liverpool: The Janus Press, 1986)

Castle, Terry, *The Apparitional Lesbian: Female Homosexuality and Modern Culture* (New York: Columbia University Press, 1993)

Cavin, Susan, *Lesbian Origins* (San Francisco: Ism Press, 1985)

Chalon, Jean, *Portrait of a Seductress: The World of Natalie Barney*, trans. Carol Barko (New York: Crown Publishers, 1979)

Chan, Sucheng, *Asian Americans: An Interpretive History* (Boston: Twayne Publishers, 1991)

Chauncey, George, Jr., *Gay New York: Gender, Urban Culture, and the Making of the Gay Male World, 1890–1940* (New York: Basic Books, 1994)

"From Sexual Inversion to Homosexuality: Medicine and the Changing Conceptualization of Female Desire," *Salmagundi* 58/59 (fall 1982–winter 1983), pp. 114–146, special issue: "Homosexuality: Sacrilege, Vision, Politics," ed. Robert Boyers and George Steiner

Chee, Alexander S., "A Queer Nationalism," *Outlook: National Lesbian and Gay Quarterly*, 11 (winter 1991), pp. 15–17, 19

Christian, Barbara, "The Race for Theory," *Cultural Critique*, 6 (spring 1987), pp. 51–63, special issue, "The Nature and Context of Minority Discourse," ed. Abdul R. JanMohamed and David Lloyd

Clifford, James, "Identity in Mashpee," in *The Predicament of Culture: Twentieth-Century Ethnography, Literature, and Art* (Cambridge, MA: Harvard University Press, 1988), pp. 277–346

Cohen, Ed, *Talk on the Wilde Side: Toward a Genealogy of a Discourse of Male Sexualities* (New York: Routledge, 1993)

"Are We (Not) What We Are Becoming? 'Gay' 'Identity,' 'Gay Studies,' and the Disciplining of Knowledge," in *Engendering Men: The Question of Male Feminist Criticism*, ed. Joseph A. Boone and Michael Cadden (New York: Routledge, 1990), pp. 161–175

"Who Are 'We'? Gay 'Identity' as Political (E)motion (A Theoretical Rumination)," in *Inside/Out: Lesbian Theories, Gay Theories*, ed. Diana Fuss, pp. 71–92

Connor, Steven, *Postmodernist Culture: An Introduction to Theories of the Contemporary* (Oxford: Basil Blackwell, 1989)

Cook, Blanche Wiesen, "Female Support Networks and Political Activism: Lillian Wald, Crystal Eastman, Emma Goldman," *Chrysalis*, 3 (autumn 1977), pp. 43–61

"The Historical Denial of Lesbianism," *Radical History Review*, 20 (spring/summer 1979), pp. 60–65

"'Women Alone Stir My Imagination': Lesbianism and the Cultural Tradition," *Signs: Journal of Women in Culture and Society*, 4.4 (summer 1979), pp. 718–739

Cory, Donald Webster (pseud.), *The Homosexual in America: A Subjective Approach* (New York: Greenberg, 1951)

Cowan, Thomas, *Gay Men and Women Who Enriched the World* (New Canaan, CT: Mulvey Books, 1988)

Crimp, Douglas (ed.), *AIDS: Cultural Analysis, Cultural Activism* (Cambridge, MA: The MIT Press, 1987)

Crimp, Douglas with Adam Rolston, *AIDS Demo Graphics* (Seattle: Bay Press, 1990)

Crompton, Louis, *Byron and Greek Love: Homophobia in 19th-Century England* (Berkeley: University of California Press, 1985)

Cruikshank, Margaret, *The Gay and Lesbian Liberation Movement* (New York: Routledge, 1992)

Cruikshank, Margaret (ed.), *The Lesbian Path* (San Francisco: Grey Fox Press, 1985)

d'Arch Smith, Timothy, *Love in Earnest: Some Notes on the Lives and Writings of English "Uranian" Poets from 1889 to 1930* (London: Routledge and Kegan Paul, 1970)

de Certeau, Michel, *Heterologies: Discourse on the Other*, trans. Brian Massumi (Minneapolis: University of Minnesota Press, 1986)

The Writing of History, trans. Tom Conley (New York: Columbia University Press, 1988)

DeJean, Joan, *Fictions of Sappho, 1546–1937* (Chicago: University of Chicago Press, 1989)

Delany, Samuel R., *The Motion of Light in Water: Sex and Science Fiction Writing in the East Village, 1957–1965* (New York: New American Library, 1988)

De La O, Maria, "Stonewall: The Queer Revolution Twenty Years Later," *Deneuve* (June, 1994), p. 30

de Lauretis, Teresa, "Sexual Indifference and Lesbian Representation," *Theatre Journal*, 40.2 (May, 1988), pp. 155–177

"The Technology of Gender," in *Technologies of Gender: Essays on Theory, Film, and Fiction* (Bloomington: Indiana University Press, 1987), pp. 1–30

D'Emilio, John, *Making Trouble: Essays on Gay History, Politics, and the University* (New York: Routledge, 1992)

Sexual Politics, Sexual Communities: The Making of a Homosexual Minority in the United States 1940–1970 (Chicago: University of Chicago Press, 1983)

"Capitalism and Gay Identity," in *Powers of Desire: The Politics of Sexuality*, ed. Ann Snitow, Christine Stansell, and Sharon Thompson, pp. 100–113

D'Emilio, John and Estelle B. Freedman, *Intimate Matters: A History of Sexuality in America* (New York: Harper and Row, 1988)

"A Response to Ann duCille's 'Othered Matters,'" *Journal of the History of Sexuality*, 1.1 (July, 1990), pp. 128–130

differences: A Journal of Feminist Cultural Studies, 3.2 (fall 1991), special issue: "Queer Theory: Lesbian and Gay Sexualities," ed. Teresa de Lauretis

Dollimore, Jonathan, *Sexual Dissidence: Augustine to Wilde, Freud to Foucault* (Oxford: Clarendon Press, 1991)

Doty, Alexander, *Making Things Perfectly Queer: Interpreting Mass Culture* (Minneapolis: University of Minnesota Press, 1993)

Dover, K. J., *Greek Homosexuality* (New York: Vintage, 1980)

Dowling, Linda, *Hellenism and Homosexuality in Victorian Oxford* (Ithaca, NY: Cornell University Press, 1994)

Duban, Jeffrey M., *Ancient and Modern Images of Sappho* (Lanham, MD: University Press of America, 1983)

Duberman, Martin, *About Time: Exploring the Gay Past* (New York: Gay Presses of New York, 1986)

Stonewall (New York: Dutton, 1993)

Duberman, Martin Bauml, Martha Vicinus, and George Chauncey, Jr. (eds.), *Hidden from History: Reclaiming the Gay and Lesbian Past* (New York: New American Library, 1989)

duCille, Ann, "'Othered' Matters: Reconceptualizing Dominance and Difference in the History of Sexuality in America," *Journal of the History of Sexuality*, 1.1 (July, 1990), pp. 102–127

Duggan, Lisa, "The Discipline Problem," *GLQ: A Journal of Lesbian and Gay Studies*, 2.3 (August, 1995), pp. 179–191

"History's Gay Ghetto: Contradictions of Growth in Lesbian and Gay History," in *Presenting the Past: Essays on History and the Public*, ed. Susan Porter Benson, Stephen Brier, and Roy Rosenzweig (Philadelphia: Temple University Press, 1986), pp. 281–290

"Lesbianism and American History: A Brief Source Review," *Frontiers*, 14.3 (fall 1979), pp. 80–85

"Making It Perfectly Queer," *Socialist Review*, 22.1 (January–March, 1992), pp. 11–31

"Queering the State," *Social Text*, 39 (summer 1994), pp. 1–14

Duyvendak, Jan Willem (ed.), *De Verzuiling van de Homobeweging* (Amsterdam: SUA, 1994)

Dyer, Wayne, *Now You See It: Studies on Lesbian and Gay Film* (London: Routledge, 1991)

Eagleton, Terry, *Literary Theory: An Introduction* (Minneapolis: University of Minnesota Press, 1983)

Echols, Alice, *Daring to Be Bad: Radical Feminism in America, 1967–1975* (Minneapolis: University of Minnesota Press, 1989)

Epstein, Steven, "Gay Politics, Ethnic Identity: The Limits of Social Constructionism," *Socialist Review*, 93/94 (May–August, 1987), pp. 9–54

Escoffier, Jeffrey, "Inside the Ivory Closet: The Challenges Facing Lesbian and Gay Studies," *Outlook: National Lesbian and Gay Quarterly*, 10 (fall 1990), pp. 40–48

"Sexual Revolution and the Politics of Gay Identity," *Socialist Review*, 82/83 (July–October, 1985), pp. 119–153

Ettorre, E. M., *Lesbians, Women, and Society* (London: Routledge and Kegan Paul, 1980)

Faderman, Lillian, *Odd Girls and Twilight Lovers: A History of Lesbian Life in Twentieth-Century America* (New York: Columbia University Press, 1991)

Surpassing the Love of Men: Romantic Friendship and Love Between Women from the Renaissance to the Present (New York: William Morrow, 1981)

"The Morbidification of Love Between Women by 19th-Century Sexologists," *Journal of Homosexuality*, 4.1 (fall 1978), pp. 73–90

Faraday, Annabel, "Liberating Lesbian Research," in *The Making of the Modern Homosexual*, ed. Kenneth Plummer, pp. 112–129

Ferguson, Ann, "Patriarchy, Sexual Identity and the Sexual Revolution," in *Feminist Theory: A Critique of Ideology*, ed. Nannerl O. Keohane, Michelle Z. Rosaldo, and Barbara C. Gelpi (Chicago: University of Chicago Press, 1982), pp. 147–161

Fone, Byrne R. S., *Hidden Heritage: History and the Gay Imagination* (New York: Irvington Publishers, 1981)

Foster, Jeannette H., *Sex Variant Women in Literature* (Tallahassee, FL: The Naiad Press, 1985)

Foucault, Michel, *The History of Sexuality: Volume One, An Introduction*, trans. Robert Hurley (New York: Vintage, 1979)

The History of Sexuality: Volume Two, The Use of Pleasure, trans. Robert Hurley (New York: Vintage, 1985)

The History of Sexuality: Volume Three, The Care of the Self, trans. Robert Hurley (New York: Vintage, 1988)

"Nietzsche, Genealogy, History," in *Language, Counter-Memory, Practice*, ed. Donald F. Bouchard; trans. Donald F. Bouchard and Sherry Simon (Ithaca, NY: Cornell University Press, 1977), pp. 139–164

Franklin, Sarah and Jackie Stacey, "Dyketactics for Difficult Times: A Review of the 'Homosexuality, Which Homosexuality?' Conference, Amsterdam, 15–18 December 1987," *Feminist Review*, 29 (May, 1988), pp. 136–150

Freedman, Estelle B., "The Historical Construction of Homosexuality," *Socialist Review*, 25.1 (January–March, 1995), pp. 31–46

Freedman, Estelle B., Barbara C. Gelpi, Susan L. Johnson, and Kathleen M.

Weston (eds.), *The Lesbian Issue: Essays from Signs* (Chicago: University of Chicago Press, 1985)

Freeman, J. E., "I Remember," *San Francisco Examiner Magazine* (June 19, 1994), p. 11

Frye, Marilyn, *The Politics of Reality: Essays in Feminist Theory* (Trumansburg, NY: The Crossing Press, 1983)

Frye, Northrop, *The Anatomy of Criticism: Four Essays* (Princeton, NJ: Princeton University Press, 1957)

Fuss, Diana, *Essentially Speaking: Feminism, Nature, and Difference* (New York: Routledge, 1989)

Fuss, Diana (ed.), *Inside/Out: Lesbian Theories, Gay Theories* (New York: Routledge, 1991)

Gallop, Jane, *The Daughter's Seduction: Feminism and Psychoanalysis* (Ithaca, NY: Cornell University Press, 1982)

Gamson, Joshua, "Must Identity Movements Self Destruct?: A Queer Dilemma," *Social Problems*, 42.3 (August, 1995), pp. 390–407

Garber, Eric, "Gladys Bentley: Bulldagger Who Sang the Blues," *Outlook: National Lesbian and Gay Quarterly*, 1 (spring 1988), pp. 52–61

"A Spectacle in Color: The Lesbian and Gay Subculture in Jazz Age Harlem," in *Hidden from History: Reclaiming the Gay and Lesbian Past*, ed. Martin Bauml Duberman, Martha Vicinus, and George Chauncey, Jr., pp. 318–331

"T'aint Nobody's Bizness: Homosexuality in 1920s Harlem," in *Black Men/White Men: A Gay Anthology*, ed. Michael J. Smith, pp. 7–16

Gates, Henry Louis, Jr., *Loose Canons: Notes on the Culture Wars* (New York: Oxford University Press, 1992)

Gates, Henry Louis, Jr. (ed.), *"Race," Writing, and Difference* (Chicago: University of Chicago Press, 1986)

Gay Left Collective (eds.), *Homosexuality: Power and Politics* (London: Allison and Busby, 1980)

Gay Rights Writers' Group, *It Could Happen to You . . .: An Account of the Gay Civil Rights Campaign in Eugene, Oregon* (Boston: Alyson Publications, 1983)

Gerard, Kent and Gert Hekma (eds.), *The Pursuit of Sodomy: Male Homosexuality in Renaissance and Enlightenment Europe* (New York: Harrington Park Press, 1989)

Gever, Martha, "What Becomes a Legend Most?" *GLQ: A Journal of Lesbian and Gay Studies*, 1.2 (May, 1994), pp. 209–219

Gever, Martha, John Greyson, and Pratibha Parmar (eds.), *Queer Looks: Perspectives on Lesbian and Gay Film and Video* (New York: Routledge, 1993)

Gidlow, Elsa, "Memoirs," *Feminist Studies*, 6.1 (spring 1980), pp. 107–127

Gilroy, Paul, *The Black Atlantic: Modernity and Double Consciousness* (Cambridge, MA: Harvard University Press, 1993)

Goldsby, Jackie, "What It Means to Be Colored Me," *Outlook: National Lesbian and Gay Quarterly*, 9 (summer 1990), pp. 8–17

Gomez, Jewelle, *Forty-Three Septembers* (Ithaca, NY: Firebrand Books, 1993)

The Gilda Stories (Ithaca, NY: Firebrand Books, 1991)

"Out of the Past," in *The Question of Equality: Lesbian and Gay Politics in America since Stonewall*, ed. David Deitcher (New York: Scribner, 1995), pp. 18–65

Grahn, Judy, *Another Mother Tongue: Gay Words, Gay Worlds* (Boston: Beacon Press, 1984)

The Highest Apple: Sappho and the Lesbian Poetic Tradition (San Francisco: Spinsters, Ink, 1985)

Gramsci, Antonio, *Selections from the Prison Notebooks*, ed. and trans. by Quintin Hoare and Geoffrey Nowell Smith (New York: International Publishers, 1971)

Greenberg, David F., *The Construction of Homosexuality* (Chicago: University of Chicago Press, 1988)

Grier, Barbara, *Lesbiana: Book Reviews from the Ladder* (Reno, NV: The Naiad Press, 1976)

Grossberg, Lawrence, Cary Nelson, and Paula Treichler (eds.), *Cultural Studies* (New York: Routledge, 1992)

Gubar, Susan, "Sapphistries," *Signs: Journal of Women in Culture and Society,* 10.1 (fall 1984), pp. 43–62

Gutiérrez, Ramón A., "Must We Deracinate Indians to Find Gay Roots?," *Outlook: National Lesbian and Gay Quarterly,* 4 (winter 1989), pp. 61–67

Haile, Mark, "The Truth about Stonewall," *BLK,* 7 (June, 1989), pp. 8–13

Hall, Stuart, "Cultural Identity and Diaspora," in *Colonial Discourse and Post-Colonial Theory: A Reader*, ed. Patrick Williams and Laura Chrisman (New York: Columbia University Press, 1994), pp. 392–403

Hallet, Judith P., "Sappho and her Social Context: Sense and Sensuality," *Signs: Journal of Women in Culture and Society,* 4.3 (spring 1979), pp. 447–471

Halperin, David M., *One Hundred Years of Homosexuality and Other Essays on Greek Love* (New York: Routledge, 1990)

Haraway, Donna, *Primate Visions: Gender, Race, and Nature in the World of Modern Science* (New York: Routledge, 1989)

"Situated Knowledges: The Science Question in Feminism as a Site of Discourse on the Privilege of Partial Perspective," *Feminist Studies,* 14.3 (fall 1988), pp. 575–600

Harding, *The Science Question in Feminism* (Ithaca, NY: Cornell University Press, 1986)

Harper, Phillip Brian, "Private Affairs: Race, Sex, Property, and Persons," *GLQ: A Journal of Lesbian and Gay Studies,* 1.2 (May, 1994), pp. 111–133

Harvey, David, *The Condition of Postmodernity* (Oxford: Basil Blackwood, 1989)

Hayes, Jarrod, Lauren Kozol, and Wayne Marat VanSertima, "Stonewall: A Gift to the World: An Interview with Tony Kushner and Joan Nestle," *Found Object,* 4 (fall 1994), pp. 94–107

Healy, Emma and Angela Mason (eds.), *Stonewall 25: The Making of the Lesbian and Gay Community in Britain* (London: Virago Press, 1994)

Hemphill, Essex (ed.), *Brother to Brother: New Writings by Black Gay Men*, conceived by Joseph Beam (Boston: Alyson Publications, 1991)

Hennessey, Rosemary, "Queer Visibility in Commodity Culture," *Cultural Critique*, 29 (winter 1994–1995), pp. 31–76

Herdt, Gilbert, "Representations of Homosexuality: An Essay on Cultural Ontology and Historical Comparison, Part I," *Journal of the History of Sexuality*, 1.3 (January, 1991), pp. 481–504

Herman, Ellen, "Scaling the Ivory Tower," *Lambda Book Report*, 3.12 (September–October, 1993), pp. 26–27

Herrell, Richard K., "The Symbolic Strategies of Chicago's Gay and Lesbian Pride Day Parade," in *Gay Culture in America: Essays from the Field*, ed. Gilbert Herdt (Boston: Beacon Press, 1991), pp. 225–252

Herzfeld, Michael, *Anthropology through the Looking Glass: A Critical Ethnography in the Margins of Europe* (New York: Cambridge University Press, 1987)

Hinsch, Bret, *Passions of the Cut Sleeve: The Male Homosexual Tradition in China* (Berkeley: University of California Press, 1990)

Hobsbawm, Eric and Terence Ranger (eds.), *The Invention of Tradition* (Cambridge: Cambridge University Press, 1983)

Hollibaugh, Amber, "Sexuality and the State: The Briggs Initiative and Beyond," *Socialist Review*, 45 (May–June, 1979), pp. 55–72

Hooker, Evelyn, "Male Homosexuals and their 'Worlds,'" in *Sexual Inversion*, ed. Judd Marmor (New York: Basic Books, 1965), pp. 83–107

hooks, bell, *Yearning: Race, Gender, and Cultural Politics* (Boston: South End Press, 1990)

Huggins, Nathan Irvin, *Harlem Renaissance* (New York: Oxford University Press, 1971)

Huggins, Nathan Irvin (ed.), *Voices of the Harlem Renaissance* (New York: Oxford University Press, 1976)

Hull, Gloria T., "'Lines She Did Not Dare': Angela Weld Grimké, Harlem Renaissance Poet," in *The Lesbian and Gay Studies Reader*, ed. Henry Abelove, Michèlle Aina Barale, and David M. Halperin, pp. 453–466

Humphreys, Laud, *Out of the Closets: The Sociology of Homosexual Liberation* (Englewood Cliffs, NJ: Prentice-Hall, 1972)

Hutcheon, Linda, *A Poetics of Postmodernism: History, Theory, Fiction* (New York: Routledge, 1988)

Hyde, H. Montgomery, *Oscar Wilde: A Biography* (New York: Farrar, Straus, and Giroux, 1975)

Irvine, Janice M., *Disorders of Desire: Sex and Gender in Modern American Sexology* (Philadelphia: Temple University Press, 1990)

Jackson, Ed and Stan Persky (eds.), *Flaunting It! A Decade of Gay Journalism from The Body Politic* (Toronto: Pink Triangle Press, 1982)

Jaimes, M. Annette (ed.), *The State of Native America: Genocide, Colonization, and Resistance* (Boston, MA: South End Press, 1992)

Jameson, Fredric, *The Political Unconscious: Narrative as a Socially Symbolic Act* (Ithaca, NY: Cornell University Press, 1981)

Jay, Karla, *The Amazon and the Page: Natalie Clifford Barney and Renée Vivien* (Bloomington: University of Indiana Press, 1988)

Jay, Karla and Allen Young (eds.), *After You're Out: Personal Experiences of Gay Men and Lesbian Women* (New York: Links Books, 1975)

Out of the Closets: Voices of Gay Liberation (New York: Douglas/Links Books, 1972; reprint edn. New York University Press, 1992)

Jenkyns, Richard, *The Victorians and Ancient Greece* (Cambridge, MA: Harvard University Press, 1980)

Johnston, Jill, *Lesbian Nation: The Feminist Solution* (New York: Simon and Schuster, 1973)

Julien, Isaac and Colin MacCabe, *Diary of a Young Soul Rebel*, with screenplay by Paul Hallam and Derrick Saldaan McClintock (London: British Film Institute, 1991)

Kader, Cheryl and Thomas Piontek, "Introduction," *Discourse: Journal for Theoretical Studies in Media and Culture,* 15.1 (fall 1992), pp. 5–10, special issue: "Essays in Lesbian and Gay Studies," ed. Cheryl Kader and Thomas Piontek

Kaplan, Caren, "Deterritorializations: The Rewriting of Home and Exile in Western Feminist Discourse," *Cultural Critique,* 6 (spring 1987), pp. 187–198, special issue: "The Nature and Context of Minority Discourse," ed. Abdul R. JanMohamed and David Lloyd

Kaplan, E. Ann (ed.), *Postmodernism and Its Discontents: Theories, Practices* (New York: Verso, 1988)

Katz, Jonathan, *Gay American History: Lesbians and Gay Men in the USA* (New York: Thomas Cromwell, 1976)

Gay/Lesbian Almanac: A New Documentary (New York: Harper and Row, 1983)

The Invention of Heterosexuality (New York: Dutton, 1995)

"The Invention of Heterosexuality," *Socialist Review,* 20.1 (January–March, 1990), pp. 7–34

Kehoe, Monika (ed.), *Historical, Literary, and Erotic Aspects of Lesbianism* (New York: Harrington Park Press, 1986)

Kennedy, Elizabeth Lapovsky and Madeline D. Davis, *Boots of Leather, Slippers of Gold: The History of a Lesbian Community* (New York: Routledge, 1993)

Kennedy, Hubert, *Ulrichs: The Life and Works of Karl Heinrich Ulrichs, Pioneer of the Modern Gay Movement* (Boston: Alyson Publications, 1988)

King, Katie, *Theory in Its Feminist Travels: Conversations in US Women's Movements* (Bloomington: Indiana University Press, 1994)

"Audre Lorde's Lacquered Layerings: The Lesbian Bar as a Site of Literary Production," *Cultural Studies,* 2.3 (October, 1988), pp. 321–342

Kinsman, Gary, *The Regulation of Desire: Sexuality in Canada* (Montreal: Black Rose Books, 1987)

Kissack, Terrence, "Freaking Fag Revolutionaries: New York's Gay Liberation Front, 1969–1971," *Radical History Review,* 62 (spring 1995), pp. 104–134

Kitzinger, Celia, *The Social Construction of Lesbianism* (London: Sage Publications, 1987)

Klaich, Dolores, *Woman+Woman* (New York: Simon and Schuster, 1974)

Klandermans, Bert, and Sidney Tarrow, "Mobilization into Social Movements: Synthesizing European and American Approaches," in *From Structures to Action: Comparing Social Movement Research across Cultures* (London: JAI Press, 1988), pp. 1–38

Koestenbaum, Wayne, *Double Talk: The Erotics of Male Literary Collaboration* (New York: Routledge, 1989)

Kuhn, Thomas S., *The Structure of Scientific Revolutions*, 2nd edn. (Chicago: University of Chicago Press, 1970)

LaCapra, Dominick, *History and Criticism* (Ithaca, NY: Cornell University Press, 1985)

Laclau, Ernesto and Chantal Mouffe, *Hegemony and Socialist Strategy: Towards a Radical Democratic Politics* (London: Verso, 1985)

Lardinois, André, "Lesbian Sappho and Sappho of Lesbos," in *From Sappho to de Sade: Moments in the History of Sexuality*, ed. Jan Bremmer (New York: Routledge, 1989), pp. 15–35

Lash, Scott and John Urry, *The End of Organized Capitalism* (Madison, WI: University of Wisconsin Press, 1987)

Lauritsen, John and David Thorstad, *The Early Homosexual Rights Movement (1864–1935)* (New York: Times Change Press, 1974)

Levine, Martin P. (ed.), *Gay Men: The Sociology of Male Homosexuality* (New York: Harper and Row, 1979)

Lewin, Ellen, *Lesbian Mothers: Accounts of Gender in American Culture* (Ithaca, NY: Cornell University Press, 1993)

Lewis, David Levering, *When Harlem Was in Vogue* (New York: Alfred Knopf, 1981)

Licata, Salvatore J. and Robert P. Petersen (eds.), *The Gay Past: A Collection of Historical Essays* (New York: Harrington Park Press, 1985)

Lipsitz, George, *Time Passages: Collective Memory and American Popular Culture* (Minneapolis: University of Minnesota Press, 1990)

Locke, Alain (ed.), *The New Negro: An Introduction*, reprint edn. (New York: Atheneum, 1968)

Lorde, Audre, *Sister Outsider* (Trumansburg, NY: The Crossing Press, 1985)
 Zami: A New Spelling of My Name (Trumansburg, NY: The Crossing Press, 1982)

Lu, Ming-Yeung, "Passion Tales: Allegories of Identity," *Lavender Godzilla* (spring 1992), pp. 6–15

Lyotard, Jean-François, *The Postmodern Condition: A Report on Knowledge*, trans. Geoff Bennington and Brian Massumi (Minneapolis: University of Minnesota Press, 1984)

MacCubbin, Robert Purks (ed.), *'Tis Nature's Fault: Unauthorized Sexuality during the Enlightenment* (New York: Cambridge University Press, 1987)

Maggenti, Maria, "Women as Queer Nationals," *Outlook: National Lesbian and Gay Quarterly,* 11 (winter 1991), pp. 20–23

Maggiore, Dolores J., *Lesbianism: An Annotated Bibliography and Guide to the Literature, 1976–1986* (Metuchen, NJ: The Scarecrow Press, 1988)

Malinowitz, Harriet, "Queer Theory: Whose Theory?" *Frontiers,* 13.2 (1992), pp. 168–185

Manalasan, Martin F., IV, "In the Shadows of Stonewall: Examining Gay Transnational Politics and the Diasporic Dilemma," *GLQ: A Journal of Lesbian and Gay Studies,* 2.4 (December, 1995), pp. 425–438

Marcus, Eric, *Making History: The Struggle for Gay and Lesbian Equal Rights, 1945–1990, an Oral History* (New York: HarperCollins, 1992)

"What a Riot!" *10 Percent* (June, 1994), pp. 48–53, 78–82

Marks, Elaine, "Lesbian Intertextuality," in *Homosexualities and French Literature,* ed. George Stambolian and Elaine Marks, pp. 353–377

Marks, Jim, "Looking for Isaac," *Outweek* (October 1, 1989), pp. 30–33

Marotta, Toby, *The Politics of Homosexuality* (Boston: Houghton Mifflin Company, 1981)

Martin, Del and Phyllis Lyon, *Lesbian/Woman* (San Francisco: Glide Foundation, 1972)

Matthiessen, F. O., *Rat and the Devil: Journal Letters of F. O. Matthiessen and Russell Cheney,* ed. Louis Hyde (Boston: Alyson Publications, 1988)

McIntosh, Mary, "The Homosexual Role," *Social Problems,* 16.2 (fall 1968), pp. 182–192

"Postscript: 'The Homosexual Role' Revisted," in *The Making of the Modern Homosexual,* ed. Kenneth Plummer, pp. 44–49

Meijer, Irene Costera, Jan Willem Duyvendak, and Marty PN van Kerkhof (eds.), *Over Normaal Gesproken: Hedendaagse Homopolitiek* (Amsterdam: Schorer, 1991)

Melucci, Alberto, *Nomads of the Present: Social Movements and Individual Needs in Contemporary Society* (Philadelphia: Temple University Press, 1989)

Mercer, Kobena and Isaac Julien, "True Confessions," in *Black Male,* ed. Thelma Golden (New York: Whitney Museum of American Art/Abrams, 1994), pp. 191–200

Merck, Mandy, *Perversions: Deviant Readings* (New York: Routledge, 1993)

Miller, J. Hillis, "Narrative and History," *English Literary History,* 41.3 (fall 1974), pp. 455–473

Mink, Louis O., *Historical Understanding,* ed. Brian Fay, Eugene O. Golob, and Richard T. Vann (Ithaca, NY: Cornell University Press, 1987)

Minton, Henry L., *Gay and Lesbian Studies* (New York: Harrington Park Press, 1992)

Moraga, Cherríe, *Loving in the War Years: Lo que nunca pasó por sus labios* (Boston: South End Press, 1983)

Moraga, Cherríe and Gloria Anzaldúa (eds.), *This Bridge Called My Back: Writings by Radical Women of Color* (Watertown, MA: Persephone Press, 1981)

Morgan, Tracy, "Pages of Whiteness: Race, Physique Magazines, and the Emergence of Gay Public Culture, 1955–1960," *Found Object,* 4 (fall 1994), pp. 108–126

Mumford, Kevin, "Homosex Changes: Race, Cultural Geography, and the Emergence of the Gay," *American Quarterly,* 48.3 (September, 1996), pp. 395–414

Murray, Steven O., *Social Theory, Homosexual Realities* (New York: Gai Saber Monographs, 1984)

Myron, Nancy and Charlotte Bunch (eds.), *Lesbians and the Women's Movement* (Baltimore, MD: Diana Press, 1975)

Naerssen, A. X. van (ed.), *Gay Life in Dutch Society* (New York: Harrington Park Press, 1987)

Nelson, Emmanuel S. (ed.), *Critical Essays: Gay and Lesbian Writers of Color* (New York: Harrington Park Press, 1993)

Nestle, Joan, *A Restricted Country* (Ithaca, NY: Firebrand Books, 1987)

Newton, Esther, *Cherry Grove, Fire Island: Sixty Years in America's First Gay and Lesbian Town* (Boston: Beacon Press, 1993)

"The Mythic Mannish Lesbian: Radclyffe Hall and the New Woman," in *Hidden from History: Reclaiming the Lesbian and Gay Past*, ed. Martin Bauml Duberman, Martha Vicinus, and George Chauncey, Jr., pp. 281–293

Nicholson, Linda J. (ed.), *Feminism/Postmodernism* (New York: Routledge, 1990)

Nietzsche, Friedrich, *The Use and Abuse of History*, trans. Adrian Collins (New York: Macmillan/Library of Liberal Arts, 1957)

Offe, Claus, "New Social Movements: Challenging the Boundaries of Institutional Politics," *Social Research,* 52.4 (winter 1985), pp. 817–868

Omi, Michael and Howard Winant, *Racial Formation in the United States from the 1960s to the 1980s* (New York: Routledge, 1986)

Omosupe, Ekua, "Black/Lesbian/Bulldagger," *differences: A Journal of Feminist Cultural Studies,* 3.2 (summer 1991), pp. 101–111, special issue: "Queer Theory: Lesbian and Gay Sexualities," ed. Teresa de Lauretis

Onge, Jack, *The Gay Liberation Movement* (Chicago: The Alliance Press, 1971)

Parker, Andrew, Mary Russo, Doris Sommer, and Patricia Yeager (eds.), *Nationalisms and Sexualities* (New York: Routledge, 1992)

Patton, Cindy, *Inventing AIDS* (New York: Routledge, 1990)

Sex and Germs: The Politics of AIDS (Boston: South End Press, 1985)

Pela, Robert L., "Stonewall's Eyewitnesses," *The Advocate* (May 3, 1994), pp. 50–55

Penn, Donna, "The Meanings of Lesbianism in Post-War America," *Gender and History,* 3.2 (summer 1991), pp. 190–203

"Queer: Theorizing Politics and History," *Radical History Review,* 62 (spring 1995), pp. 24–42

Pfeil, Fred, *White Guys: Studies in Postmodern Domination and Difference* (New York: Verso, 1995)

Phelan, Shane, *Identity Politics: Lesbian Feminism and the Limits of Community* (Philadelphia: Temple University Press, 1989)

Plant, Richard, *The Pink Triangle: The Nazi War against Homosexuals* (New York: Henry Holt, 1986)

Plummer, Kenneth (ed.), *The Making of the Modern Homosexual* (London: Hutchinson and Company, 1981)
Modern Homosexualities: Fragments of Lesbian and Gay Experience (London: Routledge, 1992)
Polan, Dana, *Power and Paranoia* (New York: Columbia University Press, 1986)
Popular Memory Group, "Popular Memory: Theory, Politics, Method," in *Making Histories: Studies in History-Writing and Politics*, ed. Richard Johnson, Gregor McLennan, Bill Schwarz, and David Sutton (London: Hutchinson, 1982), pp. 205–252
Portelli, Alessandro, "The Peculiarities of Oral History," *History Workshop*, 12 (autumn 1981), pp. 96–107
Porter, Kevin and Jeffrey Weeks (eds.), *Between the Acts: Lives of Homosexual Men, 1885–1967* (London: Routledge, 1991)
Pratt, Minnie Bruce, *S/He* (Ithaca, NY: Firebrand Books, 1995)
"Identity: Skin, Blood, Heart," in Elly Bulkin, Minnie Bruce Pratt, and Barbara Smith, *Yours in Struggle: Three Feminist Perspectives on Anti-Semitism and Racism* (Ithaca, NY: Firebrand Books, 1988), pp. 9–63
Read, Kenneth E., *Other Voices: The Style of a Male Homosexual Tavern* (Novato, CA: Chandler and Sharp, 1980)
Reade, Brian (ed.), *Sexual Heretics: Male Homosexuality in English Literature from 1850 to 1900* (London: Routledge and Kegan Paul, 1970)
Reimonencq, Alden, "Countee Cullen's Uranian 'Soul Windows,'" in *Critical Essays: Gay and Lesbian Writers of Color*, ed. Emmanuel S. Nelson, pp. 143–165
Rich, Adrienne, *On Lies, Secrets, and Silence* (New York: Norton, 1979)
"Compulsory Heterosexuality and Lesbian Existence," in *Powers of Desire: The Politics of Sexuality*, ed. Ann Snitow, Christine Stansell, and Sharon Thompson , pp. 177–205
Richmond, Len and Gary Noguera (eds.), *The Gay Liberation Book* (San Francisco: Ramparts Press, 1972)
Ricoeur, Paul, *The Reality of the Historical Past* (Milwaukee, WI: Marquette University Press, 1984)
Roscoe, Will, *The Zuni Man-Woman* (Albuquerque, NM: University of New Mexico Press, 1991)
"Making History: The Challenge of Gay and Lesbian Studies," *Journal of Homosexuality*, 15.3/4 (1988), pp. 1–40
Roscoe, Will (ed.), *Living the Spirit: A Gay American Indian Anthology* (New York: St. Martin's Press, 1988)
Ross, Andrew (ed.), *Universal Abandon?: The Politics of Postmodernism* (Minneapolis: University of Minnesota Press, 1988)
Rowbotham, Sheila and Jeffrey Weeks, *Socialism and the New Life: The Personal and Sexual Politics of Edward Carpenter and Havelock Ellis* (London: Pluto Press, 1977)
Rowse, A. L., *Homosexuals in History: A Study of Ambivalence in Society, Literature, and the Arts* (New York: Carroll and Graf, 1977)

Ruehl, Sonia, "Inverts and Experts: Radclyffe Hall and the Lesbian Identity," in *Feminism, Culture, and Politics*, ed. Rosalind Brunt and Caroline Rowan (London: Lawrence and Wishart, 1982), pp. 15–36

Rupp, Leila, "'Imagine My Surprise': Women's Relationships in Mid-Twentieth Century America," in *Hidden from History: Reclaiming the Lesbian and Gay Past*, ed. Martin Bauml Duberman, Martha Vicinus, and George Chauncey, Jr., pp. 395–410

Russo, Vito, *The Celluloid Closet: Homosexuality in the Movies* (New York: Harper and Row, 1981)

Rutherford, Jonathan (ed.), *Identity: Community, Culture, Difference* (London: Lawrence and Wishart, 1990)

Sage, Wayne, "Inside the Colossal Closet," in *Gay Men: The Sociology of Male Homosexuality*, ed. Martin P. Levine, pp. 148–163

Salmagundi, 58–59 (fall 1982–winter 1983), special issue: "Homosexuality: Sacrilege, Vision, Politics," ed. Robert Boyers and George Steiner

Sandoval, Chela, "US Third World Feminism: The Theory and Method of Oppositional Consciousness," *Genders*, 10 (spring 1991), pp. 1–25

Schuyf, Judith, *Een Stilzwijgende Samenleving: Lesbische Vrouwen in Nederland, 1920–1970* (Amsterdam: Stichting Beheer, 1994)

Schwarz, Judith, "Questionnaire on Issues in Lesbian History," *Frontiers*, 4.3 (fall 1979), pp. 1–12

Scott, Joan, *Gender and the Politics of History* (New York: Columbia University Press, 1988)

  "The Evidence of Experience," in *The Lesbian and Gay Studies Reader*, ed. Henry Abelove, Michèlle Aina Barale, and David M. Halperin, pp. 397–415

Sedgwick, Eve Kosofsky, *Between Men: English Literature and Male Homosocial Desire* (New York: Columbia University Press, 1985)

  Epistemology of the Closet (Berkeley: University of California Press, 1990)

Seidman, Steven, "Identity and Politics in a 'Postmodern' Gay Culture: Some Historical and Conceptual Notes," in *Fear of a Queer Planet: Queer Politics and Social Theory*, ed. Michael Warner, pp. 105–142

Shah, Nayan, "Sexuality, Identity, and the Uses of History," in *A Lotus of Another Color: An Unfolding of the South Asian Gay and Lesbian Experience*, ed. Rakesh Ratti (Boston: Alyson Publications, 1993), pp. 113–132

Shilts, Randy, *The Mayor of Castro Street: The Life and Times of Harvey Milk* (New York: St. Martin's Press, 1982)

Shorter, Edward, *The Making of the Modern Family* (New York: Basic Books, 1975)

Simpson, Ruth, *From the Closets to the Courts* (New York: Viking, 1976)

Sinfield, Alan, *The Wilde Century: Effeminacy, Oscar Wilde, and the Queer Moment* (New York: Columbia University Press, 1994)

Smith, Barbara (ed.), *Home Girls: A Black Feminist Anthology* (New York: Kitchen Table Press, 1983)

Smith, Cherry, *Lesbians Talk Queer Notions* (London: Scarlet Press, 1992)

Smith, Michael J. (ed.), *Black Men/White Men: A Gay Anthology* (San Francisco: Gay Sunshine Press, 1983)

Smith, Paul, *Discerning the Subject* (Minneapolis: University of Minnesota Press, 1988)

Smith-Rosenberg, Carroll, *Disorderly Conduct: Visions of Gender in Victorian America* (New York: Alfred A. Knopf, 1985)

Snitow, Ann, "Pages from a Gender Diary: Basic Divisions in Feminism," *Dissent* (spring 1989), pp. 205–224

Snitow, Ann, Christine Stansell, and Sharon Thompson (eds.), *Powers of Desire: The Politics of Sexuality* (New York: Monthly Review Press, 1983)

South Atlantic Quarterly, 88.1 (winter 1989), special issue: "Displacing Homophobia," ed. Ronald R. Butters, John M. Clum, and Michael Moon

Stambolian, George and Elaine Marks (eds.), *Homosexualities and French Literature* (Ithaca, NY: Cornell University Press, 1979)

Stein, Arlene, "Sisters and Queers: The Decentering of Lesbian Feminism," *Socialist Review,* 22.1 (January–March, 1992), pp. 33–55

Stein, Arlene (ed.), *Sisters, Sexperts, Queers: Beyond the Lesbian Nation* (New York: New American Library, 1993)

Stein, Marc, "Sex Politics in the City of Sisterly and Brotherly Loves," *Radical History Review,* 59 (spring 1994), pp. 60–92

Stigers, Eva Stehle, "Sappho's Private World," in *Reflections of Women in Antiquity,* ed. Helene P. Foley (New York: Gordon and Breach Science Publishers, 1981), pp. 45–61

Stryker, Susan and Jim Van Buskirk, *Gay By the Bay: A History of Queer Culture in the San Francisco Bay Area* (San Francisco, CA: Chronicle Books, 1996)

Sturken, Marita, "Conversations with the Dead: Bearing Witness in the AIDS Memorial Quilt," *Socialist Review,* 22.2 (April–June, 1992), pp. 65–95

Summers, Claude J., *Gay Fictions: Wilde to Stonewall* (New York: Continuum, 1990)

Symonds, John Addington, *The Memoirs of John Addington Symonds,* ed. Phyllis Grosskurth (New York: Random House, 1984)

A Problem in Greek Ethics (London: private edn., 1883)

A Problem in Modern Ethics (London: private edn., 1896)

Takaki, Ronald, *A Different Mirror: A History of Multicultural America* (Boston: Little, Brown, 1993)

Strangers from a Different Shore: A History of Asian Americans (New York: Penguin, 1990)

Teal, Donn, *The Gay Militants* (New York: Stein and Day, 1971)

Terry, Jenny, "Locating Ourselves in the History of Sexuality," *Outlook: National Lesbian and Gay Quarterly,* 2 (summer 1988), pp. 86–91

Thomas, David J., "The 'Q' Word," *Socialist Review,* 25.1 (January–March, 1995), pp. 69–93

Thompson, Denise, *Flaws in the Social Fabric: Homosexuals and Society in Sydney* (Sydney: Allen and Unwin, 1985)

Thompson, Mark (ed.), *Gay Spirit: Myth and Meaning* (New York: St. Martin's Press, 1987)

Long Road to Freedom: The Advocate History of the Gay and Lesbian Movement (New York: St. Martin's Press, 1994)

Tielman, Rob, *Homoseksualiteit in Nederland: Studie van een Emancipatie Beweging* (Meppel/Amsterdam: Boom, 1982)
"Stonewall: Amerikanisering en Nederlands Nationalisme," *Homologie: Tweemaandelijks Lesbo/Homoblad,* 16.4 (July–August, 1994), pp. 8–11
Tilchen, Maida, "Mythologizing Stonewall," *Gay Community News* (June 23, 1979), p. 16
Timmons, Stuart, *The Trouble with Harry Hay: Founder of the Modern Gay Movement* (Boston: Alyson Publications, 1990)
Touraine, Alain, *The Voice and the Eye: An Analysis of Social Movements,* trans. Alan Duff (New York: Cambridge University Press, 1981)
Troiden, Richard R., *Gay and Lesbian Identity: A Sociological Analysis* (Dix Hills, NY: General Hall, 1988)
Trujillo, Carla (ed.), *Chicana Lesbians: The Girls Our Mothers Warned Us About* (Berkeley, CA: Third Woman Press, 1991)
Turner, Frank M., *The Greek Heritage in Victorian Britain* (New Haven, CT: Yale University Press, 1981)
Umphrey, Martha M., "The Trouble with Harry Thaw," *Radical History Review,* 62 (spring 1995), pp. 8–23
Vance, Carole S., "Social Construction Theory: Problems in the History of Sexuality," in *Which Homosexuality?: Essays from the International Scientific Conference on Lesbian and Gay Studies,* ed. Dennis Altman et al., pp. 13–34
Vance, Carole S. (ed.), *Pleasure and Danger: Exploring Female Sexuality* (Boston: Routledge and Kegan Paul, 1984)
Veyne, Paul, *Writing History: Essay on Epistemology,* trans. Mina Moore-Rinvolucri (Middletown, CT: Wesleyan University Press, 1984)
Vicinus, Martha, "Sexuality and Power: A Review of Current Work in the History of Sexuality," *Feminist Studies,* 8 (spring 1982), pp. 133–156
"'They Wonder to Which Sex I Belong': The Historical Roots of the Modern Lesbian Identity," in *Which Homosexuality?: Essays from the International Scientific Conference on Lesbian and Gay Studies,* ed. Dennis Altman et al., pp. 171–198
Vivien, Renée, *A Woman Appeared to Me,* trans. Jeannette H. Foster (Reno, NV: The Naiad Press, 1976)
The Woman of the Wolf and Other Stories, trans. Karla Jay and Yvonne M. Klein (New York: Gay Presses of New York, 1983)
Warmerdam, Hans, "Een Kloon van Uncle Sam. De Amerikanisering van Homoseksueel Nederland," in *Tolerantie onder NAP: 20 Essays over Homoseksualiteit voor Rob Tielman* (Utrecht: Rijksuniversiteit Utrecht/Homostudies, 1992), pp. 217–239
"Zelfbevestiging in Apartheid: De Opstelling van het COC tegenover De Gay Pride Day 1969–1978," *Homologie: Tweemaandelijks Lesbo/Homoblad,* 11.4 (July/August, 1989), pp. 10–13
Warner, Michael, "Introduction: Fear of a Queer Planet," *Social Text,* 29 (1991), pp. 3–17

Warner, Michael (ed.), *Fear of a Queer Planet: Queer Politics and Social Theory* (Minneapolis: University of Minnesota Press, 1993)

Watney, Simon, *Policing Desire: Pornography, AIDS, and the Media* (Minneapolis: University of Minnesota Press, 1987)

Weeks, Jeffrey, *Coming Out: Homosexual Politics in Britain from the Nineteenth Century to the Present* (London: Quartet, 1977)

"Against Nature," in *Which Homosexuality?: Essays from the International Scientific Conference on Lesbian and Gay Studies*, ed. Dennis Altman et al.

Sexuality and its Discontents (London: Routledge and Kegan Paul, 1985)

Weintraub, Karl J., "Autobiography and Historical Consciousness," *Critical Inquiry*, 1.3 (June, 1975), pp. 821–848

Weiss, Andrea and Greta Schiller, *Before Stonewall: The Making of a Gay and Lesbian Community* (Tallahassee, FL: Naiad Press, 1988)

Weisskopf, Thomas, "The Current Economic Crisis in Historical Perspective," *Socialist Review*, 57 (May–June, 1981), pp. 9–53

White, Hayden, *The Content of the Form: Narrative Discourse and Historical Representation* (Baltimore: Johns Hopkins University Press, 1987)

Metahistory: The Historical Imagination in Nineteenth-Century Europe (Baltimore: Johns Hopkins University Press, 1973)

The Tropics of Discourse: Essays in Cultural Criticism (Baltimore: Johns Hopkins University Press, 1978)

Wickes, George, *The Amazon of Letters: The Life and Loves of Natalie Barney* (New York: G. P. Putnam's Sons, 1976)

Wilson, Angela R. (ed.), *A Simple Matter of Justice?: Theorizing Lesbian and Gay Politics* (London: Cassell, 1995)

Winkler, John J., *The Constraints of Desire* (New York: Routledge, 1990)

Winterson, Jeanette, *Oranges Are Not the Only Fruit* (New York: Atlantic Monthly Press, 1987)

Wittig, Monique, "The Mark of Gender," in *The Poetics of Gender*, ed. Nancy K. Miller (New York: Columbia University Press, 1986), pp. 63–73

Wittig, Monique and Sande Zeig, *Lesbian Peoples: Materials for a Dictionary* (New York: Avon Books, 1979)

Wolfe, Susan J. and Julia Penelope (eds.), *Sexual Practice, Textual Theory: Lesbian Cultural Criticism* (Cambridge, MA: Blackwell, 1993)

Woods, Gregory, "Gay Rereadings of the Harlem Renaissance Poets," in *Critical Essays: Gay and Lesbian Writers of Color*, ed. Emmanuel S. Nelson, pp. 127–142

Yoshikawa, Yoko, "The Heat Is on *Miss Saigon* Coalition: Organizing across Race and Sexuality," in *The State of Asian America: Activism and Resistance in the 1990s*, ed. Karin Aguilar-San Juan (Boston: South End Press, 1994), pp. 275–294

Young, James E., *Writing and Rewriting the Holocaust: Narrative and the Consequences of Interpretation* (Bloomington: Indiana University Press, 1988)

Young, Robert, *White Mythologies: Writing History and the West* (New York: Routledge, 1990)

Zimmerman, Bonnie, *The Safe Sea of Women: Lesbian Fiction 1969–1989* (Boston: Beacon Press, 1990)

Zinn, Howard, *A People's History of the United States* (New York: Harper and Row, 1980)

Zita, Jacquelyn N., "Gay and Lesbian Studies: Yet Another Unhappy Marriage?" in *Tilting the Tower: Lesbians Teaching Queer Subjects*, ed. Linda Garber (New York: Routledge, 1994), pp. 258–276

Index

Kaplan, Caren 101
Katz, Jonathan Ned 54–55, 130 n. 7
Kennedy, Elizabeth Lapovsky 38–42, 82,
    141 n. 36
Kerkhof, Marty PN van 137 n. 11
King, Katie 45, 133 n. 6
Kissack, Terrence 147 n. 58
Klaich, Dolores 84, 140 n. 23
Klandermans, Bert 136 n. 5
Kuhn, Thomas S. 132 n. 18

LaCapra, Dominick 135 n. 25
Laclau, Ernesto 90, 136 n. 5
Lardinois, André 139 n. 10
Lash, Scott 136 n 5
Leitsch, Dick 143 n. 2, 144 n. 12
lesbian identity 11, 41
lesbian theory 17, 18, 19
    see also queer theory
Lewis, David Leavering 131 n. 17
Locke, Alain 131 n. 17
Lorde, Audre 45, 103–107, 108, 116, 118,
    120, 133 n. 6, 150 n. 35
Love, Barbara 63, 83
Lu, Ming-Yeung 62–63, 64–65
Lyotard, Jean-François 3

Manalasan, Martin F., IV 137 n. 11
Marine Cooks and Stewards Union 42–44,
    127
Marks, Elaine 138 n. 6
Marshall, Stuart 45, 112, 130 n.4
Mason, Angela 137 n. 11
Mattachine Society 42–43, 105, 144 n. 12
Mattachine Society *Newsletter* (New York)
    77
Matthiessen, F. O. 139 n. 19
McDarrah, Fred 76, 77, 80
McIntosh, Mary 130 n. 7
McWhorter, Lucullus Virgil 148 n. 10
Meijer, Irene Costera 137 n. 11
Melucci, Alberto 136 n. 5
Mercer, Kobena 111, 149 n. 11
Milk, Harvey 146 n. 47
Mink, Louis O. 135 n. 25
Moraga, Cherríe 133 n. 6
Morgan, Tracy 132 n. 19
Morrison, Toni 110
Moscone, George 146 n. 47
Mouffe, Chantal 90, 136 n. 5
Mourning Dove 148 n. 10
Mumford, Kevin 148 n. 16

Naerssen, A. X. van 137 n. 11
Nestle, Joan 130 n. 4
New Orleans 115
Netherlands, the 137 n. 11

Newton, Esther 38–41
New York City 40, 62, 63, 71, 75, 76, 92, 94,
    106, 137 n. 11
New York Times 76, 77, 143 n. 10

Offe, Claus 136 n. 5
One, Inc. 105
Out magazine 92
Oxford University 50, 61

Parmar, Pratibha 109–111, 112–113, 118,
    120
Penn, Donna 24–26, 120, 134 n. 21
Pfeil, Fred, xii
Philippines, the 137 n. 11
Plummer, Kenneth 130 n. 6
Polan, Dana 31
Popular Memory Group 28–29, 108, 128
Portelli, Alessandro 73
Porter, Kevin 54
Pratt, Minnie Bruce 133 n. 6

queer cultural studies of history x, 13–14,
    15, 16, 25, 30–32, 38, 45, 68, 97,
    125–126, 128
queer heterosociality xii, 16, 20, 32, 38, 42,
    44, 46, 68, 81, 100, 101, 103, 113–114,
    116, 117, 126
queer theory ix, 20, 24–25, 30, 48, 128
    see also gay theory

race xi–xii, 11, 13, 47, 48, 65–67, 75–80, 99,
    100–103, 104, 109–112, 113–118, 120
Ranger, Terence 148 n. 7
Reade, Brian 139 n. 14
Redstockings 75, 143 n. 7
Reimonencq, Alden 131 n. 17
Ricoeur, Paul 135 n. 25
Riggs, Marlon 97, 133 n. 6
Rivera, Sylvia 74, 95
Rodwell, Craig 74, 89
Roscoe, Will 98, 130 n. 4, 146 n. 5, 147
    n. 10
Rubin, Gayle 58

San Francisco 62, 63, 116, 146 n. 47
Sappho 51, 55–59, 63–65
Savin, Richard 81
Schuyf, Judith 137 n. 11
Scott, Joan 73–74, 134 n. 19
Sedgwick, Eve Kosofsky 9, 16–18, 19, 21,
    22, 23
Seidman, Steven 134 n. 15
Shelley, Martha 86
Shilts, Randy 146 n. 47
Smith, Charles Michael 131 n. 17
Smith, Howard 76